MISHIMA

MISHIMA

a biography

by JOHN NATHAN

little, brown and company

boston-toronto

FIRST EDITION

T 11/74

The author is grateful to the following publishers for permission to reprint from previously copyrighted
materials:

New Directions Publishing Corporation, for selections from *Confessions of a Mask*, as translated by
Meredith Weatherby, copyright © 1958 by New Directions Publishing Corporation; and for selections from
Death in Midsummer and Other Stories, copyright © 1966 by New Directions Publishing Corporation.

Kodansha International Ltd., for selections from *Sun and Steel*, as translated by John Bester, copyright © 1970.

Jinbun Shoin Ltd., for excerpts from the poems "Song of the Plain" and "Clinging to an August Rock"
by Shizuo Ito, from *The Complete Works of Shizuo Ito*, published in 1966.

Shinchosha Company, for selections from the following works of Yukio Mishima: *Thieves*, copyright 1954
by Yukio Mishima; *Complete Essays*, copyright © 1966 by Yukio Mishima; *Kyoko's House*, copyright © 1959
by Yukio Mishima; excerpts from the story "A Forest in Full Flower" from *Collection of Yukio Mishima's
Teenage Works*, copyright © 1971 by Yoko Hiraoka; *The Defense of Culture*, copyright © 1969 by
Yukio Mishima; portions of the essay "Faith in Japan" from *King Lan Ling*, copyright © 1971 by Yoko Hiraoka.

Kawade Shobo Company, for selections from *The Voice of the Spirits* by Yukio Mishima, copyright © 1970.

Chuo Koron Company, for excerpts from the essay "My Will," which appeared in *From the Withered Fields*
by Yukio Mishima, copyright © 1967.

Kadogawa Shoten Company, for selections from *Illusory Shadow of the Flame* by Toshitami Bojo,
copyright © 1971 by Toshitami Bojo.

LIBRARY OF CONGRESS CATALOGING IN PUBLICATION DATA

Nathan, John, 1940-
  Mishima.

  Bibliography: p.
  1. Mishima, Yukio, pseud.
PL833.I7Z6984   895.6'3'5[B]   74-12184
ISBN 0-316-59844-5

Designed by Barbara Bell Pitnof.

*Published simultaneously in Canada by Little, Brown & Company (Canada)
Limited*

PRINTED IN THE UNITED STATES OF AMERICA

For Zachary and Jeremiah

I began this book while a Junior Fellow in the Society of Fellows at Harvard University; I wish to thank the society for its generosity. I am also grateful to two of Mishima's editors and lifelong friends whose help has been invaluable, Masaru Kawashima and Hiroshi Nitta.

preface

Yukio Mishima the novelist chose to die a fanatic's death, and the most Japanese death imaginable. On November 25, 1970, accompanied by four cadets from his Shield Society, he paid a visit to the commandant of the Japan Self-Defense Force. On his signal, the cadets seized the commandant and held him at swordpoint, while Mishima demanded through the barricaded office door that the 32 Regiment be assembled in the courtyard to attend a speech. At a few minutes past noon, he stepped out to the balcony and exhorted the soldiers to rise up with him against a postwar democracy that had deprived Japan of her army and her soul. He had intended speaking for thirty minutes, but since his words were inaudible above the jeers and hisses of the eight hundred angry men, he stopped after just seven. Then he withdrew to the commandant's office and committed *seppuku* (hara-kiri). When he had driven the blade into his left side and drawn it across his abdomen, he grunted a signal to the cadet standing behind him; the cadet beheaded him with a long sword, completing the ritual.

In two months, Mishima would have been forty-six. He had written forty novels, eighteen plays (all lavishly performed), twenty volumes of short stories, and as many of literary essays. He was a director, an actor, an accomplished swordsman and a muscle man; he had been up in an F-102 and had conducted a symphony orchestra; seven times he had traveled around the world, three times he had been nominated for the Nobel Prize. He was, besides, an international celebrity with a famous *zest for life*, a man who always seemed singularly capable of enjoying the rewards of his prodigious talent and superhuman will. A few days before the suicide he had been planning for fully a year, he confided to his mother that he had never done anything in his life he had wanted to do.

Despite the long tradition of *seppuku* in Japan, the Japanese were scarcely better able to fathom what Mishima did to himself than we in the West: everyone who knew him, Japanese and Westerner alike, felt compelled to attempt an explanation precisely because it was so impossible to imagine what he must have been thinking as he drove the steel into his side. Those who were able to believe that he had acted simply out of patriotic passion had their explanation ready-made: there is a long and gory tradition in Japan of hero-martyrs in the Imperial cause. Others suggested fatal disease, exhausted talent, or merely madness. A few, surprisingly few, whispered that Mishima was a masochist who might have enjoyed the pain.

It seems unlikely that any explanation can be complex enough to accommodate the reality of Mishima's suicide — I don't pretend to have one. I can only say that the story of his life as I perceive it *appears* to be principally about his erotic fascination with death. It appears, I mean, that Mishima wanted *passionately* to die all his life, and that he chose "patriotism" quite consciously as a means to the painful "heroic" death his lifelong fantasy prescribed. I don't believe necessarily that the ardent nationalism of his final years was a hoax. But it does seem to me that his suicide was in essence private, not social, erotic, not patriotic. I do not claim that my account is whole truth. I do believe it to be true.

I met Mishima in 1964 when I began to translate a novel of his called *The Sailor Who Fell from Grace with the Sea*, and for two years I saw quite a lot of him. I spent hours in his study late at night, before he began work, listening to him talk about the Japanese classics, or Oscar Wilde, or the dozen shades of red differentiated in the Chinese spectrum. I went with him to new restaurants to determine how large a bill two people could run up; I went with him to war movies, for which he had a passion. Briefly we lifted weights together at his gymnasium. And I was frequently the only foreigner at his parties, evenings at which his entire court was in attendance, young writers, boxers, movie stars, all nourishing themselves on what appeared to be his enormous vitality. It was a heady time for me: I was twenty-four, a student of literature at Tokyo University, and "friends" with the most famous novelist in the land.

Of course we weren't really friends. I was in awe of Mishima's power; he was literally a powerhouse who transmitted a palpable energy of brilliance and wit and even playfulness that was simulated but seemed real and was certainly irresistible. Mishima for his part was probably delighted with me, first because I was a good translator and he was avid for the Nobel Prize, but also because into the bargain I was capable of seeming nearly as physical as he seemed: in a word, I was the only good translator he was likely to encounter who could actually beat him at arm wrestling, and that mattered, I am certain.

Then at the end of 1965 I angered him by declining to translate his new novel when I had led him to believe I would, and he decided to have nothing further to do with me. I left Japan in April 1966, and on the way home to New York wrote a bitter article for *Life* in which I likened the experience of reading a Mishima novel to "attending an exhibition of the world's most ornate picture frames." I never saw or heard from him again, but I did learn from mutual friends that he was gravely offended.

When he died four years later and I decided to write a book I therefore assumed I would have to investigate his life without help from his family; I went to Japan in the fall of 1971 resigned to working as an outsider. Shortly after I arrived I came home one day to find I had had a call from Mishima's widow, Yoko Mishima. I was excited, and I was scared; what do you say to a woman your age whom you once knew to laugh and joke with whose husband has committed *seppuku?* I worried for a day and then I phoned. The maid got my name right the first time, as Mishima maids had always done; then she asked me to wait and switched on the music-box chimes I remembered from years before. Suddenly the music had stopped and Yoko was saying hello and asking how I had been. It was easier than I'd imagined: she didn't leave me the smallest opening to mumble condolences. She said she had a matter of business she wanted to discuss and asked if I were free later in the week. Naturally I was. Did I have a tie, she wondered, or was I as sloppy as ever. I had acquired a tie. Then I was to put it on and meet her at 8 P.M. at a restaurant called Zakuro in Akasaka. Her joshing, her preciseness, even the choice of restaurant were strikingly like Mishima; I later confirmed my feeling that Yoko had perfectly learned her husband's manner.

On the appointed day I was at the restaurant early. At 8 exactly Yoko appeared. She wore slacks and a sequined blouse, her hair in a tight permanent. The fun I remembered was vanished from her face; she looked harder, almost mannish. She led the way to a private room she had reserved, ordered dinner for us (I don't remember what) and whiskey and water for me. Once again there was no question of condolences: Yoko referred matter-of-factly to "the Incident" and "Mishima's death." Without a trace of self-pity she explained how difficult it was to manage the literary estate single-handedly, as she was doing. Then she got down to business, the translation of the tetralogy Mishima had completed just before his death. When I had known her before it had seemed to me Yoko wasn't even reading Mishima — certainly he would not have encouraged her — but now it was obvious she knew every book. We talked until midnight, then she drove me home. On the way I ventured to say what she doubtless knew already, that I hoped to write a biography. She said she would cooperate.

In the course of the year I visited Yoko half a dozen times. Usually she received me in the mid-afternoon, when she got back from school with the children. Once or twice she set the time at after ten o'clock at night, and it was my impression that she had just finished a meeting with her lawyers (the trial of the surviving cadets was in progress during 1972 and Yoko was overseeing their defense). The maid would show me into the sitting room on the first floor, Yoko would appear and pour us both a brandy. First I would present her with a list of Mishima books I had been unable to find elsewhere, and she would bring them to me from the "stacks" behind the study on the second floor. Then I would ask her to suggest new people to meet and she would add to my list of names. She declined to comment on the people she mentioned, saying only so-and-so for karate, so-and-so for Kabuki. But she did contact each of them subsequently and request them to talk to me. Without this clearance I would have been stopped in my tracks (as several other writers were), for Japan is a small and unimaginably cliquish country, and many of the people I interviewed, including an astonishing number I had never mentioned to Yoko, let me know they were acting on a go-ahead from her. About her own life with Mishima, she would not say a word. At our second meeting, as we discussed people I ought to talk to, I remarked as offhandedly as possible that I hoped also to hear "Yoko's story." She looked me straight in the face and said with a businesslike smile, "There is no Yoko story."

Nonetheless, Yoko did cooperate to the extent her feelings allowed, and I am grateful. But it was clear to me that she hated the idea of a book about her husband, that she did not want the story told. And what made it so very difficult was that I didn't blame her. For it is neither a happy nor a wholesome story, and from Yoko's point of view her two children know too much of it already, that their father abandoned them to disembowel himself. At least I imagined that was at the bottom of Yoko's stiffness as she dealt with me. It was as if she had resigned herself to someone writing the book, and decided it might as well be me, since I had known Mishima and could read him sensibly in his own language. But it was grim resignation nonetheless and, as I say, I didn't blame her.

My meetings with Mishima's parents were just as uncomfortable in their way. Since Mishima's mother, Shizue, was unquestionably the most important woman in his life, I was eager to speak with her as well as with his father, Azusa; but when I visited the parents' annex, Shizue did not appear. She was there, however, in an adjoining room, listening to my conversation with her husband and occasionally correcting him through the paper sliding doors, remarks like "*You* frightened him, that's why he cried," or "How would you know, you weren't around; you were never around when he needed you." In an American situation I would have greeted Shizue through the paper doors and asked whether she might join us, but in Tokyo that seemed unthinkable, and so I sat for several disconcerting hours, listening to the old man describe the Spartan training he had given his sons and pretending with him that Shizue wasn't there. Then, as I was leaving, with one foot out the door, she suddenly appeared, bowed to me, and said with an angelic smile and Azusa looking on, "Mr. Nathan, do you see what a sadist my husband is?" Several days later Shizue communicated to me that she would meet me secretly away from home, since she felt she could not speak freely in her husband's presence; subsequently I met her three times at a tiny kimono shop at Nihonbashi. Each time I had to sit in a corner of the miniature room, impossibly hulking and out of place, and wait for Shizue to finish examining the endless sample patterns and ask me what it was I wanted to know. When my cue came I would hurry through a list of questions which she answered laconically while the others in the room pretended not to hear. When I finished and thanked her she always murmured, "Thank goodness that's over."

I learned to expect that sigh of relief: save for the fanatics who were proud to rant about Mishima as a patriot, almost everyone was reluctant to speak about him openly. In some cases it was simply reluctance to disclose the kinds of secrets his life abounded in. But many of the people I met struck me as being guarded out of bitterness. Mishima had a great gift for making a man feel he was a closer friend than anyone else. Yet no one had even an inkling of the suicide which he had been planning for a year. When he died, each of his friends was obliged to acknowledge his ignorance to himself, and with it the cruel fact that he had known about Mishima only what Mishima had intended him to know. Most people who cared felt somehow used, even betrayed, certainly uncomfortable with their memories and loath to talk about them.

Nonetheless a picture did emerge in detail, more detail than Mishima would have forgiven. In fact, were I less profane, I would attribute the difficulty I experienced in writing every sentence to his impeding anger. I did not go so far, but I was relieved to encounter a line from Sainte-Beuve which said for me just what I would say to Mishima were he to confront me now. "When one does a study of *a considerable man*," wrote Sainte-Beuve, "one must dare to see and look at everything, and at least to indicate all that has been seen."

Jewel Farm
Princeton, New Jersey

January 14, 1974

xvi

contents

illustrations

With Kabuki female impersonator Utaemon, 1958

Wedding reception at International House, Tokyo, 1958

With his wife in their new home in Tokyo, 1959

Mishima and Yoko leaving on a trip around the world, 1958

Mishima and Yoko on the Staten Island Ferry, 1960

In his dining room, 1966

Working out at Korakuen gym, 1966

Posing in the snow, 1969

Posing with samurai sword, 1969

At Japan Self-Defense Force boot camp, 1969

At boot camp mess hall, 1969

Debating at student movement meeting at the University of Tokyo, 1969

Debating at the University of Tokyo

Mishima as Saint Sebastian (after Guido Reni), 1970

With members of the Shield Society, 1970

Addressing the Japan Self-Defense Force in Tokyo (Ichigaya), 1970

Addressing the Japan Self-Defense Force — a close-up

MISHIMA

one

1925-1937

Notwithstanding the legend he created about himself, Yukio Mishima was not "born a samurai." In fact, his forebears on his father's side were peasants of so mean a cast they lacked even a surname until the early nineteenth century. In the 1820s there appears for the first time in the temple register of the village of Shikata near Kobe in central Japan the name of Tazaemon Hiraoka and family. It is recorded simply that Tazaemon was "dispossessed" of his former home in a nearby village when his small son shot with his bow a pheasant belonging to the local lord. Thus it was that the founder of the Hiraoka house — Mishima was a pen name — came to the family seat in disgrace.

With Tazaemon's son Takichi the Hiraoka fortunes greatly improved. Takichi was a superior farmer and an entrepreneur into the bargain: by the 1850s the family had an impressively stocked warehouse and was even moneylending. But Takichi's greatest service to the Hiraoka family was sending his two sons away to get an education. The older, Manjiro, graduated from

3

the law department of the Imperial University to become a lawyer and, in 1898, a member of the newly created House of Representatives. The younger, Jotaro (Mishima's grandfather), followed his brother through the law department at the Imperial University and in 1892 entered the Ministry of the Interior at the age of twenty-nine. Jotaro Hiraoka was bright, ambitious, and very charming; he climbed the bureaucratic ladder quickly, ascending through a series of posts which culminated with his appointment in 1908 as governor of the Japanese colony on the island of Sakhalin, a post the more important since he was the first civilian to hold it.

In 1893, the year after his graduation from the Imperial University, Jotaro established what would later become Mishima's claim to aristocracy by marrying a brilliant, cultured, selfish and highly unstable young woman named Natsu Nagai. Natsu was from an illustrious samurai family; her paternal grandfather was a *daimyo*, lord of a fief, and related by marriage to the Tokugawa, for 250 years the ruling military family of Japan. Normally it would have been unthinkable that a young woman descended from the feudal nobility should marry the son of a peasant, but in this case two equalizing factors were at work. One was Jotaro's degree from the Imperial University, which admitted him to a small, prestigious elite. The other was what Natsu's family referred to as her "indisposition." Ever since childhood Natsu had been subject to fits of hysteria. In her early teens her condition had so distressed her parents that they had entrusted her to another noble family, the Arisugawas, cousins to the Meiji emperor, hoping that a change of environment would cure her. Natsu remained away until she was fifteen, but she was no better than before when she returned to her father's house. Thereafter, it was not simply that she was an embarrassment to the family;

4

since she happened to be the eldest of twelve children, the others could not properly marry before her. Thus her family was doubly anxious to have her off their hands.

It is not clear whether Natsu felt humiliated by the match her father made for her. But unquestionably the marriage itself led to a succession of humiliations public and private which taught her hatred for Jotaro and pity for herself. The trouble began in 1914, the seventh year of Jotaro's incumbency as governor of Sakhalin. Under pressure from the politicians who had secured him his appointment (notably Kei Hara of the Seiyukai), Jotaro sold some fishing and cannery licenses and sent the money to Tokyo to be used as campaign funds. Rival fishing companies leaked the news and a scandal developed; Jotaro resigned from the civil service. But his resignation was only the beginning of a dizzying descent. He had always had a taste, but no talent, for enterprise; and now disastrously he attempted to become an entrepreneur like his father before him: in ten years as an ingenuous businessman he not only lost the land and money Takichi had left the family but went heavily into debt. Old mortgages were sold, bankruptcy declared, family heirlooms tagged and carted off to auction. Finally, the mortgage on the family home in Tokyo was foreclosed and the Hiraokas had to move to the rented house where Mishima was born.

Jotaro was a failure, but he retained his gentleman's imperturbability and even his dash. He drank deeply of his beloved *sake*, sang in a fine tenor voice, and womanized indefatigably. In the words of his only son, Mishima's father, "he was absolutely unsuited for the management of a household — but an extraordinary gallant."

By 1925, when Mishima was born, Jotaro had retired loftily to the back parlor, where he spent his time receiving the former associates who had fleeced him and playing *go*. He was unique among the household in being immune to his wife's venom. And family problems were beneath him. He left his *go* board only to preside at family ceremonies such as the naming of his grandchildren.

Even before her husband's downfall, Natsu had been a selfish, haughty woman, quick to disdain and, as always, given to hysteria. Now as the family fortunes declined her wounded pride blazed ever higher and with it her extravagance. She had a passion for Kabuki theater, good restaurants, and shopping sprees; until Mishima was born she consoled herself chiefly by indulging her expensive tastes with a vengeance. To make things very much worse, she developed sciatic neuralgia, which afflicted her with spells of terrible pain and required her to live a semi-invalid life. In manic moments, when her physical pain had abated, Natsu could be a vivacious, exciting woman. She knew French and German, was a great reader, had a rich imagination and the storyteller's gift. But most of the time, essentially, she was a desperately unhappy woman whose manifold pain made her a bitter and a furious tyrant.

In the singularly unpleasant memoirs he published after his son's death, Mishima's father Azusa suggests rather coyly that Natsu's sciatica may have resulted from chronic gonorrhea caught from Jotaro. Years earlier in his autobiographical novel *Confessions of a Mask* Mishima had implied the same thing, as if the truth of it were tacitly acknowledged in the family: "Who knows but what those fits of depression she continued having until her death were a memento of vices in which my grandfather had indulged in his prime?" If this were true, and if Natsu knew about it, her bitterness and fury would require little further explanation.

Natsu's only son, Azusa, had suffered at his parents' hands

6

and had labored to become everything they were not. He was a straightlaced, unbending man, industrious and severely pragmatic. He was also something of a misanthrope, possibly because he had witnessed the results of his father's trust and pleasure in people; and this seems to have limited his success as a bureaucrat: in spite of his intelligence and all the proper credentials, including a degree from Imperial Law, he had managed by 1925 to rise only as high as deputy director of the Bureau of Fisheries in the Agriculture Ministry. The job paid moderately well but some of Jotaro's debts remained outstanding. Furthermore, Natsu saw to it that the family lived beyond its means. In the two-story house they rented in a good neighborhood in "uptown" Tokyo, the Hiraokas retained a houseboy and six maids, an extravagant number even in 1925, when girls would work for room and board. Azusa had little time in his life for anything but work and financial worry.

In 1924 Azusa married a quiet, sensitive girl named Shizue Hashi, the daughter of a middle school principal. For generations, Shizue's family had been educators and Confucian scholars; she was a lettered woman with a cultivated taste for literature (it was to his mother that Mishima would bring page by page the fiction he began to write when he was twelve, a practice he continued until the last year of his life). Naturally it was an arranged marriage: Shizue came to the Hiraoka house with no knowledge of the family situation. And her sheltered life as a scholar's daughter had not prepared her to cope. From the beginning Natsu confused and upset her; late at night the matriarch would suddenly call a cab and drag Shizue off to watch the final act at the Kabuki; the next day she would shun her. And Azusa treated her coldly when he was around, which was only late at night. Shizue spent her time

7

reading in the room upstairs where her first child was born on January 14, 1925.

That child was Mishima. When he was forty-nine days old he was formally named Kimitake, a name which reverberated with the family's aristocratic pretensions.

On Kimitake's fiftieth day of life, Natsu took him away from his mother and moved him, crib and all, into her darkened sickroom downstairs. And there she held him prisoner until he was twelve, jealously, fiercely, hysterically guarding him against his parents and the outside world. Possibly she hoped to instill in her first grandchild the values she believed were his birthright — not as a lowly Hiraoka but a noble Nagai — and thereby to live on in him. Certainly her insane possessiveness suggests that her motives were largely selfish; it was as if she wanted someone to share the burden of her physical pain, her humiliation, her comprehensive despair. Kimitake's sister Mitsuko and brother Chiyuki were raised as their parents' children: Natsu took no interest in them.

From the beginning, Natsu demanded and received what amounted to total control of her grandson's life. While Kimitake was nursing, she would ring a buzzer in Shizue's room every four hours to inform her it was time and then would limp upstairs with the baby in her arms. According to Shizue, "Mother would stand over me while Kimitake nursed, timing him on a pocket watch she always carried. When the time was up she would snatch him away and take him back downstairs to her room. I would lie in bed wishing I could hold Kimitake and feed him to his heart's content."

Shizue continues: "Even when Kimitake got to be three, permission for him to be taken out into the air was granted only when the weather was fine. He was five or six before I was allowed to go out with him alone, without the maids, and

8

only then on sunny, windless days. As long as Mother had charge of him he had to wear his winter coat and muffler and even a face mask throughout April and most of May.

"Mother thought that boys were dangerous playmates so the only friends she permitted Kimitake were three older girls she carefully selected from among his cousins. Naturally Kimitake's play was limited to dolls and house and *origami* or possibly blocks. And it had to be even quieter than girls' play normally is, because Mother's sciatica made her sensitive to noise and she insisted the children play in her room. Cars or guns or trains — anything that made a metallic noise — were absolutely taboo. Kimitake loved to take a ruler or a broomstick and swing it around over his head. I suppose he was unconsciously letting out his resentment. But these things were judged dangerous and taken away from him.

"My husband and I bought a record player which we kept upstairs in our room; but as I watched Kimitake sitting there in front of it playing children's songs for hours on end I would begin to worry about him. It was so nice outside, and so dark and damp in the house, I wanted to take him out for some sun and air. But the minute I tried to sneak him out while Mother dozed, she would wake up, confine him to the house, and lead him back into her room where the shutters were always closed. As Kimitake's mother there were so many things I wanted to do for him, but my plans were always thwarted. It was such a futile feeling."

Shizue knew that her son was being raised unnaturally, but there was nothing she could do. She was only the daughter-in-law, not even a guest so much as a stranger in the house of her husband's parents, with hardly more status than the maids. For the twelve years that Natsu maintained her fierce domin-

9

ion, Shizue was alone with her unhappiness: she tried to hide it from the boy, and Azusa would not hear of it.

While Natsu lived, Azusa seems to have been subject to his mother's will, more her only child than Kimitake's father. Unquestionably he was distressed, he admits as much; and there were times when he fought his mother for some small freedom for his son, such as going for a walk. But in general he refused to admit to himself how unnatural the situation was and forbade Shizue to speak her mind in his presence.

For what she judged to be his indifference to their child's fate, Shizue hated her husband: by the time Kimitake was returned to his parents, their marriage was badly damaged. Today, out of Azusa's hearing, Shizue says bitterly that her son's dark fate was sealed by the time he was twelve, and adds that she longed for years to leave the house and take him with her. But that was out of the question. In her dowry, in the traditional manner, her mother had packed a Japanese dagger. Its significance was that she was not to return to her own home alive, no matter what unhappiness she might encounter in her new life.

Natsu had justified her decision to move the baby into her own room on the grounds that raising a child on the second floor was hazardous. Undoubtedly the stairs were steep, as they are in all Japanese houses. And when Kimitake was two he did fall backward from the third step. Shizue's recollection of the incident evokes the atmosphere in the house during the early years: "One day when Mother was at the Kabuki and the whole household was having a festival in her absence, Kimitake started up the stairs when no one was looking and tumbled backward, cutting his forehead. It wasn't a bad fall but there was a surprising amount of blood, so we took him to a nearby clinic and had Mother paged at the theater. She came rushing home and stopped just inside the door. She was making an effort to control herself, but I could see the state she was in by the color in her face and by the way she gripped the handle of her cane. There was a moment of silence, we were all too frightened to speak. Finally Mother walked over to my husband and said very slowly and clearly, 'Is he dead?' My husband shook his head; and without another word or a glance at anyone Mother walked past us down the long corridor to her room, where Kimitake was already asleep, and very quietly closed and locked the door." Thereafter Kimitake was forbidden to climb the stairs without permission from Natsu. The new rule not only assured her of his safety but guaranteed he would not be upstairs with his mother when she was out of the house.

Kimitake's response to the circumstances of his childhood was frighteningly internal. His parents agree that he accepted Natsu's rule without protest or even apparent emotion. When Natsu stormed out of her room to confiscate a "hazardous" or a "noisy" toy Shizue had bought for him, he would surrender the toy without expression, even if Shizue was in the room; when Natsu forbade him to play out-of-doors, or later, to join his class on excursions, he would sit playing quietly in her room for as long as she kept him there. Nor did he ever complain to his mother when he was with her, or in any way attempt to enlist her aid in opposing his grandmother. On the surface, Kimitake appears to have been a small boy resigned to his fate.

Shizue insists that her son deferred to Natsu because he understood by the time he was three that the slightest truculence would result in misery to her. At least a part of this seems to have been objective truth. So advanced was Natsu's jealousy that she interpreted any disobedience from Kimitake as evidence of his preference for his mother, and found endless vengeful ways to retaliate — against Shizue. If Kimitake relied on his mother for anything, however trivial, without asking Natsu first, she would fly into one of her "rages" and scold both her grandson and his mother.

Shizue implies that Kimitake's principal allegiance was to her. But it is more likely that he was in love with both the women in his life, felt compelled in a child's way to keep peace between them, and judged, under the circumstances soundly, that the way to accomplish this was to defer to Natsu on the one hand and at the same time to conceal his anxiety from his mother in her presence. What this performance required of him was that he conceal his feelings from both women, at an enormous emotional cost to himself. Reality was cruel, demanding, unspeakably difficult. And all the evidence argues that at a very early age Kimitake created an alternative to which he withdrew when he was alone.

In *Confessions of a Mask*, Mishima portrays himself at five as a child with a developed antipathy for reality and an irresistible fantasy world to pose against it. It is a world of "Night and Blood and Death," of beautiful princes being slain or devoured or lovingly executed, of "the most sophisticated of cruelties and the most exquisite of crimes." The child feels vaguely guilty about his immersion in these fantasies; and although he is not aware of their significance, they frighten him. Yet they are far more beautiful, and even more real, than reality itself; and he is helpless to resist them.

From the beginning the boy views reality as an invading enemy. At four he is uneasily in love with a picture in one of his books, of a beautiful knight astride a white horse. He spends whole afternoons gazing at the knight and rapturously imagining the death he is about to confront. One afternoon his "sicknurse" catches him dreaming over the picture and informs him that the knight is Joan of Arc, not a He but a She. The child is thunderstruck: "This was the first *revenge by reality* that I had met in life, and it seemed a cruel revenge, particularly upon the sweet fantasies I had cherished concerning *his* death. From that day on I turned my back on the picturebook." At four the child lacks the strength of imagination to defend his fantasies against the invader. But he quickly learns to "edit" reality to accord with his fantasies. At five,

the things that were happening before my eyes — my grandmother's spells or the petty family quarrels — and the fanciful events of the fairytale world in which I had just become immersed seemed to me to be of equal value and like kind. I could not believe that the world was any more complicated than a structure of building blocks, nor that the so-called 'social community,' which I must presently enter, could be more dazzling than the world of fairy tales.

There is no knowing whether the fantasies Mishima attributes to himself were truly in his head when he was five. But it seems certain that he did develop formidable defenses against reality at a very tender age. His father relates a little episode which suggests how advanced these defenses had become by the time he was four: "On one of the many occasions when I had fought with my mother and finally pulled Kimitake away from her and taken him out for a walk, we came to a railroad crossing just as a steam engine was roaring down the tracks toward us belching black smoke and making a terrific racket. There was a fence separating us from the tracks, but the engine passed so close you could touch it if you put out your hand. I thought to myself, Here is a perfect chance for some spartan training. I lifted Kimitake and, shielding his face with my hat, held him out toward the engine and said 'Are you scared?

13

Don't worry — and if you cry like a weakling I'll throw you in a ditch.' As I spoke I looked down at Kimitake's face and was astonished to see there was no reaction. I waited for the next train and tried again, but the result was the same, no effect! Was he like a puppy I wondered, too young to know fear, or had the schoolgirl training he was getting from my mother made him insensitive to this kind of turbulent, masculine experience? I felt deflated. The next day I came back and tried with a quieter train. But Kimitake's face was the same Nō mask as before. I gave up. I couldn't solve the riddle."

Azusa swears every word of this is true and repeats his own bewilderment each time he tells the story. The episode antici-pates the insensitivity that would characterize him as a father when he came into his own after Natsu's death. And it sug-gests about Kimitake that he was close to autistic. That was not the case, however: most of the time he was all too painfully in touch with reality, acutely conscious of its demands and laboring to meet them.

Just before his fifth birthday, Kimitake vomited something "the color of coffee" and went into a coma. The diagnosis was autointoxication, the prognosis negative. Relatives gathered in the house; Shizue quietly collected the toys and clothing she intended to place in Kimitake's coffin. Natsu locked herself in her room. Late that night, Shizue's brother, a professor of medicine, announced that the crisis had passed. In a week Kimitake was well again, but for more than a year the attacks recurred once a month, hospitalizing him each time. The condition disappeared when Kimitake began to go to school, as if all his system wanted was temporary liberation from the two women in his life.

In April 1931, Kimitake entered the first grade at the Gakushu-in, the Peers' School. The school had been established in the 1870s as a private institution for children of the Imperial family and the new aristocracy. Originally a child had to be from a titled family to qualify for admission. But by 1931 roughly a third of the students were commoners, including Kimitake Hiraoka. To be sure, Natsu's ancestors had been feudal aristocracy, but their loyalty to the old regime had discredited both her grandfathers with the new government, and neither side of the family had been granted peerage under the new system.

Inasmuch as Kimitake was not only a commoner but middle class he had no business being at the Peers' School, which remained distinctly aristocratic. But given Natsu's obsession with her past and the family's pretensions, it was the inevitable choice. Noblemen's sons were admitted without an entrance examination, but Kimitake had to take one. The whole family, including Jotaro, accompanied him to the auditorium and waited outside until the test was over. Kimitake passed easily: he had been reading and even scribbling poems since he was five.

Kimitake's first six years of school were mostly miserable. Possibly he felt humiliated by the humbleness of his background and home. Even the commoners in his class tended to be wealthy children who lived in large, grand houses. And the young aristocracy treated their commoner classmates and even the teachers with aristocratic hauteur. They went to school tuition-free and were excused from all examinations. In the teachers' rollbook (known as "the devil's log") there were circles entered alongside their names; teachers addressed them in polite forms. It was common to hear the eight-year-old son of a duke inform his friends loudly and in the man's presence that his teacher was "an old retainer," meaning that his ancestors had been family vassals.

But Kimitake's major problem was that he had no notion of how to behave with boys. He was frail, shy, girlish in his manner. Naturally his classmates made him suffer for it. He was known as "asparagus child" or "snake-belly" and treated as the class runt. And Natsu's protectiveness reinforced his isolation. After his preschool illness and a recurrent lung infection which kept him out of school on and off throughout the first grade, she doubled her watch over his health. She restricted his diet to the blandest kinds of whitefish, which meant he was not allowed to eat in the school cafeteria. She saw to it that he was excused from the physical education program. And until he was in the fourth grade she would not allow him to accompany his class on excursions.

The earliest Mishima prose I have seen is a composition he wrote in the second grade, called "Excursion to Enoshima":

I didn't go along on the excursion.
When I woke up on the twentieth I thought, everybody must be at Shinjuku station by now, or already on the train.
Those were the first thoughts in my head.
When I have time I go to my grandmother's or my mother's room to talk.
When I thought of everybody arriving at Enoshima I wanted to go so badly I could hardly stand it.
I have never been to Enoshima so I wanted to go even more.
I thought about it from morning to night.
When I went to sleep I had the following dream.
I went along with the others on the Enoshima excursion.
And I had a good time but there were rocks and I couldn't walk.
That is when I woke up.

Kimitake's loneliness is clear in this and so is his dependence on the two women. But the saddest thing is his resignation, as if it were only natural that he should be forbidden to go along.

Except in a dream. Kimitake spent his time indoors, playing quietly with his girl cousins, reading fairy tales, and dreaming beautiful, frightening dreams.

In 1934, when Kimitake was nine and had just entered the fourth grade, the family moved a few stations down the line into two small houses on the same street. In the smaller, darker house lived Kimitake's parents and the two younger children. Kimitake lived with Jotaro and Natsu in a house two doors away. One reason for this drastic move seems to have been Azusa's promotion to section chief. In his new post he was obliged to have his subordinates home from time to time, but the only parlor in the Yotsuya house was occupied day and night by Jotaro and his "associates." Since it was unseemly that the two sets of guests should run into one another, it was decided to separate. Such is the official family explanation; but according to Mishima's brother Chiyuki, the move was at least partly financial. Azusa's promotion was an increase more in status than in salary. And as Japan prepared for "expansion" in China, the cost of living was going up. Possibly the family was finding it difficult to afford the big house, the six maids, the new children and Kimitake's tuition, not to mention Jotaro's outstanding debts. There is no proof of this. But it is a fact that the new houses were "shabby" and that three of the maids were let go.

During the three years the family lived apart, Kimitake was in his parents' house infrequently. Shizue walked him to school in the morning and in the afternoon brought him back, to Natsu's house. Natsu awaited him with the three o'clock snack she prepared with her own hands every afternoon and served him in her room. When Kimitake had eaten and recited his lessons for an hour or so, he was generally permitted to visit Shizue, but never to stay for dinner. When for whatever reason Natsu's jealousy was enflamed or her sciatica was acting up, she would forbid Kimitake to visit the other house for three and four days at a time. Chiyuki, who was only five when the family separated, remembers that he and his sister Mitsuko took it for granted that their brother was someone they rarely saw. They were free to visit their grandmother's house, but she treated them coldly and they preferred to play together at home. Shizue could have spent more time with Kimitake herself if she had visited him but says she couldn't bear to be with her son under Natsu's possessive eye.

These were the cruelest years for Shizue, who insists that Kimitake suffered unspeakably with Natsu and lived for his brief visits with her. She describes him as "overjoyed the minute he was in the door, laughing and running around the house and doing all the things he couldn't do with Her." She adds, sadly, that "he would stop what he was doing the minute it was time to leave without a word of complaint, and when he said goodbye he was always smiling." Shizue interprets his "cheerfulness" as an act Kimitake put on for her benefit; and to a degree this may have been true. But his life with Natsu was probably not the unrelieved horror Shizue imagined it to be. Chiyuki remembers his brother at eleven and twelve talking fondly of Natsu and excitedly retelling her tales. "I could never understand what Kimitake liked about that ferocious old woman," he told me, "but he definitely loved her." Undoubtedly he did, in an anxious, devastating way. His physical separation from his mother may even have made it easier for him to be his grandmother's child.

But there was one aspect of Kimitake's life with Natsu which unquestionably was a nightmare. Her sciatica was worse, and complicated now by stomach ulcers and kidney disease. Kimitake was still living and sleeping in her room, and when

he was home, nursing her. Natsu would take her medicine
only from her "little tiger," as she called him; Kimitake had to
sponge her brow and massage her back and hip; and it was
Kimitake who led her by the hand on her frequent trips to the
toilet. The worst times were at night. When Natsu's pain was
bad she would cry and tear her hair, imploring Kimitake to
comfort her. At least once she seized a knife and held it to her
throat, screaming she would kill herself. These moments must
have been torture to the boy. Shizue says the only complaining
she ever heard from him was when he would tell her that he
didn't know what to do when Grandmother cried.

Kimitake's situation during these years was close to unimaginable, and it is hard to be precise about his feelings with
any confidence, particularly since he never spoke about this
period in his life or wrote about it at any length. There is,
however, a passage embedded in a long story he wrote when he
was sixteen, two years after Natsu's death, which seems to
express his anxiety during these years of separation. It begins
with a reconstruction of the physical reality:

My father was rarely in the main house. He built a kind of
retreat for himself in a corner of the garden, alongside the greenhouse, and lived in it. . . . In the main house lived my grandmother
and my mother. In my child's way I was puzzled by my parents'
separation. At night, when my grandmother's pain had exhausted
her and she was deep asleep and I was breathing as though fast
asleep myself (in fact I was observing my mother's movements
through half-open eyes) I would see my mother step into garden
sandals and hurry away through the moonlit orchard to my father's cottage, pulling with her a shadow so long it reached even
to where I lay. At such times — was it an evil reaction, I wonder?
— my only feelings as I watched my mother's receding form were
of pleasure and approval.

19

Surely the author has in mind his own passage back and forth between Natsu's house — the "main house" — and his mother's. The furtiveness of the rendezvous and the narrator's fear that it is evil of him to observe them with "pleasure and approval" reflect the guilt Kimitake associated with his longing for his mother, and, more generally, his anxiety at being caught between the two women in a tug-of-war for his love and allegiance. The passage also suggests that he longed for his father to play a more central role in his life, or at least that he was moved to normalize his situation in some way. Kimitake continues with a telling "description" of life with Natsu:

My grandmother suffered from neuralgia and was constantly having spasms. They began suddenly, as if something had possessed her. As her subdued moaning became audible the spasm would spread across the room like an invisible undulation, across the cigarette tray, the incense burner, the medicine chest, and for just an instant the room would go numb, as though paralyzed. But that sudden tension would dispel as quickly as mist and in the next instant everything in the room would be permeated with her grieved, monotonic moaning. This groaning of the room itself is probably unimaginable to someone who has not experienced it. But when the spasms continued for an entire day, or at times for nights on end, a more distinct sign would appear: "disease" would occupy the house as if it were the owner.

"Pour my medicine, little friend," my grandmother said to me in a just-awakened voice. The sound came entirely from her aged throat, soft, blurred, like the trailing of a brush stroke. But because she had tried to sit up as she spoke she began to groan again. She always drank her medicine from a wineglass with a stem. Sitting straight up with my knees together, just the slightest bit nervous about my important task, I opened the medicine bottle. I still remember the sound of the cork as it was liberated, a flat, spiritless, now that I think about it, portentous sound. I tilted the bottle of thick, wine-colored medicine and carefully lifted it to the glass.

I knew from experience that the glass would take only a small quantity, and my deliberateness should have been almost unconscious. But I still remember feeling this particular time a peculiar awkwardness — nothing flowed from the bottle, as if the liquid were being blocked by something the same color. I held the bottle up to the light and shook it gently. It was empty. Again I tilted the bottle. Nothing. Suddenly I realized. Like the hinges on a door that will open no farther, the bones in my wrist would not bend past a certain perilous angle. It seemed to me this must be a superstition, I sensed it was ridiculous. At the same time I could feel myself becoming terrified. Now the trembling of my hands made it impossible for me to tilt the bottle safely. Just then I saw very clearly one creature, one "disease" in the bottle. He was small, like a dwarf, and he was sleeping with his chin on his knees, as if totally unaware of the sea of medicine washing his body.

To the old rooms at the back of the house I went to see the helmets and the armor and the large swords like black hairy legs. The way back! The maid would leave me at the hall that led to the toilet and say, as she went away, "You won't be afraid from here." The truth is that the most frightening part still lies ahead, from here to my grandmother's room three or four rooms away. There is one long hall and three turnings — shaking with fear I run down the dark hall. And at every turning I meet at least one "disease." They are in a great hurry too. They are much taller than I. Some have no faces and some do. One who had a face — he was smiling innocently. He must have been a "disease" not intimate with "death" yet. He must have been taking news to a "disease" more intimate with "death." One day the little finger on my right hand just brushed that slimy, invisible presence. All day long, whenever I had a minute, I washed that finger. I scrubbed it so hard that the tip swelled painfully and the fingerprint, which I had never noticed, appeared with a curious, clean distinctness. The fingerprint made me think of the grain in the ceiling of the room where I could not sleep, and also of the hieroglyphics habitually employed by "disease."

This speaks eloquently for itself. It is morbid, and so at sixteen was its author. Small wonder. For twelve years he had lain awake studying "the grain in the ceiling" of Natsu's sickroom, while at his side his grandmother moaned like one possessed.

In March 1937, one month before Kimitake entered the seventh grade, Natsu suddenly announced it was time for him to rejoin his parents. She was sixty-two and very ill; Jotaro had been trying to persuade her for a year to release her grandson. The minute she heard the news, Shizue rushed out to look for a larger house. Three weeks later, the younger Hiraokas and their three children moved to a modest but comfortable house in the Shibuya district. It was a happy moment for everyone, but particularly for Shizue and Kimitake. Now for the first time in his life he had a room of his own where he was free to study — and to write. For the first time in his life, as Shizue put it, he had come home.

two

1937-1945

The move away from Natsu's insane bedside was a relief, but no sooner had the family reunited than Azusa revealed himself as a martinet with a temper to match Natsu's and none of her imagination. As he explains today, "A parent has to apply pressure. You squeeze and you squeeze, and any child that collapses is better off dead."

In fact Azusa had always been an unsympathetic husband and a frightening father. But until Kimitake joined the family he had not been in the house enough to realize how very unhappy his parents were, nor had he been under his father's jurisdiction. Now for the first time he witnessed Azusa's cruelty to Shizue; at the same time he found himself the principal object of his father's severity. Azusa was strict with all the children (Chiyuki was regularly reviled and punished for being "a dullard") but with Kimitake in particular he was tyrannical, as if driven by guilt to undo what he considered the "girlish" effects of life with Natsu. In the beginning he concentrated his attack against Kimitake's "bookishness."

23

Although Kimitake was now free to go out of doors when he liked, he preferred to stay in and read; as a twelve- and thirteen-year-old he was discovering Oscar Wilde, Rilke, the court classics and the great Japanese decadent Jun'ichiro Tanizaki; and he was rarely without a book. This seems to have infuriated Azusa. He would snatch books out of Kimitake's hands, verify that they were literature, tear them or hurl them across the room, and send Kimitake upstairs to bed. In Azusa's immovable view, literature was lies and corruption, girlish nonsense at best, and he would not stand for it.

In January 1938, less than a year after the family had moved to Shibuya, Azusa was promoted to director of the Bureau of Fisheries, which had its offices in Osaka, three hundred and fifty miles west of Tokyo. Since this was a considerable pro-motion, there was no question that he would make the move. But because Shizue's health was poor and Natsu was against taking the children out of school, it was decided that he would go alone. From 1938 until he resigned from the civil service in 1942, Azusa was in the house only two or three nights a month. He had a vague idea that Kimitake was writing a "bit of poetry" and this displeased him. He did not suspect how far things had gone, and Shizue had no trouble keeping him in the dark.

When Azusa was home the house was stormy. When he was away, which was most of the time, Shizue and the children lived together happily. Kimitake was fond of his brother and adored his sister Mitsuko. But Chiyuki remembers that it took him and his sister a long time before they began to feel that their older brother was more than a guest in the house. He and Mitsuko liked to gang up on Kimitake for the pleasure of watching how quickly he would flee to his own room. There he spent most of his time, reading and writing, and there he was happiest.

It was during this period that a passionate bond developed between Kimitake and his mother. The first summer the family was together, Shizue took the three children for a month at the beach. Azusa had decided it was time for Kimitake not only to get some real sun but to learn to swim. Ever since he had contracted adenitis of the lung in the first grade, the family doctor had advised against exposing him to direct rays of the sun and Natsu had interpreted this to mean that daylight was deadly. Kimitake had grown up almost entirely indoors: at twelve he looked no more than eight or nine; he was thin as a reed, weak, pale as the underbelly of a fish. He did not learn to swim that summer. In fact his first encounter with the ocean disturbed him deeply. But he did fall in love with his mother. This was the first time in his life he had been free to depend on Shizue without interference or internal conflict; one month was all he needed to discover that she was the woman for him. From then on no other woman ever really mattered. Shizue, on her part, free at last to express the love pent up in her for twelve years, adored and continued to adore Kimitake in a manner almost too ardent to be called motherly.

Not that Natsu had dropped from the picture. When she released Kimitake she made him promise to telephone her every afternoon when he returned from school and to spend one night a week with her. This he did faithfully until she died two years later. She also retained the final vote in important decisions about his life. For example, the Peers' School required middle form students to live in the campus dormitory for at least one year. Shizue wanted Kimitake to have this experience, but Natsu ruled against it and Azusa followed suit. Natsu was afraid dormitory life would be injurious to

Kimitake's health and an unwholesome influence on his "moral development." When he was twenty, Mishima would write sardonically, "But I was able to fly at the Hell in my mind no matter how closely my grandmother and my father clipped my wings."

But there was at least one respect in which Natsu now contributed positively to Kimitake's pleasure and development. Shortly after he moved to Shibuya, she began taking him with her to the Kabuki theater. For years she had been priming his interest with souvenirs she brought home from the theater, accounts of the plays, and backstage gossip about her favorite actors. And she chose his first play well; it was *Chushingura — The Tale of the 47 Ronin —* a celebration of feudal allegiance which is perhaps the most exciting of the great Kabuki classics. From the moment the curtain went up Kimitake was captive. And very quickly he became a real aficionado. He read the entire repertoire, copied lines in his notebook, and even learned to imitate the deliveries of the most famous actors. For the rest of his life, Mishima went to the Kabuki at least once a month. He wrote eight plays for the Kabuki stage in the traditional Kabuki style, the last of which he directed himself shortly before his death. Kabuki actors agree that he was the only contemporary playwright capable of handling "grand Kabuki" conventions and language authentically.

In January 1939, a few days after Kimitake's fourteenth birthday, Natsu died of hemorrhaging ulcers. According to Azusa, Kimitake's face when he heard the news was the same "Nō mask" that had distressed his father years before at the railroad crossing. Shizue's explanation is that Kimitake was so attached to her by this time that his grandmother's death had not affected him. That is unlikely, but it does seem that whatever Kimitake was feeling he was careful not to show it. Nor did he ever talk or write about Natsu except to note in passing that he had been raised "a grandma's boy."

Nonetheless it is scarcely possible to exaggerate Natsu's effect on Kimitake's life. Very likely the domestic situation . she created was the basis for the latent homosexuality already beginning to trouble him as he grew into pubescence. But her influence on his life was even more comprehensive: by whispering into Kimitake's ear for all those years her profound dissatisfaction with herself and her wildly poetic longing for a distant past, an elegant past, a past of beauty, she can be said to have afflicted him with "the romantic agony." Surely he was in its grip by the time he was a twelve-year-old, longing like a true romantic for purity and beauty and possessed by a fierce impossible desire to be other than himself.

All this and more — the sum of which might be called Natsu's legacy — is clear on every page of the first fiction Kimitake wrote, in the summer of his twelfth year. The first thing he did when he entered the seventh grade in April 1937 was to join the large, active literature club, which boasted an entire school of famous writers as alumni (the White-Birch School) and consequently was highly serious about itself. Throughout elementary school, Kimitake's composition master had tried to cure his "unpleasant precociousness" with poor marks. Fortunately his new teacher recognized his talent and encouraged him to join the club and to begin writing in earnest. In November 1937 he submitted "Six Poems on Autumn" to the club's biannual journal, and these appeared in the December issue. The next issue carried more of his poetry and his first short story. Called "Sorrel Flowers — A Memory of Youth," it described a six-year-old's encounter with an escaped convict. The boy is forbidden by his mother to play on a hill near his house, because a convict is known to have escaped from the prison on top of the hill. But the season is early summer, and the hill is on fire with blooming sorrel. The boy sneaks out of the house and goes to play on the forbidden hill:

He took from his pocket a white ball and threw it high into the air.

Blue sky.

The sky clung to the ball, rose, then fell with terrible swiftness. He caught the ball and rejoiced, as if he had captured the blue sky. Then he breathed the air, deeply, deeply. Not in rooms or in the streets had he ever breathed such air. It was more like eating than breathing. Into his mouth he stuffed the air with its strange taste and fragrance, the blue sky, the clouds. Whence came their flavor and fragrance he did not know.

Yet he did know, he felt he understood the source.

Joy welled in him again. To have verified the source of the air's flavor and fragrance was the greatest joy.

Now he perceived the vitality of the earth.

The earth began a dance like the pounding of a heart; and his feet naturally took up the step. The woods and everything in them began a musical accompaniment.

The music — the song — he understood it all. The woods were singing, and the sea of green fields to the north of the hill. Small birds were singing.

At that moment he could even have spoken with the little birds.

Exuberant, the boy wanders into the woods at the foot of the hill and loses his way. The moon rises. Suddenly a man steps out of the shadows:

"Where . . . are . . . you . . . going?"

"I started on a journey but I forgot something at home."

"You mean the gray house on the hill? The one they call the prison?"

"That's right. My house is called the prison." The man was surprised.

"Then you must be the convict. And you've forgotten something in the prison. And when you get it you'll come back out again."

The boy pursued and held the man's eyes with his own.

The boy's eyes were an autumn lake, so clear you could count the grains of sand on the bottom. What frightful purity! It was that perfect clarity that was frightening. When you see a perfect pearl you cannot bring yourself to touch it for a time. Ah, how frightening, how majestic. . . .

"Yes," the man murmured, and as he spoke the godlike boy rushed at him and buried his face in the arms outstretched to him and wept. A *nightingale* high in a tree wept too.

"You mustn't come back out. We'll be forbidden to play on the hill again. Go straight back to your gray house!"

. . .

The man sighed. He looked up at the moon. Now his own eyes were as clear as Akihiko's.

"I had a child. A pretty little boy just like you."

"Where is he now?"

"Now he is a seagull flying above the vast sea. And when he spies the silver glitter of scales among the waves he thrusts his neck into the water and he says, I was murdered on the gray evening sea. My murderer sank to the dark, dark bottom. Until he floats to the surface I must remain suspended here on these white wings in the low clouds of the sky."

"What do you mean?"

The man continued: "But the devil who killed that poor poor seagull has found his way up to the surface. And you know who showed him the way — it was you. So I'm going to make you happy. I'll go back to prison."

The convict leaves the boy at the edge of the woods and climbs the hill to the "gray house." A year passes. As the sorrel begins to bloom again the convict emerges from the prison gates a free man. The boy and his friends are waiting for him:

29

His face appeared. The man came out.
His face glowed — the light was everywhere.
Ah, the children flew to him. They sat on the green.
Radiance!
Sorrel,
Sorrel!
The sorrel flowers here, there —
The children glanced down at the foot of the hill. A black, small mass was approaching — women.
Akihiko's mother, Toshiko's mother, three, four. . . .
Their footsteps were chill. When they approached they took their children by the hand. "Touching a convict! How dirty!"
With their handkerchiefs they wiped their children's hands. The handkerchiefs fluttered. The man's eyes watched.
The women shouted fiercely at the man. In silence the man stooped and picked the sorrel flowers. And when he had given one to each child, he walked quickly away without looking back.
Each child had a flower in his right hand.
"Throw that away!"
The mothers' voices were sharp. The sorrel flowers dropped to the ground glowing with the setting sun.
Ah, the sorrel flowers burned with red heat.

Like all fantasy, "Sorrel" originates in longing. But it is important to see that the ecstatic identification with nature the boy achieves on the hill is sham, the earliest example of Mishima disguising his desire. There is no question that the young author was feeling irresistibly drawn to a dance *like the pounding of a heart*. But it is equally certain that the dance climaxed not amid the bright flowers on the hill but in the dark, forbidden woods, at the moment when the boy throws himself into the arms of a filicide while high in a tree a nightingale weeps. It is in this unmistakably erotic, vaguely homosexual embrace that the author seeks the ecstasy he is helpless to resist. It is the beauty of this moment, not of the dance on the hill, that grips his heart. The essential elements are a dark woods, a beautiful, weeping boy, and a murderer. Here is a model of the beauty which would compel and terrify Mishima all his life.

The principal object of longing in "Sorrel" is the ecstatic dance beginning to beckon Kimitake. But there is something more. At twelve he contemplates with awe the "frightful purity" of a "godlike" boy with eyes as "clear as an autumn lake." Surely his awe of the boy's purity is engendered by the feeling that he has lost his own. In a poem written just before "Sorrel" he says as much:

ECHO

People say this cave
(Leads to Hell)
Into this finely darkly excised devil's mouth
No one has entered.
It is a cave which guards an eternal riddle and mystery.
Yet I stood before that insistent cave
And called out in gentle words of love.
But the answering echo
Was not my present voice:
It was the innocent voice of years gone by.

The innocence in the poem and the purity of the godlike boy are identical; the Hell to which the cave is access corresponds to the ecstatic dance evoked in "Sorrel." The story demonstrates Kimitake's awareness, only semiconscious perhaps, that the dance is forbidden, accessible only in the violation of a taboo. It also reveals him beginning to identify the dance as erotic and specifically homosexual: it is no accident that the agents of reality who interrupt the boy's forbidden dream are women. Finally "Sorrel" betrays the anxiety that accompanied Kimitake's awakening, his sense of having lost his innocence. Like the cave in the poem, the dance beckons irresistibly. But the voice of gentle love in which the poet responds is a voice of innocence no longer his own. The poet is awakening to the nature of the "riddle and mystery" the cave guards: innocence (purity) has been banished by consciousness, which gives rise to shame and to fear. Yet the cave remains "insistent."

Until he was sixteen, Kimitake considered himself primarily a poet, and poetry poured from him to fill a notebook a week. Generally it is bad poetry, self-consciously precocious, the work of a brilliant adolescent seeking refuge from experience in words. Much of it has in common a dank, unwholesome eroticism, the result of the poet's disguising his fantasies to accord with his notion of "normal" desire. Beginning in 1940, as Kimitake turned fifteen, the verse becomes more overtly homosexual and more troubled:

> Your hand trembles in mine
> Like a frightened pigeon. I fear
> Your pink beak will peck
>   My youth, the only fruit.
> Morning.
> The forest shadows on this side of the forest.
> The fountain gushes and quickly subsides.

(1940)

At the Peers' School Kimitake's poetry was fulsomely admired by students and faculty alike. The first to recognize his talent was a nobleman's son named Toshitami Bojo. In the fall of 1937, when Kimitake submitted his first poetry to the journal, Bojo was in his last year at school (the fourteenth grade) and had just retired as editor. He was twenty years old, eight years Kimitake's senior, but was so impressed by the poetry that he set out at once to meet the poet. His account of their first meeting (written after Mishima's death) is redolent of the atmosphere at the Peers' School in the prewar years:

Picking out the first-year middle-formers in the rooting section was an easy matter: no matter how they tried to dirty them the cherry blossom insignia on their school caps and uniform buttons retained their metal brightness. And there were their shrill voices, like small birds — first-year boys were not allowed to stop cheering for even a minute; and they were more afraid of upperclassmen than teachers. . . .

I walked up to the first year bunch and tapped one on the shoulder. He turned around and snapped to attention.

"Is Kimitake Hiraoka here?"

"Yes, Sir —"

I followed his gaze to the first row of benches.

"That's him — that pale one."

"Call him, will you."

A minute later a fragile looking lad made his way through the crowd to me. His neck was slender, his skin pure white. Under the cap he wore pulled down over his forehead, his eyes were huge.

"I'm Kimitake Hiraoka."

I liked his voice, neither high nor low.

"I'm Bojo. On the Edit Board."

He must have recognized my name; his eyes relaxed.

"You submitted some poems, 'On Autumn.' I recommended them for the next issue."

I didn't use the familiar form *kisama*, in vogue at the Peers' School: he seemed too young.

"Here's one of our magazines. You'll find a story of mine — read it. I've included some comments on your poetry too."

Embarrassment in his every feature, Mishima took the magazine.

I nodded slightly. It was a signal he was free to go.

Mishima hesitated, then saluted me. In his awkward salute and in his embarrassment I glimpsed the gentle spirit of a young boy.

I turned and walked away, but I was aware of Mishima being questioned by his classmates behind me.

"Are you his fag?" — I could almost see that pale, frail boy making his way past questions half mocking, half envious, back to the first row of benches.

Thus began an assiduously literary friendship which thrived for roughly four years, the time it took Kimitake to outgrow Bojo. The boys met seldom. Occasionally Kimitake visited Bojo at his stately home where they read the court classics together. But for the most part they communicated in voluminous letters which they exchanged nearly every day. These began with criticism of new poetry received in the previous dispatch and went on to poetry, book reports (Bojo introduced Kimitake to Cocteau and Huysmans and Villiers de L'Isle Adam), family episodes and dreams in color. Frequently the boys met by arrangement simply to hand one another letters. As Bojo explained, "We felt we could express ourselves better in writing."

Bojo remembers Kimitake at thirteen and fourteen as a "quiet, fragile boy with exquisite but somehow feminine manners." He recalls passing Kimitake and his mother in the street one day. Kimitake was in Peers' School uniform; standard Peers' School decorum required that he salute his senior and then tip his cap. Instead, in an "altogether unexpected manner," he bowed! It was Bojo's strong feeling on this occasion and at other times that "Mishima's mother had trained him to behave girlishly."

Considering they were in correspondence for four years, Bojo has little to say about Kimitake as an adolescent. He admits as much, and reflects that Kimitake was careful not to expose himself in any essential way. He would not speak about his family, for example, nor did he invite Bojo to visit him at his home. Bojo, on the other hand, says that he was "lured" into revealing all that was of concern to him and describes Kimitake, somewhat bitterly, as a "compelling listener." The picture that emerges is of a brilliant, very private youth feeding his curiosity about the outside world and his colossal vanity on the passion of a rather spellbound twenty-two-year-old.

There is little question that Bojo's friendship was of large importance to Kimitake in the years when he was discovering himself as a writer. Shortly before his death he recalled his excitement each afternoon as he rushed home from school to see if a letter from Bojo had come. "In those apricot envelopes of yours," he wrote, "was a literary nectar sweeter than any I have had since." But his progress was dizzyingly swift, and Bojo inevitably was left behind. What seems to have happened, and would happen again, was that Kimitake decided one day that his friend was no genius after all but "mediocre." At that time, the summer of 1941, he took steps to terminate his friendship with the older boy. Bojo had sent him a short story about an unhappy love affair between a university student and a married woman. In an appended note he explained that the story was a faithful account of his own experience, and asked for Kimitake's comments. Kimitake did not answer the letter. Bojo wrote again, asking Kimitake to meet him at a coffeehouse near the Imperial University. Kimitake kept the appointment but said nothing about the story. Finally Bojo asked for his opinion, and he replied only that the dialogue was "unnatural." When Bojo protested that the lines were a verbatim record of conversations between himself and his lover, Kimitake replied that it was bad dialogue for just that reason, and proceeded to criticize the prosaicness of the narrative, which he likened to a newspaper article. Bojo was stunned, but failed to realize the affront was intended until the following spring, when Kimitake began a coterie magazine called *Red Pictures* and did not invite Bojo to participate. Although the boys corresponded occasionally until the end of the war, they did not meet again.

The coeditors of *Red Pictures* were two upperclassmen whom Kimitake had met through Bojo and who had replaced Bojo in his esteem. One was a poet and painter named Tokugawa who was to design the cover of Kimitake's first book. The other was a writer five years older named Fumi-hiko Azuma. Azuma was slowly dying of tuberculosis. In 1939 the disease had moved into his throat and confined him to his bed where he lay for four years until he died, writing tirelessly on a tablet he held above his head. His fierce devotion to his art and the fact that he was destined to die an early death made Azuma a hero in Kimitake's eyes, perhaps the first indelibly important figure in his literary life. In the eulogy he published in the school journal when Azuma died in 1943, Kimitake re-counted "staggering" into the rain on the night he received the news and rushing blindly through the streets with no idea of where to go. Years later, a few months before his own death, he asked one of his publishers (Kodansha) to bring out a vol-ume of Azuma's work, promising to write an introduction. The publishers agreed, although they were confused by the abrupt request to publish an unknown author. No one realized until later that this was one of the final gestures Mishima wanted to make before he died.

As tuberculosis of the throat was highly contagious, Azuma was not allowed visitors: Kimitake spoke with him in person only once. But from January 1941 until Azuma died at twenty-three in 1943, the boys corresponded constantly. Unfortunately Azuma's letters to Kimitake have been lost. But Azuma's father, a lawyer and judge who adored his son, has saved nearly two hundred long letters from Kimitake. Many of these are purely literary. But here and there they open like small windows on a painfully self-conscious young man who is profoundly troubled about himself. This is clear in Kimitake's very first letter to Azuma, a note he wrote on January 14, 1941, his sixteenth birthday. At the time he was studying poetry with a well-known but unimportant poet named Gyuko Kawaji who was a friend of Shizue's father. Apparently Kawaji responded both to Kimitake personally and to his poetry with something close to physical revulsion: one day after they had been working together for nearly a year he complained to another disciple, "He's not precocious and he's not a genius; he's just a profoundly unpleasant freak!" This had come back to Kimitake, and he reported it to Azuma, adding, "Perhaps he is right. . . . If only I could regard the world with more child-like ingenuous eyes. I have a feeling I won't be writing poetry very much longer." In a longer letter written at the end of January, he makes even clearer his anxiousness and even disgust at what he senses to be his own unwholesomeness. It is a curious, saddening letter in which he apologizes to his friend for knowing as much as he does, and then describes himself perpetrating just the "masquerade of normalcy" he would later detail in *Confessions of a Mask*:

You call me a head full of facts and I want to explain how this came about. It is entirely due to my surroundings. My father pressed me with books about the Nazis doing this, the Nazis doing that; and so I began reading only such books in his presence, as a kind of *camouflage*. But gradually I became interested, and began reading essays on the Jewish problem and on Japanism by choice. For some time I read the Bible and biblical commentary with a passion. Before that I read books on insects and animals. I have also been exposed to the Chinese classics by my grandfather (maternal) who is a Confucian scholar. But it is not only reading that has affected me: the only people I ever meet at my house are "empiricists"; and this too has gradually influenced me, not in my writing necessarily, but in my approach to daily life. I look in the mirror, and think, imagine someone as sickly pale as you able to talk about nothing but literature — self-hatred of this kind leads me when I am speaking with adults to choose topics of conversation which befit a middle-school student, such as current events and politics. Accordingly, the conversation partner I have come to consider ideal has no knowledge that I am a writer of fiction and poetry, does not notice how wan I am, and in short permits me to behave very much like an ordinary middle-school boy, who speaks in a lively healthy way about school life etc. But the truth is that I have become a creature utterly withdrawn who cares only for writing.

By 1941 Kimitake's writing had carried his star high into the sky of Peers' School prestige. In 1940, at fifteen, he became the youngest member of the editorial board in the literary club's hundred-year history. The following year he was elected editor of the journal, replacing Azuma, who had just graduated, as the central figure in literary activity on the campus. Then in the summer of 1941 his mentor Fumio Shimizu invited him to serialize a story in the coterie magazine Shimizu coedited with three other academic critics. This was an unprecedented invitation and, even for Kimitake Hiraoka, an intoxicating one. *Bungei-Bunka (Art and Culture)* was no student publication but a real literary magazine. Not only was Kimitake the first student the editors had ever asked to contribute, this was the first time they had ever solicited fiction rather than critical essays. Kimitake agreed at once to write a story "at least one hundred pages long" and informed Shimizu "unhesitatingly" that the title would be "A Forest in Full Flower." Then he asked his teacher to help him select a pen name. There is no special significance in the choice of Yukio Mishima. Shimizu says that Kimitake wanted a first name three characters long, and that he took the hint for Yu-ki-o from a poet named Sa-chi-o Ito.

"A Forest in Full Flower" was a tour de force, dazzlingly accomplished for all its determined precociousness and elaborate artificiality. Moreover, it was quintessential Mishima, a lyric exposition of longing penetrating very nearly to the heart of the anxious, erotic romanticism which Kimitake had first expressed three years earlier in "Sorrel":

I know where my longing resides. Longing is like a river. No part of the river *is* the river. For a river flows. The river yesterday is no longer the river today, yet the river is there eternally. We can beckon but cannot describe it. My longing is much this way, and the longing of my ancestors. In my family's past are both samurai and court nobles. When we set out for either homeland, a beautiful river winds in and out of sight along our way. To ensure the peerless elegance of our journey. Ah, that river! I understand it, it is an unspoken pact between my grandfathers and myself. In places this longing lurks just out of sight, but it is not dead. As roses on an old hedge still live today, in my grandmother and mother the river flowed underground. In my father it became a murmuring brook. In me — ah, how can it become other than a swollen mighty river, like a song of blessing by the gods.

Here the world-weary (sixteen-year-old) narrator exalts the implacable longing within himself into a personal and a privileged destiny. He has inherited his longing from the past; it is a pact between his (noble) ancestors and himself — his birthright. Moreover, he is *the* heir in whom the tradition is destined gloriously to culminate in a "song of blessing by the gods." Then what is the object of this quest the young artist conceives as his special destiny? It is nothing less than Beauty:

Now Beauty is a gorgeous, runaway horse. But there was a time when it was reined in and stood quivering in its tracks and neighing shrilly at the misty morning sky. Only then was the horse clean and pure, graceful beyond compare. Now severity has let go the reins; the horse stumbles, regains its footing, plunges headlong. It is no longer immaculate, mud cakes its flank. Yet there are times even now when a man will see the phantom of an immaculate white horse. It is just such a man that our ancestors are searching for. Gradually, they will come to abide in him.

Like all rivers, the river of longing empties into the sea: the sea pervades "A Forest in Full Flower" as it would pervade all of Mishima's writing, a symbol in its "terrible repletion" of the source of longing. Having established himself as the heir to a longing for beauty, the narrator offers three episodes from his family's past as "proof of the affinity of [his] bloodline for the sea." In the first, a Christian noblewoman beholds a miracle from the parapet of her husband's castle. In a field of flowers which borders on the beach she sees the figure of a woman in gleaming white with something glistening at her breast. The woman understands that the figure is the Holy Mother, and that the golden fire at her throat is the sun glinting off the cross she wears. Almost at once the apparition vanishes and the lady swoons. Six months later, she dies. The narrator explains: "The miracle was prepared by the lady's noble longing. What she beheld was one of the beautiful measures taken by longing in times of crisis. The life force within her risked a grave danger and as a result the lady died." Implicit in this are several associations fundamental to Mishima's romanticism. Longing is equated with nothing less than the life force itself and thus becomes central to existence. Longing creates or leads to beauty, whose essence is ecstasy, in this case religious ecstasy. Finally, the ecstasy sought results in death. By the time he wrote "A Forest in Full Flower," Mishima was well on his way to evolving an esthetic formula in which Beauty, Ecstasy, and Death were equivalent and together stood for his personal holy grail.

The second episode is closest to the author's heart: its nuances are erotic, and it uncovers the fear inherent in his longing for "the sea." It is set in the Genji Period, the eleventh century, and "quoted" from the heroine's diary in the elegant classical style of the eleventh-century romances. (This in itself is a technical feat equivalent, say, to writing fluently in the style of Fielding.) A young woman in attendance at the court is driven by her lover's coldness to run away from the capital with a man who recently has become a monk. He takes her to his uncle's village, which happens to be on the sea. But the sea terrifies the woman. For three days she lies in her room with the shutters closed against the sound of the surf. On the morning of the fourth day, she resolves to confront her terror:

So that her frenzy would not be observed, the woman set out for the beach alone when her husband was not at home. In the distance the sea glittered like a narrow satin ribbon. But the thunder of the waves reached her where she stood. Covering her face, she raced toward the beach. The sea breeze beat at her ears and the waves roared at her. When she felt warm dry sand beneath her feet her body trembled. She took her hands away from her face.

Now for the first time the whale-rich sea engraved its image on the woman's heart. As pain rarely accompanies a violent wound at the moment it is inflicted, the woman's feelings in that instant bore no resemblance to the fear she had expected. From that moment of impact against her breast, the sea god lived inside her.

She was enfolded in the mysterious ecstasy of the moment just before the murderer strikes, when we are conscious that we are about to be murdered. It was a moment of unmistakable premonition, but a premonition which held no meaning for the present. It was a beautifully isolated present, a moment disconnected and pure as anything in the world. While the moment lasted the woman's stance, her attitude, was passive beyond compare, hers was the pure mindlessness of a collapse, accepting all and becoming nothing. Perhaps her pose there on the beach resembled the "maternal" breast. But almost at once, she was ejected from the ecstasy of enfoldment. An unbearable heaviness and awe descended upon her.

This is clear enough despite its preciousness: the ecstasy the woman experiences at the hands of the sea god is the ecstasy of ravagement, of erotic death. And it is this moment which is the imagined, the irresistible destination of the "elegant journey" on which the author's destiny leads him. What Mishima wants in "A Forest in Full Flower," and would want all his life, is the ecstasy of death. At the heart of the esthetic he is already developing at sixteen, in which death is equated with supreme beauty, is this erotic need.

"A Forest in Full Flower" earned Kimitake Hiraoka, now and forever Yukio Mishima, full membership in the Shimizu coterie. The story was serialized in four issues of *Bungei-Bunka*, from September to December 1941, and lavishly admired by the adult editors. Thereafter, until the magazine was discontinued in August 1944, Mishima was a regular contributor of fiction, poetry, and criticism. He was also welcomed at the monthly gatherings of the coterie at Shimizu's house.

Meanwhile things were very bad at home. Azusa had returned from Osaka and was determined to stop his son from becoming a writer. The storm had been building for some time; Kimitake had chosen to write "A Forest in Full Flower" under a pen name because he wanted to conceal his identity from his father. Later he would "explain" that he had taken a pen name at this time because he had been afraid the school administration might disapprove of a student publishing in a coterie magazine. But a letter to Azuma dated December 19, 1941, even while "A Forest in Full Flower" was being serialized, is evidence that it was Azusa he was really afraid of:

I am treated like a heathen! I have had to promise my father that I will write no more fiction. And I have agreed to read only the books he recommends. My mother, who understands me better than anyone, knows the truth. But from my father, who is still in Osaka, I must keep my writing a secret of secrets.

On February 22, 1941, Kimitake again complained to Azuma about his father:

Where my writing is concerned, he is the embodiment of every imaginable handicap and obstacle. In a word, he is a bureaucrat frozen stiff with the bureaucratic spirit. He has never read anything of mine. But he is free with his criticism: "the practice of literature," he informs me, "befits only the people of a degenerate nation." As you can imagine, magazine serialization, book reviews, private editions, etc. are not subjects which can be mentioned in my father's hearing. He harps on one string only: Nazis, Nazis, Nazis.

Azusa's own point of view is clear in a letter he wrote to Kimitake from Osaka, probably in the fall of 1941:

I want you to keep me well informed about Mother's health. I hear that some high and mighty writers speak of you as a genius, or precocious, or some kind of deviate, or just unpleasant. I think it's high time you took stock of yourself.

Mother is angry with me about all this and says it's the fault of
your upbringing. But there's no use talking about the past. Just
think about how to improve the present and the future. Son, leave
literature for a while and use the good head you're lucky enough
to have for something that will do you some good, for physics, or
engineering, or chemistry. If you could just turn the energy you
devote to literature to one of these areas I know you could make
something of yourself. I want you to think hard about this. Your
Mother and I are worried to death about you and you should
know that. Can't you find it in yourself to convert? . . .

There's no point in talking now about how bad your upbringing
was. Don't you want to become a straightforward youth? When I
see a cheerful and upright and guileless young fellow the same
age as you it makes me so sad I can hardly speak. Write me your
intentions, son.

Possibly the answer to this letter was the promise Mishima
never intended to keep. But once Azusa was back in the
Shibuya house, it was impossible to keep the secret. Mishima
was writing furiously every night until dawn, and when Azusa
discovered how "grave" the situation really was, he became
uncontrollable. In his own words, "I immediately adopted a
countermeasure, a policy of search and seize." Several times a
week, as he freely admits, he "forcibly entered" Kimitake's
room and destroyed whatever manuscript he cound find while
Kimitake looked on. Shizue says she was helpless to intercede:

I would look into his room after his father had left and find
him staring down at his desk with his eyes full of tears. I confess
my husband was hateful to me. But I couldn't permit myself to
speak ill of his father to Kimitake. So I would simply bring him
tea and cake, wipe his tears away with my handkerchief, and leave
the room without a word.

According to Shizue, the damage was extensive: "I know there were whole stories he tore to bits. And often Kimitake was too upset to rewrite them so they were just lost for good."

Although the situation in the Hiraoka house was extreme even in the Japanese context, it was not so unaccountable as it appears. Like any upstanding gentleman of his day, Azusa was morally a Confucian. In the Confucian view, fiction was mendacity and nothing more, one manifestation of moral degeneracy. Writing, therefore, was considered a dishonorable avocation (a view which remains prevalent in Japan today). Kimitake's forbearance is at least partly accountable in terms of the same ethic, which held "filial piety" to be perhaps the highest virtue of moral man. Given Natsu's obsession with her feudal past, he must have been inculcated with Confucian values from early childhood.

Kimitake would not openly disobey his father, but neither would he stop writing. Eventually he began carrying his manuscripts with him to school or entrusting them with a classmate of his sister's who lived in the neighborhood. From 1942 until he graduated from the Peers' School at the end of 1944, he managed to produce eight novellas, three long essays on classical literature and a slim volume of new poetry, in spite of Azusa's unrelenting attacks. And if he had only half an audience at home, he was also secure in the knowledge that whatever he put down on paper would be energetically appreciated by the adults in his coterie.

The four adult regulars in the coterie which nourished and protected Kimitake during the war years were academics and not, properly speaking, "knights of the pen." But they considered themselves apostles of a group of recognized writers and critics known as the Japan Romantic School, and it was to the influence of this "school" primarily that Kimitake was exposed during his years as the coterie wonder child.

45

The Japan Romantic School had emerged in the mid-thirties, just as Japanese fascism was winning a decisive victory over the Proletarian Movement. Its leaders, men like Hojuro Yasuda and Fusao Hayashi (who years later would introduce Mishima to the young men who became the first "cadets" in his Shield Society), were apostate Marxists who had established the basis for a new identity by "converting" their faith in Marxism to a faith in national tradition. In an essay written in 1941 about his own "conversion," which typically occurred during his imprisonment for communist activity, Fusao Hayashi stated the case succinctly:

Marxism cannot possibly function as an everlasting support of the Japanese spirit. It is nothing more than an arbitrary theory based on western class society of the nineteenth century. It is an ideology, but it can never be a cause for which the [Japanese] people can joyfully die. . . . The foundation or support of national spirit must be discovered within the people. Tradition, the product of three thousand years of culture, is the only cause for which the people can die.

Building on this conviction, the Japan Romantics fabricated a fantastically complex and, indeed, impenetrable esthetic ultra-nationalism in which everything traditional was exalted into an absolute, a supreme ideal. Naturally, the divinity of the emperor was an article of faith. And so, by extension, was the peerless beauty of the traditional literature. The beauty of the classics was seen as a reflection and a corroboration of the emperor's divinity, which in turn provided a cause — and this is important — "worthy of dying for." Not only were the Romantics obsessed with purity and bloodline, they cherished a death wish. After the war, a leftist critic characterized these writers severely but not inaptly as "men who were eager to race to the Front and their deaths, the great Classics tucked under their arms."

After the war, when Mishima was bent on disavowing the "romantic" in himself, he repeatedly vilified the Romantic School as being "the most serious illness of youth" and "an insidious influence which encouraged and justified the indulgence of adolescent sensibility." Presumably by "adolescent sensibility" he meant the exalted equating of personal Destiny with Beauty and Death to be found in "A Forest in Full Flower"; and there is no question that this tendency was "encouraged and justified" by the Japan Romantics. The most zealous nationalist in the coterie, for example, the thirty-seven-year-old critic Zenmei Hasuda,* was constantly exalting death in imponderable epigrams such as "To die is to know culture."

Then there was the death-obsessed poet Shizuo Ito, one of the coterie's heroes:

> Oh vision of high peaks
> I implore you:
> In readiness of that beautiful day when I shall die
> Melt not away your white snow.

* Zenmei Hasuda was Mishima's most ardent admirer among the adults. Both his zealous nationalism and the maternal possessiveness with which he claimed Mishima as kin are clear in the now famous editorial postscript he appended to the first installment of "A Forest in Full Flower":

The author is very young in years. I prefer not to disclose just what sort of person he is, for I believe it best not to. For those who insist on knowing, I will say only that he is *one of us, a youthful version of ourselves.* That young men like this are emerging in Japan is a joy too great for words. And for those with no confidence in our national literature, his advent will come as an overwhelming surprise. But there is no cause for surprise: the truth is that this young man is heir to Japan's everlasting history. Though far younger than we, he emerges fully mature. And it is *from ourselves that he is born.* (Italics in original.)

Clinging to an August rock
The favored butterfly
Now perishes;
Who, having learned his fate,
Could live in the ardent light
Of the summer sun?

Throughout the war, Kimitake read Ito religiously. Later he would characterize verses like these as "lucid projections of a Nietzschean love of destiny" and speak of the poet as "the mentor of [his] adolescence."

But the romantic influence should not be exaggerated: the erotic longing for death which underlay Kimitake's "adolescent sensibility" was nearly congenital. Certainly there is evidence before he had been exposed to the Romantic School that he was beginning to view death, or something equally engulfing and fatal, as a privileged destiny which he awaited impatiently. The following poem, for example, written in March 1940:

CATASTROPHE

Evening after evening
Standing at the window I await
An accident,
A baleful sandstorm of catastrophe
Whirling toward me from beyond
The night rainbow of city streets.

There was also his instant obsession with the French enfant terrible Raymond Radiguet, when he read Radiguet's novel *Le Bal du Compte d'Orgel* shortly after his fifteenth birthday. In that year, 1940, Mishima's principal reading was the Japanese classics, Tanizaki, Rilke, Proust, and Cocteau. Then

48

he discovered Radiguet, possibly was led to him by Cocteau who was his champion and lover, and for a time all else was forgotten. Later Mishima would describe reading *Le Bal du Compte d'Orgel* over and over, finishing the last page and going back to the beginning again, "gnashing [his] teeth in envy." *Le Bal du Compte d'Orgel* is a remarkable work for a writer of twenty. But as Mishima himself was perfectly aware, his enthrallment was principally with the author, who had died at twenty after finishing the book, as if, in Mishima's words, "he had been consumed by his own brilliance." In a later portrait of himself during this period called "The Boy Who Wrote Poetry," Mishima described the exalted notion that must have prompted his veneration of Radiguet and his desire to emulate him:

He liked Oscar Wilde's short poem "The Grave of Keats." — "Taken from life when life and love were new/ The youngest of the martyrs here is lain. . . ." The youngest of the martyrs here is lain. It was so surprising how catastrophe assailed these poets *like a benefaction*. He believed in preestablished harmony. The preestablished harmony in the biographies of poets. Belief in that was the same as believing his own genius.

It gave him pleasure to think about the long speeches that would be delivered at his funeral, and about fame and honor after death. But the thought of his own corpse made him uncomfortable. "Let me live like a sky-rocket. Let me color the night sky for an instant with all my being and then burn out." *The boy thought hard, but could think of no other way to live*. But he ruled out suicide. Preestablished harmony would do him the favor of killing him.* (Italics mine.)

* While this passage is clear enough as it stands, it assumes an even fuller significance when the phrase Mishima quotes from the Wilde poem is completed: "Taken from life when life and love were new/ The youngest of the martyrs here is lain,/ *Fair as Sebastian, and as early slain*." The figure of Saint Sebastian pierced by arrows was the central image in Mishima's sadomasochistic eroticism.

Here the equation implicit in "A Forest in Full Flower" is fully formulated: *Destiny* (Genius) equals *Beauty* equals *Death*. The poet believes that his death has been ordained in the same preestablished harmony which has endowed him with genius. Genius and death are therefore consubstantially his destiny. Death is a *benefaction* because it is proof of the poet's genius and because, as his destiny, it is the aim and object of his life. The death the boy anticipates is a skyrocketing, incandescent death: Beauty itself.

There is no question that the atmosphere within the Shimizu coterie was highly congenial to the kind of fantasy Mishima recreates in "The Boy Who Wrote Poetry." But his writing during the war years argues that an even more decisive "encouragement and justification" was the reality of the war itself. For although death does cast a shadow on the stories he wrote in 1941 and 1942, it is not until the middle of 1943, when the tide of battle suddenly turned against Japan, that he began consciously to define his destiny as the attainment of beautiful death. The point is that by the end of 1943 death was for *all* young Japanese an inescapable reality. The young poet's conclusion that *"he could think of no other way to live"* but to die was therefore realistic. Mishima was no realist. But the exalted fantasy in which he transformed death into a "benefaction" certainly fed on the wartime reality.

The real war he hated. In letters to Azuma written in 1943 he consistently deplores his father's admiration for the Nazis and the Imperial Japanese Army, and refers to the battle as "vulgar" and "mediocre." But in his private fantasy the reality was transfigured. Later he would speak of the war years as "a time, the only time in my experience, when death was a rite and an intoxicating blessing."

In September 1944, Mishima graduated the higher form

(fourteenth grade) at the head of his class and was awarded the traditional silver watch by the emperor personally. Azusa was delirious with pride. And even Kimitake, for all his formidable skepticism, seems to have been touched by a sense of honor and of awe: years later, addressing an auditorium full of hostile leftist students, he would suddenly speak of his "personal gratitude" to the emperor and recall that His Majesty had been "splendid" on graduation day.

A silver watch from the emperor was a thrilling reward, but it is unlikely that anything Mishima felt on graduation day can have equaled his excitement the following month, when his first book of short stories was published. In a later reminiscence he summed up his feelings on that occasion in one line: "Now I was ready to die."

It was no easy matter to be published in October 1944, as Tokyo began to burn. First a petition for paper had to be filed with the government. Mishima had begun his "in a modest attempt to preserve the literary tradition of the empire," and it had been granted. Next a publisher had to be found; for weeks a friend of Shimizu's named Masaharu Fuji had made the rounds of small publishers with Mishima and finally they had found one willing to do a book of fiction. It was a cause for celebration; a small party was held in Mishima's honor. Shizue prevailed on Azusa to contribute some whiskey he had brought home from a business trip to Europe in 1938, but he declined to attend the party. The guests were Shimizu and two other members of the coterie (the zealot Hasuda was in Manchuria), several young writers associated with the Japan Romantic School, and, representing the Hiraokas, Shizue:

The sight of Kimitake sitting there among all those older gentlemen, looking so small in his student uniform and being

51

treated so respectfully, was a thrill I shall never forget. It was a time when you could never know when the air raid alarms would ring. Stepping outside was like stepping into reality out of a dream.

Possibly because it aspired to a gorgeous alternative to reality when reality was fire and death, *A Forest in Full Flower* sold out its first edition of two thousand copies shortly after it appeared. At another moment in literary history, this commercial success would certainly have been accompanied by an official reaction from the cliquish literary establishment. But in 1944 there were no literary prizes or even book reviews. *A Forest in Full Flower* was an event in the coterie which had nourished Mishima, but it was not his debut as an acknowledged writer.

The week after his book appeared, Mishima entered the Imperial University as a first-year student of German law. The choice was Azusa's. Everyone else who knew Mishima urged him to study literature, and certainly that was what he would have chosen. But Azusa was adamant:

A large number of the men in our family, including myself, had studied law at university. And no matter how hard you searched the family tree there wasn't a single performer or author to be found. This gave me the advantage. I forced Kimitake into the study of law, and I should say into the most orthodox branch of law, German law, because I wanted desperately to tear him away from literature once and for all.

Although Mishima was acting under orders, it seems he was not particularly upset about having to enroll. In the first place he expected, indeed hoped, to die. Moreover, there were no classes to interfere with his writing; no sooner had the term begun than his entire class was "mobilized" and assigned to an airplane factory on the outskirts of Tokyo. Mishima contrived to get a medical excuse from physical labor — he never had any trouble looking ill — and was given an office job which took little of his time. By noon each day he was free; the rest of the day he wrote. By February 1945, he had completed a long novella called *The Middle Ages*. The hero, with whom he obviously identified, was an aristocrat-general of the fifteenth century who was famous for his personal elegance and patronage of the arts and who died a hero's death in battle at the age of twenty-four.

It was during these months at the airplane factory, as he worked on the book he spoke of as his "last novel" and waited for his draft summons, that Mishima's fantasies of Beauty, Death, and Destiny seem to have possessed him entirely. As he would later reflect, with the wonderful accuracy he was sometimes capable of:

The narcissism at the border separating adolescence from adulthood will make use of anything for its own ends. Even the annihilation of the world. At twenty I was able to fancy myself as anything I liked. As a genius destined for an early death. As the final heir to the tradition of Japanese beauty. As a decadent among decadents, the last Emperor of an age of decadence. Even as Beauty's *kamikaze* squad!

In February 1945, this wartime fantasy was momentarily interrupted by the reality of war: Mishima received his draft notice, known as the "red paper" because the form was blood red. This was a grimly appropriate touch; in 1945, a draft notice was tantamount to an imperial command to die.

Shizue was distraught. At the time she was sick in bed, but she came to the door to see Kimitake off when he left with his father. According to Chiyuki, fifteen at the time, "She came

53

down the hall sobbing, in a long robe and her hair all disheveled. She looked like a woman possessed, a madwoman from another world. I've never seen anything like her distraction, particularly after they had left. She knelt down by herself in front of the [Buddhist] altar and began to pray as if in a trance, as if she were mad. To watch her made me so afraid I wanted to run away."

Kimitake's induction center was in Shikata village, the Hiraoka family seat. The previous May, Azusa had sent him there to register on the assumption that Kimitake would have a better chance in a country town than in Tokyo. He had been classified 2B, which meant that he had a record of illness but was eligible for active duty, health permitting.

The Hiraokas arrived in Shikata the evening before Kimitake was due to report. (This was the last time Mishima would visit his ancestral home.) Kimitake had a cold and a slight fever. Late that night he developed a cough and his fever went soaring up. A doctor was called and he was given an injection and ice packs for his head to bring the fever down. In the morning he was still sick; Azusa helped him dress and took him to the induction center. The arrival of a chalky-white boy from Tokyo seems to have created a stir among the farmers' sons waiting in line. There were whispers of "Tokyo!" and even "the Peers' School!" Finally it was Kimitake's turn for the perfunctory medical checkup that preceded the "glorious signing" of the papers which amounted to the signing away of life. But when the doctor listened to his chest, he shook his head and wrote across the medical form "unfit for military service; immediate return for convalescence." To Azusa he explained, "Severe *Rassel* [German for lung-rasp], probably advanced tuberculosis." When Kimitake was reexamined in Tokyo by a "proper doctor," this was found to be a mistaken diagnosis of "severe bronchitis." In Chiyuki's opinion, the army doctor had mis-read the symptoms intentionally: "I think the doctor took one look at my brother and realized he was too frail to survive more than a few days of life in an army barracks. I think he let him off because he was sorry for him; he was pale as death in those days and so thin, only a monster would have inducted him."

When he had dressed, Kimitake was herded into a room with other rejects and admonished not to forget his duty to sacrifice himself for the empire with the same fervor as those actually fighting at the front. Meanwhile Azusa waited ner-vously outside, anxious to be away. When the lecture was over he hurried Kimitake out of the barracks. In his own words, "As we stepped outside the sky seemed so high and so bright it was dizzying. The minute we were past the gate I took Kimitake's hand and broke into a run. How we ran! I don't remember how far but it must have been quite a distance. And the whole way I kept looking back, for all I knew a soldier would come after us shouting 'It was all a mistake, Congratu-lations on qualifying!' and that possibility had me scared to death. . . . When we got home we went into the living room and had some green tea and I remember how delicious it tasted. My wife had with her the will and the nail clippings [a traditional memento] Kimitake had placed in her room secretly before he left. As we gradually relaxed everyone began to feel exhilarated.

"My wife wandered around the house as if she were too happy to keep still. Kimitake's brother and sister were jubilant. Every kind of joy was displayed. But I cannot for the life of me remember Kimitake's expression. I know he cannot have been unhappy; but I have no memory that he displayed any clear reaction that would have indicated what he was really thinking. I remember deciding later that he was probably just worn out after his high fever and that frantic trip we took."

Azusa asserts that Kimitake "cannot have been unhappy" and undoubtedly he is right; yet it is unlikely that he can have been happy either. What is more probable is that he was confused primarily, about his rush *away* from death; almost certainly the questions whirling in his head at the time were similar to those he would later attribute to the hero of *Confessions of a Mask*:

> Why had I looked so frank as I lied to the army doctor? Why had I said that I'd been having a slight fever for over half a year, that my shoulder was painfully stiff, that I spit blood, that even last night I had been soaked by a night sweat? (This happened to be the truth, but small wonder considering the number of aspirin I had taken.) Why when sentenced to return home the same day had I felt the pleasure of a smile come pushing so persistently to my lips? Why had I run so when I was through the barracks gate?
>
> I realized vividly that my future life would never attain the heights of glory sufficient to justify my having escaped death in the army, and hence I could not understand the source of the power which had made me run so rapidly away from the gate of the regiment. And that completely automatic reaction which always made me dash so breathlessly for an air-raid shelter — what was this but a desire to live?

There is, however, a perfectly obvious answer to questions like these. The "natural, spontaneous suicide" the narrator (and Mishima) desires, the beautiful death ordained in the pre-established harmony, is death in a fantasy. But the Imperial Army was reality with a vengeance, and death as a soldier was therefore death as reality, violent, vulgar, incontestably medi-ocre: loathsome and terrifying. Whether Mishima really lied to the army doctor is impossible to know, but certainly he might have, in a "completely automatic reaction" to the threat of *real* death.

The intrusion of reality in the form of a draft summons may have torn Mishima away from his fantasy momentarily. But the war raged on. In fact the most fiery air raids on Tokyo began only in March of 1945. And these furnished his imagination with all the incendiary fuel it required to exalt death once again into a glorious and privileged destiny. In *Confessions of a Mask* the narrator "realizes" in February 1945 that he has no desire to die. By May, however, the force of his fantasy world is once again insulating him against the threat of real death:

There was a rumor that the enemy would probably make a landing soon in S Bay and that the region in which the arsenal stood would be overwhelmed. And again, even more than before, I found myself deeply immersed in a desire for death. It was in death that I had discovered my real "life's aim." . . .

I was hoping — no, it was more than mere hope, it was a superstitious certainty — that during that month the Americans would surely land at S Bay and we would all be sent out as a student army to die to the last man. . . .

In May 1945, Mishima's class was transferred to the navy arsenal at Zama, thirty miles southwest of Tokyo. The law students lived in a navy dormitory and worked as a maintenance crew. Mishima, however, on grounds of poor health, not entirely false, managed once again to be excused from physical work and was placed in charge of the "library." This was a cubbyhole in a corner of the arsenal where the university kept a few volumes to permit the class to "maintain" its law studies. In fact, only three weeks of classes had been held since Mishima had entered the university in October 1944, and no one used the library. Mishima was free to read and to write. In a postcard written from the arsenal in May, he informed his mentor Fumio Shimizu that he was reading eleventh-century court diaries, the ancient creation myths which establish the divinity of the emperor, fourteenth-century novels and the romantic novelist Kyoka Izumi (Natsu's favorite). He added that he was using the classical epistolary style to translate an unnamed one-act Yeats play. Years later he would reflect, "It is not easy to imagine how Yeats can have been related in any way to that final year of the War. It wasn't that I was striving to connect things that had no connection, *I was intent on abstracting the reality of the time,* engrossed in a private, isolated world of beauty as small as I could make it. The air raids on the distant metropolis, which I watched from the shelter at the arsenal, were beautiful. The flames seemed to hue to all the colors in the rainbow: it was like watching the light of a distant bonfire at a great banquet of extravagant death and destruction."

Just as Mishima entered the dormitory at the arsenal, Shizue and the children moved to the relative safety of a cousin's house in Gotokuji, a residential suburb surrounded by paddies and fields. Most families who could manage it were evacuating as far to the north as they could get, but Azusa maintained that Gotokuji would be safe enough. As for himself, he chose to remain alone in the Shibuya house to guard against vandalism.

From May to August, Mishima visited the Gotokuji house whenever he could get a "day leave," which was generally after a severe air raid. Shizue remembers that the first thing he would do when he had determined that everyone was safe was to show her proudly how much manuscript he had produced since his last visit. During these last months of the war he was writing furiously.

58

Then, on August 15, Japan surrendered unconditionally and the emperor himself went on the radio to command his subjects to lay down their arms. A week earlier, Mishima had developed a high fever again and had been sent home to recover: he listened to the broadcast with his family at the house in Gotokuji. When the emperor had finished speaking, after a moment of silence, Azusa turned to Mishima and said: "Now we enter an age of culture, so if you really want to be a writer, go ahead." Later he thought better of this rashness and retracted it.

It is hard to say with any confidence what Mishima was feeling as he listened to the emperor declare the war at an end. The tempting assumption is that he shuddered with the existential horror of feeling bereft of identity and deprived of destiny. Certainly that is the assumption which he would encourage again and again in essays and novels written *after* the war:

The war ended. All I was thinking about, as I listened to the Imperial Rescript announcing the surrender, was the Golden Temple. The bond between the temple and myself had been severed. I thought, now I shall return . . . to a state in which I exist on one side and beauty on the other. A state which will never improve so long as the world endures.

Severance and disintegration: death as "an intoxicating blessing and a rite" now eternally unattainable.

But it is unlikely that Mishima's perception of the new reality was so sharply focused as this at the time. Unquestionably the surrender was a blow, but it seems to have struck him with the somehow unidentifiable force of a presentiment.

There is evidence of this in a story which he was writing when the war ended called "A Tale at the Cape." The story is about an eleven-year-old boy whose mother takes him to the beach one summer to learn to swim. He does not learn to swim, but he discovers, in the sea,

the source of something which had long attracted me but which I had never known where to look for. It terrified and rejected me, but for just that reason I felt the more strongly compelled. . . . As I confronted the sea I was aware of something calling to me from the offing. It seemed to me that to respond to that call would be something extremely beautiful but something no man must do.

One day, when the boy has wandered off by himself, he encounters "a beautiful person, a girl not more than twenty," and her lover. The girl invites the boy to join them in a walk along the cliffs and the boy is ecstatic: "How to describe the innocent happiness of that walk." Suddenly the older youth suggests they all play hide-and-seek. The boy covers his eyes and counts as slowly as he can, "the least I could do for that beautiful person whom I felt I loved with a passion new to me." As he counts he hears footsteps "dancing" away from him and then, "Could it have been my imagination? I thought I heard a voice or cry too solemn and beautiful to be a scream, more like a god laughing." The boy opens his eyes and searches the cliff for the young lovers but cannot find them. Vaguely frightened, he walks to the edge of the cliff:

It was as if a magnetic force were drawing me toward that beautiful abyss which was the sea. I managed to retreat a few steps. Then I threw myself to the ground and, as I tried to quiet the pounding of my heart, peered down into the abyss. What was it that I saw this time? Perhaps I should say I saw nothing; for what I saw was the same as before. Pine trees in the sun, rocks, a small inlet, waves which never ceased their white activity. *All that appeared was a seashore so still and so tranquil I found it hard to believe.* I thought for a minute about the meaning of that cry so like the laughter of a god. But it struck me as too large in importance for me to comprehend as yet. (Italics in original.)

Surely the voice the boy *thinks* he heard, which so resembles the mocking laughter of the gods, is his presentiment that he will now find himself deprived of the possibility of fulfillment. The "beautiful girl" and the youth have committed love suicide; they have answered the call of the sea, something "beautiful but which no man must do." In them the longing for "Beauty and Death" has been realized, fulfilled. But the boy has been left behind. Moreover, he senses that there is no longer any possibility that he will follow them. How else to explain his incredulity when he observes that the world *appears* to be "the same as before!" His sense of existential derangement leads him to expect a visible change in the physical world. In fact he knows somehow that there is a change, but he cannot discover it.

In a brief reminiscence written in 1955 Mishima represented his uneasiness at the end of the war in terms of this same conviction that the physical world must be altered:

A summer meadow stretched in front of me. In the distance I could see the barracks. And above the woods sailed quiet summer clouds. If the war had really ended, that scenery would suddenly have altered its significance. Perhaps I couldn't have identified just how it had changed, but the meadow, those woods and those clouds must now have become part of a world we had never before experienced. In that instant, I felt I had glimpsed a world of a different sensuous dimension.

The world Mishima glimpsed, the world the boy in the "Tale" expects to find and senses must be there although he cannot "identify" it, is a world which lies beyond beauty, death, destiny itself. From within the dream made possible and real by the war, it is a world impossible to conceive. Yet it is a real world, a tangible negation of a dream. Mishima was aware of this, however vaguely, in August 1945. But he managed not to face up to it for some time. The war was over, but Yukio Mishima managed to dream on.

three

1946-1949

Mishima cannot have known in August 1945 that adapting to the postwar reality would prove an impossible task. Neither was he conscious, as he would be by 1949, of the threat to survival he carried within himself. But in at least one important respect it was undoubtedly true, as he was later to write so often, that the end of the war was accompanied by "a sudden assault of unhappiness." While Tokyo burned, he had managed to feel a correspondence between his private, internal world and external reality: "it was a rare time [1944-45] when my personal nihilism and the nihilism of the age and of society at large perfectly corresponded." But now that the fires were out and death was no longer a reality in the air, the dream that had permitted him to believe that he was symbolic of the age had vanished, and with it his confidence in his genius. As he would later reflect at the height of his fame, when he could afford to be accurate about at least this aspect of his past, "I could not avoid the bewildering discovery that at twenty I was already an anachronism. My beloved Radiguet, and Wilde, and

Yeats, and the Japanese classics — everything I had valued was now suddenly offensive to the tastes of the age. . . . The boy who had carried on like a genius within a small group during the war was now a helpless student taken seriously by no one."

In November 1945 Mishima took "A Forest in Full Flower," "The Middle Ages," "A Tale at the Cape" and five other manuscripts to the one-room "editorial offices" of the publishing house Chikuma Shobo, which was preparing, as was everyone, to publish a new literary magazine. The man who had been designated "adviser" to the new magazine was the critic and translator of Gide, Mitsuo Nakamura, later to be a friend of Mishima's, and today the "Boss" critic of the literary establishment. Mishima had never met Nakamura nor had Nakamura heard of Mishima. The twenty-year-old writer had chosen to submit his work to Nakamura simply because he had heard that the tiny company which had published his first volume of short stories had been purchased by the larger Chikuma Shobo.

Mishima had nowhere else to go. His most ardent supporter during the war years, the fanatic Zenmei Hasuda, was dead by his own hand. And the other adults who had nourished and protected him, all affiliated with the Japan Romantic School, had been among the first to be purged, first by the newly liberated community of leftist writers and then by Occupation Headquarters (GHQ). The critic and ideologue Hojuro Yasuda, whom Mishima had visited in 1943, the poet and novelist Haruo Sato with whom Mishima had been associated in 1944, and the writer and publisher Yoichi Nakagawa, from whom Mishima had received his first commission in February 1945, were at the top of a list designating "literary war criminals" drawn up in October by a committee of leftist writers and critics. By late November all had been purged by GHQ and had withdrawn, blacklisted, into enforced isolation. The poet Shizuo Ito had saved himself by a quick shift to liberalism (as had many others) and Mishima did publish two poems in a short-lived magazine Ito began in May 1946. But Shizuo Ito was one of those who seems to have found Mishima physically and artistically repugnant, and this Mishima must have sensed, for he quickly dissociated from the older poet.

A question worth asking is whether Mishima avoided the men who had sponsored him during the war because they were no longer in a position to help or because the Japan Romantic School was now anathema. There are those who were in a position to know who accuse him to this day of having dissociated from the Romantics with icy calculation. One is a pediatrician and occasional poet named Fujima Hayashi, who when he first met Mishima late in 1943 was a disciple of the poets Ito and Sato, major figures in the Japan Romantic School. According to Hayashi, Mishima spent "numberless evenings" at his home during 1944 and 1945, discussing literature, eating, playing with his children; and then in November 1945 he suddenly failed to answer a letter and was thereafter "unimaginably cold" whenever they chanced to meet. Hayashi explains, "Mishima was always the first to say goodbye in any relationship. He couldn't use me anymore, he had outgrown me, so he cut me off. And the main reason was that he wanted to get away from the Romantic School." As proof Hayashi points to Mishima's "sudden switch of mentors," from Haruo Sato to the novelist who was to become Japan's first Nobel laureate in literature, Yasunari Kawabata. He says that Mishima had asked Sato to accept him as a disciple in the winter of 1945 and that Sato had agreed. For this there is only Hayashi's word. But it is history that Mishima visited Kawabata, who had not been purged, on New Year's

65

Day 1946, and that this was the beginning of a not uncompli
cated relationship in which, officially, Kawabata remained
Mishima's mentor all his life.

There is no question that Mishima was capable of discard
ing people abruptly, for whatever the reason. Fujima Hayashi
is only one in a long line of "associates" strung across his life
who were confounded by his sudden change in attitude. But in
this case it is not certain that he was acting on a desire to
dissociate from the Romantic School, as Hayashi claims. In
fact, his presence at a memorial gathering held for Zenmei
Hasuda in November 1946 is persuasive evidence to the contrary. Hasuda had died a fanatic's death. When the war ended
he was stationed in Manchuria; three days after the surrender,
he had shot his commanding officer to death and then killed
himself. Earlier in the day the officer had expressed the view
that there would no longer be any distinction between the
emperor and the common people. In the suicide note he
clutched in his fist, Hasuda accused the officer of being a spy
"with Korean blood in his traitor's veins," and finished, "I am
honored to become a stone cast away in service of the empire."
When news of Hasuda's suicide finally reached the mainland
his friends gathered to honor his memory. Present were the
three academics from the *Bungei-Bunka* coterie, the publisher and purged "red-hunter" Yoichi Nakagawa, and Yukio
Mishima. Poems written for the occasion were collected in a
pamphlet illustrated by Shiko Munakata. Had Mishima been
concerned with dissociating himself from the Japan Romantic
School he would hardly have participated.

More likely Mishima discarded Hayashi as he had discarded
Bojo and would discard others, because he had decided that
Hayashi was "mediocre," ever an unforgivable failing in
Mishima's eyes. And if he chose not to seek help from the

writers of the Romantic School, it was probably because he had judged, dispassionately to be sure, that these men were no longer in a position to help him. In any case, in November 1945, there was no one to whom he wanted to show his manuscripts who was likely to welcome him particularly or even to know him.

For four weeks Mishima was on tenterhooks waiting for a decision on his stories. Finally they were returned, rejected. What Mishima did not know, and was not to learn until years later when he had become a friend of Nakamura's, was that the critic had awarded the eight stories a total grade of "minus one hundred and twenty points." Nakamura's evaluation proved to be representative of the response to Mishima's work throughout 1946, 1947, and much of 1948. In view of the chasm that separated the concerns of the age and his hopelessly private fantasies, this was not surprising.

In the early postwar years, thought and literature were dominated by the Left. Among the first steps taken by GHQ in October 1945 were the release of political prisoners and the abolishment of the secret police, the Propaganda Ministry, and the Board of Censors (the occupation practiced its own brand of censorship). For many Marxist intellectuals and writers who had spent the last years of the war either in prison or in hiding, these directives were literally a new lease on life. Released from prison and also, for the first time since the early thirties, from the fear of arrest, they poured into the shambles that was Tokyo from all over the land, renewed old ties, founded new magazines, and began to write with a passion bred of ten years of hardship and enforced silence.

Nor was it only the Communists who were liberated. By 1943 censorship had become so severe and paper so scarce that silence was enforced on less political writers as well, including the so-called "elder statesmen" of the literary establishment, men like Shiga, Hakucho Arai, Tanizaki and Kafu. Space in wartime magazines had always been available to established writers, so long as they festooned their work with convincing enthusiasm for the war effort. And most well-known writers (indeed, nearly all of them with the exception of Kafu, who maintained stony silence throughout the war and was consistently critical in his diaries) did write in support of the Imperial War, some opportunistically and others out of real conviction. But the Propaganda Office was a dispiriting obstacle to all but a few; and it is safe to say that nothing of lasting importance made its way into print during the war years, though a number of significant books were written in secret. A good example was Tanizaki's *The Makioka Sisters*, a long, dark study of the breakdown of traditional family values set in the middle and late thirties. When a part of the book appeared serially in January and March of 1943, it was declared "inappropriate" wartime material and banned. Tanizaki, fifty-six at the time, exiled himself to the country where he continued work on the book for the rest of the war. In July 1944 he published Volume One privately and circulated it among his friends. Early in 1947 he resumed serialization and the book was finally published in December 1948.

The flood of literary energy liberated by the occupation and the nation's pent-up hunger for the written word are reflected in the extraordinary proliferation of new magazines which began in January 1946. In that month alone thirteen major literary and cultural monthlies were founded; by the end of 1946 more than sixty new magazines were on the market.*

* Since the last decades of the nineteenth century the principal arena of Japanese literature and criticism (and, indeed, of all intellectual writing) has been the monthly magazines. This is no less true today than it was in 1946: there is no such thing as a first book; all debuts must be made in the maga-

Naturally, competition was severe. And from 1945 through 1946 and into 1947, it was the older, established writers who were being competed for. Many a new magazine sank after an issue or two because it failed to induce the old guard to publish in its pages; and all new magazines had to be careful not to allot too much space to the new writers clamoring to be heard. One result was that the literary scene in 1946 was dominated by men in their fifties and sixties. As the leftist critic Shugo Honda put it, "Beginning with the surrender we all felt like singing but certainly not war songs. But there were no new songs to sing; so for a long time we sang the old songs."

By the summer of 1946, however, new voices were beginning to attract the attention of the critics; and by the end of 1947 a group of four or five young writers were being styled "the Postwar School." Naturally, interpretations of the past and programs for the future were various. But there was a prevailing attitude about the present in 1946 and 1947, leftist-oriented to be sure, but extending into "liberal" circles as well. In February 1946, the leftist critic Masahito Ara characterized it beautifully in an essay called "A Second Prime of Youth":

When I first read that Dostoevsky had been condemned to death and then reprieved only a moment before his execution, I was filled with envy close to despair. It was not his genius I envied so much as that abnormal experience of his that not one in a thousand or even a hundred thousand can have. . . . However, what we have just experienced with the Defeat has been in no degree less traumatic or profound than that great Russian writer's experi-

zines. Until 1957, and to a lesser extent even today, relatively few novels were commissioned and written before publication. Everyone serializes, and it is the installments which are scrutinized by the critical establishment. By the time a work is bound between hard covers, whether it be a novel, a short story, or critical essays, its value has been assessed. Therefore, what happens in the magazines was, and remains, what is happening in literature.

ence. Until the emperor announced the unconditional surrender, the men and women of Japan were prepared for collective suicide. During the air raids they had entrusted their precious lives to some corner of an air-raid shelter not fit to be called a garbage can. For years they had been obliged to consider the severance of all bonds of love and affection for a scrap of red paper [i.e., draft notice] the highest honor. . . . For those incapable of ending their lives with the slavish cry Banzai for His Imperial Majesty, it is no exaggeration to reflect that the thousand days now over were a living Hell.

Looking back, it is clear that the past year has been an Annus Mirabilis. We have seen Hell, we have known Heaven, we have heard the Last Judgment, witnessed the fall of the gods and witnessed before our eyes the creation of the heavens and the earth. We have accumulated incredible experiences rarer even than Dostoevsky's.

For the new writers who were to hold the stage during the postwar years, the incineration of Hiroshima and Nagasaki and the unconditional surrender were simultaneously Judgment Day and the first day of Creation. It was impossible not to despair at what they beheld on Day One — and, indeed, for many days to follow. Tokyo, like all Japan's major cities, was a junkyard; the most conspicuous objects in the cityscape were metal safes, all that remained of households when the fires had died out, and the tall chimneys of public bathhouses, which American bombardiers had assumed were small factories. In the severe winter of 1946 and again in the winter of 1947 thousands who were living in the parks died of cold. For those who had homes there was not enough to eat; in May of 1946 the rice ration, which was always late and never sufficient, was replaced in Tokyo by a "caloric equivalent" in scarcely edible yams and soybeans. Until the middle of 1948 the papers were filled with stories about citizens who had died of starvation because they refused to patronize the black market and had tried to survive on their weekly allotments. By the winter of 1946, a terrible inflation was on the land; the cost-of-living index was forty times what it had been in 1937. And there were no jobs. Families with possessions survived by selling them, "peeling off" a layer at a time like the layers of an onion or, in Japan, a bamboo shoot; this became known as "bamboo shoot existence."

Inevitably severe economic hardship was accompanied by social chaos. In 1946 and 1947 eight hundred thousand repatriated troops from His Majesty's Imperial Army poured into Tokyo alone. These unhappy men were received coldly: the city couldn't bear to be reminded of the war. Many were maimed and became beggars on the streets in tattered military uniforms. Those of able body found they were discriminated against when they sought employment and had to join the gangs which ran the black market. On every Tokyo street-corner hoods with belly bands and American pennies in their ears "peddled" food and clothing (shoes were not manufactured domestically until 1948; an American pair cost $60 in a store, $5 on the street), toilet paper (the government ration was twelve sheets a week per family), and whiskey. It was a time not only of domestic hardship and social mayhem but profound humiliation. The Japanese diet was so low in sugar that a whiff of the tinfoil wrapping from a stick of chewing gum was enough to cause dizziness: a few sticks of gum tossed into the street from a jeep were sufficient to create a small riot. In many neighborhoods GIs, including blacks (who struck fear into the hearts of most Japanese), were "shacked up" with local girls won over by stockings and lipstick, known as *onlys* and recognizable in the streets by their cosmetic attempts to

71

look as "western" — heavy rouge and lipstick, blowzy clothes — as possible. Speakers at train stations blared American boogie-woogie.

In every respect it was a nightmarish time, and the writing of the period is dark and sorely wounded. But however grim the reality appeared and was, the young writers of the Postwar School shared with the critic Ara the unshakable conviction that life was precious and to be affirmed. This group — Hiroshi Noma, Haruo Umezaki, and Rinzo Shiina, to name the principals — were all men in their early thirties, men who had been "baptized in Marxism" as students before the war. Moreover, all of them had fought in the Imperial Army. For them death was not merely a concept to be sublimated into a fantasy. Their death had been assured, and miraculously, like Dostoevsky, they had been reprieved. By no means was their writing optimistic. Hiroshi Noma's "A Red Moon in Her Face" (April 1946), for example, expresses his fear that the war experience has so dehumanized him that he is no longer capable of caring about other people. The hero has sacrificed a comrade during a battle to save his own life. He meets a young woman who has lost her husband in the war and is drawn to her by her sad and needful beauty. He wants to fill the emptiness of her life with himself but finds he has only emptiness to offer her. And the image of his sacrifice of his comrade in battle recurs to mock his charitable impulse. The conclusion, that love is no longer possible after the war, is despairing, forlorn. Yet the story is animated by a will to care and to love, a passionate desire to recover. In this it is representative of postwar writing.

For Yukio Mishima, the surrender was no reprieve but a sentence to life. In August 1944 he had written "The murderer," meaning *the artist*, "had less use for recovery than for any illness. He disdained passion directed toward recovery." These lines expressed many things for him, but in essence they meant that for the young artist, death was more beautiful and more precious than life. It was not that he wanted to die in any conventional sense: when he was finally confronted with death as a reality in 1944 he ran from it as fast as his legs would carry him. But he was captive to a romantic longing for death as an esthetic ideal which originated in his erotic nature, his very sexual identity. And changes in external reality could neither release him from his longing nor alter its nature: the emperor had announced Japan's surrender, but death remained his "life's aim."

From 1946 through 1948 Mishima remained engrossed in his private reality. The difference was that he was now forced to the realization that his passion was carrying him directly away from the concerns of the postwar age. The wartime reality had been congenial; it had offered itself to him for abstraction, fed his passion, and permitted him to feel in "correspondence." But the new reality he found alien, intractable, forbidding. Like "The Boy Who Wrote Poetry," he "cast a cold eye on it, considering it unworthy of a poem," and resolutely turned to a passionate affirmation of his private reality. Later he would characterize these years more than once as a "time of brutal lyricism":

Summer has come again. As I walk through this stinging light, this dizzying glare, the early years of the postwar period are renewed in me with a curious vividness. The decadence which followed that destruction, that grotesque life which had been placed back to back with death — for me, that was summer. The glistening putrescence and the season of rebirth, that was summer. I have the feeling that for me, midsummer continued without a break from 1945 through 1947 and into 1948. It was for me a

73

period of the most violent, the most vicious lyricism. . . . During those years which, in view of my age should have been my most vital, I was in fact closest to death. . . . I felt that somehow I must affirm all of myself and my life.

Mishima's "violently lyrical" attempt at self-affirmation in spite of reality is best observed in his first novel, *Thieves*, about a young couple who commit love suicide on their wedding night, but not for love of one another. Mishima began the book in January 1946 and wrote most of a first draft by June of that year, when he seems to have reached an impasse. In 1947 he resumed it, revising and publishing chapters out of order in several small magazines. The completed novel appeared in November 1948 and, despite a glowing preface by Mishima's new mentor, Yasunari Kawabata, was ignored. This was inevitable, for *Thieves* was an excruciatingly private book and the times demanded social vision. As one critic put it, "In that period of social tumult the pressing problem was to build a foundation for a new building; at a moment when the major concern was where to select a vacant lot to break ground, no one could be bothered about the quality of the lace for the window curtains."

The hero of *Thieves* resembles Mishima as he must have seen himself in 1946. Akihide Fujimura, a recent graduate of the Peers' School and the Imperial University, the son of a nobleman, is a "dreamer" of such intensity that he has "lost the yardstick for measuring present reality." He is also possessed of a nearly superhuman capacity to deceive others *and himself* about his real feelings. So far, the self-characterization is not unironic. But in the first pages of the novel the narrator asserts that Akihide's very capacity to deceive himself, to maintain an illusion in the face of whatever the reality, qualifies him uniquely as a hero of modern tragedy, which originates not in "external events in the manner of classical tragedy but in internal developments." Thus Mishima exalts his incapacity to face reality into a requisite for tragedy.

Summering with his mother at a fashionable resort, Akihide conceives a "grand passion" for a beautiful debutante, Yoshiko. They have an affair and are discovered by their parents. At summer's end, Akihide's family petitions Yoshiko's family for her hand in marriage; Yoshiko refuses. Akihide, a master at self-deception, is at first unaware of pain at having been rejected. Then, as he stands at the sea one day, he "realizes" that "his longing for Yoshiko had been magnificently converted to a longing for death." It is not that Akihide has chosen death because he has been rejected; if that were the case he would be drawn away from death by the possibility of reconciliation. But reconciliation clearly is *not* what he longs for:

Suddenly Akihide considered telling his friend all about what had happened between himself and Yoshiko. Arakura, who was without equal in his capacity to be moved by a confession, would weep tears with Akihide, wring his hand, and then jump up and force his way into Yoshiko, whom he had never met, with the story. Yoshiko would be moved and would come here to see him. Crying!

At this point Akihide regained his senses. How could he even have considered such foolishness! He wondered if such insanity might not return; and the thought filled him with fear.

What Akihide wants is "Death,

which, like a flower that has now forgotten the time when it was a seed above the ground, was free of the strictures of cause and effect, a glittering entity unto itself, independent and complete.

75

Confronted as he looks out over the sea by "death as a glittering entity" — an end unto itself — Akihide resolves to die. The resolution is exalting:

> Akihide could hear the light footfall of destiny. All phenomena extended a quiet hand and gently recommended him to death. Suddenly pride rose in him, as if he were destiny's favorite child.

Here again, as in Mishima's wartime writing, death is exalted into destiny. The difference is that self-deceit has now become essential to perceiving and attaining that destiny:

> He must have realized the last time he saw her that he was ardently desiring death. Had he not deceived himself about his longing all this time in order to nourish his resolve as secretly as possible, without exposing it to the wind! Was it not the deceit he had practiced on himself which now permitted him to feel so keenly the strength of his resolve, this intimacy with it, its inevitability! . . .

While Tokyo burned, reality could be used to reinforce illusion. But now that the flames were out, it was possible to perceive death as personal destiny only by practicing self-deceit, resolutely disregarding reality and affirming illusion.

In the second half of the novel Akihide enters a "lover's pact" with another girl, Kiyoko, who has also, independently, resolved to die after having been spurned by her lover. The two are united by their mutual resolution to die and by their discovery that they can serve one another as mirrors in which to behold their private illusions of the lovers who have rejected them. The key word is *illusion*: both Akihide and the girl revel in the knowledge that the images they see in one another are illusions, meaningless glorifications of their former lovers. The labored, paradoxical point is that the fulfillment of death is obtainable only when illusion can be sustained in the face of reality. By permitting one another to sustain their illusions, the "lovers" are permitted to sustain their will to die. And on their wedding night they do achieve death, by double (lovers') suicide.

It is possible to read *Thieves* as a sardonic commentary on love: certainly there are places in the novel where Mishima is ironic about his hero:

> The drastic measures that other young men would undoubtedly have considered — for example, lying in wait and, when the girl finally appeared, holding her until he had spoken his heart — were to Akihide like dreams within dreams. How could I do anything as unreal as that — like a character in a novel! His own fantasies, which he projected on everything he did, made even realities which ordinary people would have achieved seem like hardly more than dreams themselves.

But the ironic impulse is occasional. Mishima wrote *Thieves* intending from the beginning to vindicate his heroes (and himself) in their stubborn adherence to illusion. If his intent is often obscured in the main body of the novel it is clear in the short coda. At a Christmas Eve party sometime after the "lovers" have died, the original villains of the piece, the "heartless boy" and the "beautiful girl" who have spurned Akihide and Kiyoko, ignorant of any connection between themselves, meet for the first time:

> "This is Mr. Saeki."
> "This is Miss Harada."
> "How do you do."
> "Pleased to meet you."
> Yoshiko lifted her face and for the first time peered at this mar-

velously handsome young man. To an onlooker their eyes met
sweetly. But in that instant, as if they had discovered in one
another's faces a terrifying devastation no one else could understand, both tried desperately to avoid the other's glance . . . and
for just a moment stood motionlessly, paralyzed with fear. It was
Yoshiko who first backed off trembling.

At the same moment both of them had been struck by an impulse to speak in front of others of this fearful discovery. What
they had discovered was that the true beauty and everlasting
youth within them had been uprooted and borne away by some
exceedingly skillful thief.

There is nothing remotely ironic about this; it proclaims
that the young heroes have achieved, in death, "everlasting
youth and true beauty," and it vindicates their rejection of
reality in favor of illusion. Of course, it also conveys Mishima's
total engrossment in his own fantasy world and his anxious
need in 1946 and 1947 to affirm that world in the very teeth of
an uncongenial reality.

In the same 1955 reminiscence in which he wrote that he
was "closest to death" during these years, Mishima attributed
his "brutal lyricism" to two incidents in his personal life which,
he reflected, "must have been the propellant force behind my
literary passion in the years that followed." The first was the
death of his sister Mitsuko in October 1945:

Japan's defeat was not a matter of particular regret for me. A
far more sorrowful incident was my sister Mitsuko's death a few
months later. I loved my sister. I loved her to an inexplicable degree. At the time she was a student at Sacred Heart Women's
College; one day when she had been helping classmates move
books back into the library, which had been evacuated, she suddenly developed a fever. The doctor said it was flu; but the fever
stayed high and she lost her appetite. She was taken to Keio Hospital and very quickly went into a coma. As soon as the diagnosis

of typhoid fever was confirmed, she was transferred to a smaller hospital for infectious diseases [Keio's infectious diseases annex had been burned].

My mother and I took turns nursing her; but she began intestinal hemorrhaging and soon died. A few hours before her death, when she was quite delirious, I heard her say clearly, "Brother, thank you," and I wept.

Shizue confirms this account of Mitsuko's death. She says that Mishima would come to the hospital straight from his lectures at the university, draw up a chair to his sister's bed, and sit with her motionlessly through the night, never taking his eyes from her, sponging her brow and spoonfeeding her sugar water. Apparently the hospital in Okubo to which Mitsuko was transferred was understaffed, dark, and squalid. Watching his sister die in such surroundings undoubtedly contributed to the morbid darkness which deepened in Mishima during these postwar years.

To the second incident, which in the long run had a more decisive effect on him, Mishima refers more cryptically: "There was another postwar incident in my personal life. A girl with whom I had associated during the war and to whom I would shortly have been engaged, because of my indecision, married someone else." Unquestionably this girl was real, but I have failed to uncover her identity. Those who know, Shizue for one, and the woman who later would introduce Mishima to his wife, have refused to name her or to say anything about her except that she was a classmate of Mishima's sister. The only available information is therefore Mishima's brief reference in the above essay and *Confessions of a Mask*, of which the final third is devoted to Mishima's relationship with Sonoko, as he calls her.

79

Pressed for details of what actually happened, Shizue would say only that the story was just as Mishima recorded it in *Confessions*. In the novel, the hero meets Sonoko late in 1944 and for the remaining months of the war attempts agonizingly but without success to experience physical desire for her and thereby prove to himself that he is normal. His efforts to fabricate "normal" passion culminate when finally he brings himself to kiss Sonoko and feels nothing. Sonoko is ignorant of this, supposes her own excitement to be his, and begins hinting about marriage. Shortly before the surrender, the hero receives a letter from Sonoko's brother urging him to name a date for the engagement. As he reads the letter, he is elated by the thought that he has "become a man who can entice a woman without even loving her and then, when love blazes up in her, abandon her without thinking twice about it."

The hero knows that he is lying to himself about not loving Sonoko, but his fear drives him to maintain the pretense. He calls to his mother who is gardening just outside his room; the scene is set in Gotokuji, in the suburban house where Shizue and the children moved for safety in the spring of 1945. Shizue remembers the conversation, and says it was just as Mishima described it. The hero tells his mother about the letter and suggests hesitantly that the time is not right for marriage in view of the uncertainty of the future. When his mother presses him he "admits" that he is not certain that he loves Sonoko. Naturally, his mother advises him to call the marriage off. That night the hero writes "a letter of indirect refusal, which sounded artificial even to me."

In *Confessions of a Mask* the Sonoko episode does not end with this. More than a year after the war, in the spring of 1947, the hero runs into Sonoko in the street and feels that he still loves her: "To me she appeared the incarnation of my love of normality itself, my love of things of the spirit, my love of everlasting things." Every few months through the summer of 1948 he manages to meet Sonoko for an innocent hour or two of pretending to sustain a "chimerical love like a gas" that exists when you believe it and disappears when you don't. In fact he has never believed so much as desperately wanted to; inevitably, the time comes when Sonoko also begins to doubt. In the last, brilliant scene of the novel, on a hot day in September 1948 (when in fact Mishima was just beginning to work on *Confessions of a Mask*), they wander into a cheap dance hall. The hero is transfixed by the sight of a young tough naked to the waist with a peony tattooed on his chest. He loses himself in one of his "bloody, brutal visions" and realizes only when Sonoko's "high, sad voice" calls him back that he has forgotten utterly her existence. The implications are as terrifying as they are unmistakable:

At this instant something inside of me was torn in two with brutal force. It was as though a thunderbolt had fallen and cleaved asunder a living tree. I heard the structure which I had been building piece by piece with all my might up to now collapse miserably to the ground.

The danger of using *Confessions of a Mask* as a biographical document is that Mishima imposed an interpretative scheme on his experience which essentially eliminates what must have been the dominant grays of confusion and ambivalence and makes of every moment a startling epiphany. It is unlikely, for example, that his first glimpse of Sonoko filled him with "remorse as prelude to sin," by which the hero means that he knew at once that he would be impelled to entice the girl on false grounds. So is it unlikely that after one kiss "he knew everything." Unfortunately there is no way of knowing whether Mishima continued "playing with fire" with Sonoko after the war, but even assuming that he did, it is also improbable, particularly as late as the fall of 1948, the date the novel establishes for the last scene, that a decisive lightning bolt illuminated the impossibility of his masquerade of normality. Nonetheless there is no reason to assume that Mishima exaggerated the impact upon himself of Sonoko's marriage, however he may have overclarified its significance in *Confessions of a Mask*. Once Shizue let slip in a kind of aside that "Kimitake" had drunk himself into a stupor for the first and only time in his life the day he heard the news of "her" marriage.

Possibly a more realistic representation of the immediate effect on Mishima of "Sonoko's" marriage is implicit in *Thieves*. (It is not impossible, as *Thieves* might be read as suggesting, that it was *Mishima* who was rejected; but in either case the final implication of the rift, that he was not capable of a "normal" relationship with a woman, would have been the same.) In *Thieves*, when the hero learns that the girl has spurned his offer of marriage,

He couldn't believe that what was now before him was the loss he had been fearing since the moment he had met Yoshiko. *This languorous suffering which in the beginning was not accompanied by any symptoms he could feel was beyond his understanding.* (Italics mine.)

Adding to this the hero's subsequent "discovery" that his longing for the girl has been converted to a longing for death may provide a replica of the immediate effect on Mishima of "Sonoko's" marriage. Very likely it produced in him a "languorous suffering" which he could neither account for nor was prepared at the time to examine. The effect of this anxiety was to reinforce his withdrawal into the "brutal lyricism" which characterizes his writing during these years.

Throughout the writing of *Thieves* Mishima depended for encouragement on Yasunari Kawabata. Mishima went to see Kawabata for the first time on New Year's Day 1946, at the author's home in Kamakura, thirty miles south of Tokyo. Later he would "fail to remember" what if anything had given him the courage to visit the older man, and no one has claimed credit for having introduced him. Whatever the details may have been, Mishima in his quest for a new mentor could not have made a more appropriate choice than Kawabata. In November of 1945 the forty-six-year-old novelist had declared in a short essay his disinclination to continue living in the postwar age:

I have the strong, unavoidable feeling that my life is already at an end. For me there is only the solitary return to the mountains and rivers of the past. From this point on, as one already dead, I intend to write only of the poor beauty of Japan, not a line else.

Assuming that Mishima had read this, which is likely, it must have provided all the reassurance he needed to take to Kawabata unsolicited the same manuscripts which Mitsuo Nakamura had just rejected.

Not surprisingly, Kawabata liked what he read and strongly recommended Mishima's stories for publication in a new magazine called *Ningen* (*Man*) which he had just founded with a group of other writers also resident in Kamakura. In fact Kawabata was vice-president of the small founding company called the Kamakura Library (originally a lending library to which the Kamakura writers had all contributed during the war), and so his recommendation was decisive. When Mishima learned several weeks later that one of his stories was scheduled for publication in *Ningen* he was jubilant. His brother Chiyuki recalls that it was as if "the hand of God, who was of course Kawabata, had suddenly reached down from Heaven and taken him onto its palm."

As it turned out, Mishima was hard-pressed to sustain his excitement: publication of "Cigarette," a reminiscence about his early days in the literary club with delicately homosexual undertones, was repeatedly postponed at the last minute to make room for more established writers. Each month Mishima rushed out to buy the new issue of *Ningen* only to discover that his story once again had been "held over." When "Cigarette" finally appeared in the June issue of *Ningen* no critic of importance paid it any attention; Mishima's official debut in the postwar literary establishment passed unnoticed. In November, Kawabata arranged to have "A Tale at the Cape" published in the major literary monthly *Gunzo*, and it was similarly ignored.

Throughout 1947 Mishima fared no better with the critics. In fact he fared not at all. In April he published a new story in *Gunzo*, a lush, antique celebration of the earliest lovers' suicide in Japanese recorded history, "Prince Karu and Princess Sotobori." In August and again in December he published novellas in *Ningen*. The first, "Preparations for the Evening," was a "psychological study" of high society carryings-on during the final months of the war; the second, "Haruko," was an impressively detailed portrait of a lesbian. In the writing of both these long stories Mishima had help from the editor of *Ningen* who had commissioned them, Tokuzo Kimura. Kimura went over the manuscripts sentence by sentence, demonstrating to Mishima the prolixity and preciousness that would always be his weakness; Mishima was sufficiently impressed to make revisions on the spot. In the case of "Preparations for the Evening," he whittled the hundred-page manuscript down to eighty pages in the course of one afternoon's session with Kimura; later he would say that all his stories during these years were in effect "collaborative efforts." Unquestionably Kimura's guidance resulted in a tighter construction and a less indulgent style than Mishima had been capable of previously; "Preparations for the Evening" was his most mature work to date. But with the notable exception of Kawabata and a very few others, no one who mattered was impressed. In November a small publisher brought out Mishima's second volume of short stories, A *Tale at the Cape*. The book was not reviewed. At the end of 1947, Mishima was still essentially unnoticed.

In these early postwar years, Mishima was a writer only at night; in fact he was Yukio Mishima only at night. By day he was Kimitake Hiraoka, a law student at the Imperial University. From October 1945, when classes resumed, until he graduated in November 1947, Mishima attended lectures faithfully, in an old Peers' School uniform. "I was too absorbed in my writing to make a thorough study of the law," he would later write, "but I did get as far as the heretical discovery that a Law lecture could be listened to as literature. I was fond of criminal law, of criminal and civil suits. Until then I had been infatuated with the Romantic School (that worst disease of youth) and now for the first time I discovered the appeal of dry-as-dustness."

At school Mishima kept to himself. At the end of the day he went straight home, ate with the family, then went upstairs to his room where he wrote until far into the night. Saturday nights were a curious and seemingly uncharacteristic exception: he would leave the house at eight, occasionally with his brother Chiyuki in tow, to join a group of wealthy young aristocrats on a round of "dance parties" and barrack nightclubs.

Although the Hiraokas were better off than most Tokyoites (the Shibuya house had not been damaged in the air raids, and Azusa had managed to put away enough money so that neither of the boys had to help out with part-time jobs), Mishima was far from wealthy; his connection with this set was a carryover from his days at the Peers' School. It was a small, highly exclusive group with a limited territory isolated like an island in the sea of ruin that was Tokyo. There were several, no more than half a dozen, barrack nightclubs which had been thrown together to accommodate primarily officers with the occupation. The most famous was the Latin Quarter, which still stands on the same site in Akasaka. In 1947 it was merely a barrack building with a dance floor, a Japanese band playing American tunes, and a bar stocked with black market whiskey. Although wealthy young Japanese were admitted, it was clear that American servicemen and their "ladies" were preferred: the tuxedoed Japanese at the door greeted his countrymen in English, "Good evening, sir."

Mishima's crowd gathered every week for parties at the Latin Quarter or at private homes in Karuizawa, a fashionable resort several hours north of the city which had not been bombed. There was a lot of drinking and, in the American style, promiscuity. Mishima neither drank nor smoked at the time; certainly he was not promiscuous, not yet, never in a circle like this. But he did accommodate himself to the extent of taking dancing lessons in the summer of 1946. Perhaps, as he always maintained, Mishima truly loved to dance. Or perhaps the "zest" for dancing he began to display as early as

86

1946 was one of his earliest simulations of normalcy. I have seen Mishima "lose himself" to the Monkey or the Watusi in the mid-sixties and it was like watching a studied imitation of a dancer; he always looked horrifyingly sober, though clearly his movements and expressions were intended to create the effect not merely of spontaneity but enthrallment. In any case, he was a bad dancer, uncoordinated and apparently deaf to music. In 1946 and 1947, when he was still a wan, emaciated figure, his jitterbug must have been an awesome sight.

None of Mishima's debonair friends during these years had any reason to suppose that he was feeling "closest to death" even as he madly danced with them. Possibly he was not fully conscious himself of how deeply he had withdrawn into his private reality. But however innocent he may have been of the nature of his "brutal lyricism," he cannot have believed for very long about himself, no matter how authentically he behaved, that he was really one of the crowd. The clearest indication that he was not at home with his friends or their way of life was his abrupt farewell to them in the summer of 1947. At that time, five months before he was to graduate from law school, Azusa confronted him with a new demand, that he take the "higher civil service examination." This was a test designed to intimidate all but the brightest and most ambitious candidates for a career in the civil service. A student was guaranteed a good bureaucratic career simply by virtue of having graduated from Tokyo Imperial University. But those who had hopes of reaching the highest rungs, of becoming ministers, for example, also had to pass the "higher civil." Always in character, Azusa was determined that Kimitake should go to the top and therefore demanded that he prepare for the examination. To Azusa's surprise Mishima agreed without protest. Possibly he was sufficiently discouraged by his failure to gain recognition as a writer to have considered seriously at this point a career as a bureaucrat. Possibly this was simply another instance of his inability, or disinclination, to cross his father. At any rate, he said yes and proceeded immediately to take leave of his friends at a party. Chiyuki was there and remembers his brother moving from couple to couple, shaking hands and announcing that he must retire from social life "for a time" to prepare for the exam. Though he would renew these acquaintances from time to time when it suited his purposes, he was never again a regular member of the group.

Mishima passed the difficult "higher civil" effortlessly and in November 1947 graduated from the Law Department of Imperial University (since October 1, 1947, officially renamed the University of Tokyo). He now possessed all the credentials necessary for an elite bureaucratic career and applied at once for a position in the Finance Ministry. The choice of ministries was also Azusa's. Evidently Azusa had been made to feel and resent the power of the Finance Ministry, particularly the Budget Bureau, during his years as a bureaucrat, and it was to the source of power that he directed his son.

Unquestionably the Finance Ministry was for the cream of the elite, the ministry most difficult to enter. Having acceded to his father yet again, Mishima proceeded to pass the entrance examination and on Christmas Eve 1947 formally received his first (and only) bureaucratic appointment, to the national savings section of the Banking Bureau, Ministry of Finance.

Mishima was a bureaucrat for nearly nine months, from January to mid-September 1948. During this period he survived on three or four hours' sleep a night, for he had to be at work at eight-thirty and invariably he wrote until three in the morning. According to one of his colleagues, he was "cautioned" more than once by his section head for sleepily miscopying figures. But as with all his many roles he seems in general to have succeeded in playing and looking his part: the same colleague remembers him as a "bright-eyed boy bureaucrat in a neatly pressed suit." A few of his fellow bureaucrats knew that Hiraoka was also the writer Yukio Mishima; and once he was even asked to draft a speech for the finance minister. His section head returned the draft, covered with corrections in red ink, with a note saying it was "far too elaborate."

When Mishima resigned after nine months at the ministry it was with his father's permission. One rainy September morning shortly after he had left the house for work he came back and reported to his parents that he had slipped from the platform onto the tracks while waiting groggily for his train at Shibuya station, just managing with someone's help to climb back in time. Perhaps this had really happened, and perhaps it was Mishima's way of making an effective appeal to Azusa. Given his determination to leave the job, he might well have resigned eventually even if it had meant defying his father. But that turned out to be unnecessary. When Azusa heard the story, he said to his son, "Then quit the job and become a novelist, but make very sure you become the best in the land." Mishima is said to have answered merely, "Yes, I will." The following day he submitted his resignation, explaining to a friend who shared a desk with him that he had hoped "like many French novelists" to support himself some other way since writing novels for a living was so difficult, but had discovered that this particular job made it impossible to keep "both rivers flowing." On September 13, 1948, his resignation was accepted; from that day on Kimitake Hiraoka was never more than a legal name on contracts.

In view of Mishima's background, the family emphasis on

conventional success, and the time he had devoted to acquiring his credentials, his resignation from an elite bureaucratic post to become a novelist was a drastic step, particularly since he was by no means a widely recognized writer in September 1948. He had managed to publish an even dozen stories during his nine months at the Finance Ministry, several of them in major literary magazines. He knew that his first novel, *Thieves*, would be published in November and that his third volume of short stories, *Preparations for the Evening*, would be published in December by Kawabata's publishing house, Kamakura Library. But since only two of his 1948 stories had been reviewed at the time of their original publication in magazines, he had no reason to expect that these new volumes would bring him acclaim. In spite of his dazzling talent and his prolificness given the schedule he had been forced to keep, the fact was that Mishima's special preoccupations had deprived him of any sort of general recognition.

No doubt he was apprehensive about his prospects for the future when he resigned: he had, and would always have, his practical, even calculating, side. But if his resignation was a courageous step it was also a desperate one, necessitated by his sense of personal crisis. The autobiographical novel he had well in mind at the time he quit, *Confessions of a Mask*, was to be a therapeutic effort. It was a book Mishima felt certain he must write in order, quite literally, to survive.

It is impossible to know what it was precisely that brought Mishima in the fall of 1948 to the writing of *Confessions of a Mask*, itself a drastic step. Possibly, as the novel suggests, the termination of his relationship with "Sonoko" opened his eyes to the direction in which his fantasy life was leading him. But for this there is only Mishima's word, Mishima's interpretation. Possibly there were no specifically isolatable forces at work; the natural evolution of Mishima's consciousness may have brought him to a realization of the danger to himself of his esthetic involvement with death and destruction.

Yet if any single incident was likely to have contributed to Mishima's awakening, not from his fantasies but to their significance, it was the suicide of the novelist Osamu Dazai in June 1948. Dazai was a brilliant and above all a passionate writer bent from the beginning of his career on self-destruction. His fundamental despair about himself led him in the course of his life to a passionate indulgence in every brand of dissipation; he was a notorious womanizer, an alcoholic, a drug addict. Into each of his weaknesses he flung himself headlong, hating himself for his indulgence and unable to abstain, repeatedly reaching the conclusion which was the title of his last book, that he was *No Longer Human*. From his very first work in the mid-thirties, in which he wrote of his affair with a Tokyo bar girl and their attempted lovers' suicide, in which only the girl died and Dazai survived to shame his family and hate himself, his theme and method were the passionate documentation of self-despair. For the devoted millions who read him amid the rubble of their own lives, Dazai more than any other writer was the spokesman of the age, a popular hero who, albeit he always reached the same desperate conclusion about himself, continued to struggle against his fate. In June 1948, having published a series of best-selling novels, Dazai finally did what all his heroes had either attempted or seriously considered; he tied himself to his mistress with a kimono sash and jumped into the Setagaya Reservoir, leaving behind a wife and three children.

Mishima's only meeting with Dazai, in January 1947, is now a famous incident in Japanese literary history. A circle of fledgling writers had persuaded Dazai to join them for an

91

afternoon of talk and drinking. At a time when the only alcohol available was a murderous rice whiskey distilled from dregs, a young poet in the group had obtained several half-gallon bottles of rice wine (*sake*) and this was the bait. Dazai appeared at the poet's shabby room with the essayist Katsuichiro Kamei (one of the first of the writers to have been purged). Mishima went along with a young playwright named Yashiro, an avid admirer of Dazai's. The bottles were passed from mouth to mouth, Dazai proceeded to get quite drunk at once, and the others followed. Mishima, who did not drink, sat stiffly apart watching in silence. Abruptly, during a drunken lull in the conversation, he moved forward to confront Dazai, looked him straight in the eye and said, smiling, "I don't like your writing." According to Mishima, describing the encounter sixteen years later, "Dazai peered at my face and then drew back slightly, looking as if he had been caught off his guard. But he recovered instantly and, turning halfway toward Kamei, said to no one in particular, 'But he's here, isn't he, so he must think I'm pretty good; he must like what I do or he wouldn't be here.' "

The playwright Yashiro says that this exchange, or one very like it, did occur. He remembers that Mishima left shortly afterward and that a few days later he came to tell him that his association with "a man like that" could only do him harm.

In Mishima's account he writes that he had gone to see Dazai expressly to tell him to his face that he disliked him, and describes himself arriving "with a dagger hidden in the folds of [his] robes, like a terrorist." Specifically he abhors Dazai's "shameless self-caricature," the "affected Christ-like face visible" behind every page, his "confident pride that he was representative of the malaise of the Age," in short, Dazai's "glorification of despair." But Mishima does not stop with listing the qualities in Dazai he cannot abide; he seeks to explain why they so repulsed him:

Naturally I recognize Dazai's rare talent; and yet I know of no other writer who from my very first contact with him filled me with so violent a physiological revulsion. Possibly . . . this was due to my immediate sense that Dazai was a writer at pains to expose precisely that which I most wanted to conceal in myself.

What this suggests — very likely the truth — is that Mishima was beginning to locate in himself the same self-destructive impulses he saw in Dazai and was converting the terror of this self-awakening to a hatred of the other man. Mishima declared he hated Dazai because he glorified his weakness, the destructive addictions he was helpless to resist. And what was *Thieves* if not a glorification of Mishima's addiction to fantasies whose luminous object was death! If it was true that he was beginning to identify a similarity between himself and Dazai even before the latter writer's suicide, then he also must have been approaching an awareness of his own addiction and its implications for himself. There is evidence that such was the case in an essay called "A Lethal Weapon for the Seriously Wounded," which Mishima wrote in March 1948, only three months before Dazai's death. His intent was to "prove" that for his generation, suicide was impossible. He began with what he claimed was a new "logic" unique to his generation:

Can suffering kill a man — Nay!
Can ideological anguish kill a man? — Nay!
Can grief kill a man? — Nay!
East and West, now as ever, nothing can kill a man except *death*.

93

To conclude this is to make of life a matter very simple, very clear. I intend to devote my life to believing in this clarity.

To maintain that only death can kill is to assert the impossibility of dying for something. This "logic of health," as Mishima called it, was designed to lead to the following conclusion:

The war did not wound us in spirit. Moreover, it toughened our skin. Our undamaged souls are now wrapped in toughened skin. We are virtually impervious; like the sideshow performers at local fairs, we do not bleed though our chests, our hands and feet be pierced by knives. Those who bleed at the slightest wound curse us as cold-blooded. But they do not consider the plight of a virtual immortal for whom suicide will never be possible.

"A virtual immortal for whom suicide will never be possible"! This is what Mishima intends to tell us and himself in March 1948. Surely it is an uneasy assertion. And surely Dazai's love-suicide three months later was a terrifying warning to him. It can hardly be coincidence that so soon afterward he took the first step toward what he hoped would be recovery.

Mishima knew when he left the Finance Ministry in September 1948 that his next book must not indulge in fantasy but dispel it. In a note dated November 2, 1948, he informed his new editor of his intentions:

This will be my first "autobiographical novel." I don't mean the conventional *ich-roman* we have grown so accustomed to. I will turn upon myself the scalpel of psychological analysis I have sharpened on fictive characters. I will attempt to dissect myself alive. I hope to achieve a scientific accuracy, to become, in the words of Baudelaire, both the condemned and the executioner. It requires determination, but I will hold my nose and write ahead.

Mishima was not speaking lightly: in *Confessions of a Mask* he did dissect himself alive. What he hoped to find was the source of his fascination with death, in his own words, "the root source of [his] reckless, nihilistic estheticism." What he discovered was his homosexuality.

Reliving his life in *Confessions of a Mask* through his first-person hero, Mishima drove himself remorselessly to the recognition that he was a latent homosexual and, worse, a man incapable of feeling passion or even alive except in sado-masochistic fantasies which reeked of blood and death. There is no drama in this history of sexual awakening: the hero knows when he begins his story what its conclusion will be. On page 14 of the novel he tells the reader as much:

Ever since childhood my ideas concerning human existence have never once deviated from the Augustinian theory of predetermination. . . . I had been handed what might be called a full menu of all the troubles in my life while still too young to read it. But all I had to do was spread my napkin and face the table. Even the fact that I would now be writing an odd book like this was precisely noted on the menu, where it must have been before my eyes from the beginning.

Mishima's determination in *Confessions of a Mask* to derive from his past a proof of abnormality is easily discerned. The difficulty is understanding what he hoped to accomplish. The answer is suggested by his method in this book, the manner in which he discloses the truths of his past. Consider the passage in which the hero confesses that he was incited at age twelve to his first *ejaculatio* (the word Mishima uses) by a reproduction of Guido Reni's *Saint Sebastian*. He begins by describing the picture — "The arrows have eaten into the tense, fragrant youthful flesh and are about to consume his body from within with flames of supreme agony and ecstasy." — and the act

95

of masturbation his excitement leads him to. He then interjects in a long parenthesis a psychiatric observation by one Hirschfeld:

(It is an interesting coincidence that Hirschfeld should place "pictures of Saint Sebastian" in the first rank of those kinds of works of art in which the invert takes special delight. This observation of Hirschfeld's leads easily to the conjecture that in the overwhelming majority of cases of inversion, especially of congenital inversion, the inverted and the sadistic impulses are inextricably entangled with each other.)

And this in turn is followed by an "unfinished prose poem on Saint Sebastian," which the hero claims to have written when he was fifteen. It is offered as proof that "[his] own rapture before the legend, before the picture," was a "fiercely sensual thing":

This was Sebastian, young captain in the Praetorian guard. And was not such beauty as his a thing destined for death? Did not the robust women of Rome . . . quickly scent his ill-starred fate, as yet unknown to him, and love him for that reason? His blood was coursing with an even fiercer pace than usual within his white flesh, watching for an opening from which to spurt forth when that flesh would be torn asunder. How could the women have failed to hear the tempestuous desires of such blood as this?

His was not a fate to be pitied. In no way was it a pitiable fate. Rather was it proud and tragic, a fate that might even be called radiant.

When one considers well, it seems that many a time, even in the midst of a sweet kiss, a foretaste of the agony of death must have furrowed his brow with a fleeting shadow of pain.

And he must have foreseen, if dimly, that it was nothing less than martyrdom which lay in wait for him along the way; that this brand which fate had set upon him was precisely the token of his apartness from all the ordinary men of earth.

Mishima is a marvelous mimic of himself: the passage might have appeared in almost anything he had ever written *previous* to *Confessions of a Mask*. Blood and the sea, the special beauty which destines the hero for death, his "radiant destiny" — all the elements of Mishima's esthetic are assembled here. But there is a crucial difference. Until now, this kind of *homage* to beauty and death was the *subject* of his art. But in the context of *Confessions of a Mask* it is *objectified*, offered as a clinical example of what no less an authority than "Hirschfeld" has just explained as *merely* the sadomasochism frequently encountered in "inverts." Thus Mishima's heretofore mysterious and terrifying sexual fascination ·with the "Martyrdom" is rationally accounted for; and this same "rational accounting" occurs, or rather is engineered, throughout the book. It is as if Mishima hoped that by explaining his "estheticism" he could escape or at least defuse it. Years later, describing his state of mind at the time of the writing, he implied just that:

I had taken secretly to jotting down epigrams such as "Whether another A-bomb falls or not is no concern of mine. All that matters to me is whether the shape of the globe would become even a little more beautiful as a result." I knew I couldn't continue in this vein; sooner or later I felt I would have to analyze comprehensively the root source of this desperate, nihilistic estheticism of mine.

Mishima often said that analysis is not possible until a conclusion has been reached. In the *Confessions* he begins with the conclusion — or possibly the hypothesis — of the essential homosexuality to which he leads his hero. Accordingly, the "mask" of this confession is no ordinary mask designed to hide the speaker's face from the confessor. On the

97

contrary, this mask of sexual perversion is donned by the confessor in an attempt to discover his real face.

The problem the book presented was not how to end it but how to substantiate its foregone conclusion. As he channeled his past into the book, Mishima was obliged at every turn to shape it in accordance with that conclusion. Not that he fabricated his homosexuality, or, properly speaking, his latent homosexuality: the data was all there in the chaos of his past. But until the writing of *Confessions of a Mask* his past, like any past, was rich with ambiguity — to say the least, inconclusive. When he finished the *Confessions*, he had more than just a past; he had a history.

Toward the end of the novel, when the hero drags himself to a brothel and demonstrates to his satisfaction (but not the reader's) that he is impotent with women, he tastes

the temporary relief a man feels when the incurable disease he has lived in fear of is finally diagnosed in him and named. Of course he knows the relief is only temporary. And in his heart he awaits a still more inescapable, hopeless, and for just that reason more lasting relief. I too had probably come to expect a blow even more impossible to parry, or, to put it another way, a still more inescapable feeling of relief.

The relief of hopelessness, then, is what the hero gains(!) from his heterosexual failure. And by implication the final moment of the novel, in which he "recognizes" the impossibility of his masquerade, will afford him the *lasting* relief of total inescapability, utter hopelessness:

At this instant, something inside of me was torn in two with brutal force. It was as though a thunderbolt had fallen and cleaved asunder a living tree. I heard the structure, which I had been building piece by piece with all my might up to now, collapse miserably to the ground.

Mishima's intent in *Confessions of a Mask* is not to confess to sexual perversion but to verify it. What he wants, requires, is a definition, a diagnosis however hopeless, so that he will be able, in the most literal sense, to live with himself. Not that any diagnosis would have sufficed. In order "rationally to account" for the "nihilistic estheticism" that was leading him to the brink of death, it was necessary to derive sexual perversion.

Artistically, *Confessions* was a success: it is one of Mishima's finest novels. But in a crucial personal sense it was a resounding failure. In his Notes to *Confessions of a Mask* Mishima wrote, "This book is a last testament I want to leave behind in the domain of death, where I have resided until now." And he consistently referred to the book as a "closing of accounts" of his twenties. The truth was otherwise; for the process by which Mishima verified a hypothesis about himself was also a process of self-discovery, an *opening* of accounts. The confession which issued from Mishima's hypothetical mask was not so much an account of the past as a prophecy of the future.

four

1950-1956

Confessions of a Mask established Mishima as a star. With a sale of twenty thousand copies in hardcover it was a best seller for 1949. And throughout the summer and fall it was discussed in all the newspapers and literary monthlies. Many critics were shocked or even disgusted by Mishima's explicitness.* But those who mattered all acknowledged, in some cases in spite of themselves, that this was a brilliant and an important book. One of several critics to admit that he had underestimated Mishima previously was Mitsuo Nakamura. Yasunari Kawabata was speaking for the establishment when

---

* The response of critic Shugo Honda was typical of this:

> The books abounds in episodes I fail to understand. For example, the hero having his first *ejaculatio* when he sees Saint Sebastian with the arrows sticking into his young body, or his becoming excited to the point of an *erection* at the sight of the dark hair in the armpits of his older, delinquent friend. And when I read the passage where he sits on a rock at the sea and commits his "bad habit" with his own armpits as an erotic object —I threw in the towel. . . . Episodes like the one in which he strangles his friend, places his body on a large western platter, and carves into his heart are just too preposterous even as imaginary games and devoid of interest for me.

he titled a short article in December "Mishima: The Hope of 1950."

In *Confessions of a Mask* Mishima had taken a giant step toward a definition of himself, but accepting that definition was no easy matter. In the fall of 1949 he asked his first editor, Tokuzo Kimura, to recommend a psychiatrist. He told Kimura he was suffering from stomach spasms and from nightmares "in sleep and in wake." Apparently he meant the sado-masochistic fantasies that fill the *Confessions*. Kimura did recommend a psychiatrist and Mishima saw him, but only once or twice.

Mishima's writing during 1950 confirms that it was a troubled year. His short stories in particular were gratuitously ugly, like screams of anguish that died in his throat. "Fruit," for example, is about a lesbian couple who decide they must have a child to be a real family. Someone leaves an unwanted infant with them and, when they have verified that it is a girl, they smother it with love. Mishima's description of their attentions to the infant manages to be as horrid as anything he wrote: one of them douses the baby's "evil-smelling" diapers with her favorite perfume; then the girls lovingly caress the infant with their lips until "her tiny chest" is left "bright red with their lipstick." Shortly the infant falls ill and dies, and the "parents" seclude themselves in their grief. Several days later a neighbor breaks into their room and discovers they have committed suicide. The little tale ends: "Like fruit left in a greenhouse to ripen and to rot, their bodies had already begun to decay. The fierce summer sun pouring through the skylight had accelerated the process."

Another example is "Sunday," about a very ordinary young couple who work at the same office and are nicknamed "Sunday" because they always spend their day off together. Mishima

101

follows them on an excursion into the country, never missing an opportunity to disdain their conventionality. At the end of the day the couple stand on a crowded platform waiting for the train to take them back into the city. Suddenly the crowd behind them pushes them onto the track in the path of the oncoming train:

Since their arms were linked together there was no danger they would have to die separately. The boy fell, and the girl was dragged down with him. Here again they were favored, for the wheels of the train sliced cleanly, accurately, through the two necks perfectly aligned on the track. Now, the train began to back up and as it did so deposited neatly side by side on the gravel between the tracks the lovers' heads. All who observed it were impressed by this trick, and felt moved to praise the engineer's curious skill.

Thus ends a brief but effective vendetta against healthy mediocrity.

Mishima's major novel for 1950, *Thirst for Love*, was at least as unwholesome as the short stories. The heroine, Etsuko, a woman consumed by a need to be adored, loses her husband to typhoid and becomes the mistress of her aging father-in-law. At the same time she conceives a passion for the stolid farmhand Saburo. When Saburo becomes involved in his "dumb, animal way" with a peasant girl on the farm, Etsuko begins to suffer the agonies of jealousy, a state she seems to require for survival. She forces Saburo to meet her in an orchard late at night, confuses him with questions about whom he truly loves, and finally drives him to reach for her. For just a moment she revels in the feeling of his heavy body on top of hers, then she screams. The old man comes out with a mattock in his hand and stands "irresolutely" looking from one to the other. Etsuko seizes the mattock and slices through the peasant's neck. This is of course the moment the novel has been racing toward; it recalls a statement Mishima made in December 1948, while he was writing the *Confessions*: "I am desperate to kill a man; I want to see red blood. An author writes love stories because he isn't popular with women; I began writing novels so I wouldn't end up with a death sentence. . . ."*

The heroine of *Thirst for Love* never comes to life because she is not really a woman at all but a subterfuge to enable Mishima to focus on the peasant lad who is the object of her passion — and his. At the same time she becomes a vehicle for realizing those obsessive impulses (including the homicidal) which her creator was able to enact only in fantasy. This is best observed in a scene at a temple festival. The entire household goes down to the village to watch "the demented spectacle" of one hundred young men abandon their nearly naked bodies to the intoxication of the festival dance. Only Saburo, who attracts Etsuko (and Mishima) because there is no consciousness interceding between his impulses and his actions, plunges into the wild dance and becomes indistinguishable from the others. Etsuko watches with envy; then abruptly she "relinquishes" all power over her legs and throws herself into the dance. She discovers Saburo and perceives his naked back as a bottomless ocean into which she longs to throw herself. The mob presses her against him, "causing her fingernails to gouge into his back. He did not even feel it. . . . Etsuko felt his blood dripping between her fingers." Thus Mishima "relin-

---

* In *The Sailor Who Fell from Grace with the Sea*, Mishima described with clinical detail the vivisection of a cat. Sometime in 1964 as I worked on the translation he told me that he had actually killed and vivisected a cat (with a writer friend formerly a medical student) before attempting the description. He added, "I can't write something I haven't seen with my own eyes and it's a problem because I want to do a homicide!" Then he laughed loudly. I remember feeling distinctly that he was only half joking.

quishes" himself, through Etsuko, to the frenzy of the forbidden dance that has called to him since childhood and will continue to call.

While Mishima worked on *Thirst for Love* he was also serializing a novel for the first time; *Whitest of Nights (Junpaku no yoru)* was the first of seventeen serial novels (in twenty years) that he referred to as "minor works."* Essentially these were potboilers; at best they were worthless stones skillfully cut and polished. Mishima himself had only contempt for them, and when he had finished one he was impervious to criticism about it. He wrote them to read easily and sell well and he adjusted his style accordingly, avoiding complexity and even trimming his vocabulary, by far the richest of any writer in his generation. Astonishingly, he was able to work simultaneously on these books and the novels to which he gave his best. Toward the end of his career he would interrupt work on a major novel and incarcerate himself in a hotel room, complaining bitterly to friends and editors, for the ten days or so it took him to complete a novel to be serialized later. But there were times when he divided his working night in half, dashing off page after popular page for the first few hours and then slowing his pace for more serious work until dawn.

Whitest of Nights was so successful that it was made into a film at once, the first of fifteen Mishima novels to be filmed; and *Thirst for Love* had a colossal sale of seventy thousand copies, earning Mishima a considerable sum of money for 1950 (approximately 1,400,000 yen or $4,000). In August of

* *Natsuko's Adventures* (1951), *Made in Japan* (1953), *The Capitol of Love* (1954), *Goddess* (1955), *The Happiness Sets Sail* (1956), *Too Much of Spring* (1957), *Lectures in Immoral Education* (1959), *Continued Lectures . . .* (1960), *Mademoiselle* (1960), *Stampede of Love* (1963), *Body School* (1964), *Music* (1965), *College of Unchasteness* (1966), *That Complicated Guy* (1967), *Evening Dress* (1967), *Life for Sale* (1968).

that year, three months after the book had been published, he moved his family, of whom he was now the sole supporter, into a larger house in a residential neighborhood to the southwest of Shibuya called Midorigaoka. In this roomy, two-story Japanese house the Hiraokas lived for eight years, until Mishima married and moved his parents and bride into a house he designed and built.

The Midorigaoka years seem to have been the most tranquil period in Mishima's life at home. Although Azusa had been appalled by what he called "the preposterous nonsense" in *Confessions of a Mask*, the success of that book and of *Thirst for Love* had more than reconciled him to Mishima's choice of careers. He now became arrogant about his famous son, carrying on as if he were the novelist, and after the move to the new house he even began to act as Mishima's agent. Shizue also contributed to easing the tension in the house by reconciling herself to life with Azusa. During the period just after the war she had spoken often of divorce. Now the Hiraokas settled into a relationship which was civil if not entirely happy.

Late in the summer of 1950, Mishima began to frequent the homosexual bars and cafés which had materialized all over Tokyo immediately after the war. (There were no "gay" bars in Japan before the war. Their sudden appearance afterward is attributable to the large foreign homosexual community, including significant numbers of soldiers, which gathered in Tokyo during the occupation.) His favorite place was a "gay" café on the Ginza called Brunswick. This was a coffeehouse and bar which employed attractive young waiters and was patronized by a rather bizarre combination of older, well-to-do Japanese and foreign businessmen, GIs, and Japanese hustlers. At night the waiters doubled as stars in the famous Brunswick floor show. One of the performers was a then unknown "gayboy" named Akihiro Maruyama, later to become a "chansoneuse" in drag, often styled the Edith Piaf of Japan, and still later an "actress" who would play the leading role in Mishima's play *The Black Lizard*. As Maruyama recalls Mishima in those early days, "He was pale as death, so pale his skin had a purplish tint. And his body seemed to float in his clothes. And yet he was a narcissist, that was clear, and he had a true eye for beauty. The key to him in those days, before he began the body building and all that, was that when he looked at himself with those eyes that could really perceive beauty, and he was looking at himself constantly, he was filled with disgust at what he saw."

Anyone who knew Mishima in 1950 and 1951 found himself accompanying him at one time or another on a round of gay bars which invariably ended at Brunswick. Ostensibly he was gathering background material for his new book, *Forbidden Colors*, and, as he insisted, was afraid to go into such places alone. Inside he behaved like a spectator. He made no effort to hide the fact that he knew the denizens of the place. But he never let on that he was a participant in the world he was sketching on the note cards he always carried, and apparently his friends did not suspect him.

There is no evidence that Mishima had become actively homosexual until his first journey to the West in 1952; but clearly the writing of *Forbidden Colors* led him deeper into the homosexual world than he had dared to venture before. One thing he discovered was its ubiquitousness. The hero of *Confessions of a Mask* was convinced that he was alone in the world with his "perversion"; in *Forbidden Colors* it is revealed that almost everyone is afflicted. In a typical scene at "Rudons" (Brunswick), an old foreigner comes in with his male secretary and sits down with the hero. As the secretary makes overtures, presumably for his employer, he wraps his feet around the hero's ankles underneath the table. The book is filled with somehow triumphant revelations of this kind. But if there is a certain jubilance in the book there is also deep-seated anxiety. The hero himself is rather a mindless young man, more or less untroubled by his double life as a married man and a homosexual. But there is a siren which recurs throughout the book as a signal of the author's foreboding; and more than once the narrator voices fear. In a passage which reads like Mishima himself speaking from the page, he refers to the homosexual world as a "jungle of sentiment" which holds a man entangled in its vines no matter how he struggles:

From the damp familiarity he feels for creatures of his kind no man has been able to sever himself decisively. There have been numberless attempts at escape. But in the end there is only the return to this damp handshake and this sticky meeting of glances. Men like this, essentially incapable of maintaining a home, discover something vaguely like a hearthfire only in the gloomy eyes that say "You, too, are one of us."

Mishima's editor on *Forbidden Colors* was a young woman named Michiko Matsumoto. Actually she was not an editor in the western sense: in Japan a manuscript by an established author is rarely edited by anyone except in the most mechanical way. Her job as *tantōsha* (responsible party) was to visit Mishima's home once a month at a time appointed by him to pick up that month's installment.* From January to Novem-

---

* The job is not the simple delivery-boy operation it sounds; if the author does not feel he can discuss his work with the "responsible party" when he chooses, if he is not comfortable with him generally, he will have second thoughts about doing another book with the same publisher. The *tantōsha* must therefore secure the author's confidence and at the same time insure that he writes to deadline—no easy task. Matsumoto succeeded admirably: later Mishima would say that she knew more about literature than any woman in Japan.

ber 1951, while *Forbidden Colors* was being serialized, she
saw Mishima at least once a month; the first thing she noticed
was his intimacy with his mother. Whenever she visited the
house to pick up manuscript, Shizue was there, hovering over
Kimitake, "overprotecting" him. Mishima habitually referred
to Shizue, even in her presence, not as *o-fukuro* (my old lady)
or simply *haha* (mother) but *o-kaa-sama*, a rather effeminate
and far too decorous appellation meaning roughly *chère ma-
man*. (At the Bungaku-za Theater, where Mishima's first
"modern Nō play" had just been performed, the young actors
referred to him among themselves as "Mother dear.") Matsumoto remembers thinking to herself that the woman who
came into this house as Mishima's bride would not have an
easy time.

She was also impressed by Mishima's lack of "characteristic
affectations." To begin with, he was punctilious about deadlines. Established authors — and Mishima was established by
1951 — customarily informed their "editors" just before a deadline that work had been going badly for the past week, or that
someone or other had insisted on "one more round" the night
before. Mishima never missed a deadline in his entire career.
As Matsumoto was only the first to attest, he would designate
a certain hour of a given day, often weeks and even months in
advance, and at that hour precisely he would deliver the
finished manuscript, in Matsumoto's words, "in sickness or in
health, even if it killed him." Generally Mishima met a number of deadlines in a given month; it was not unusual for
several "editors" representing various publications to encounter one another at his front door, where a maid would deliver
to them the addressed envelopes Mishima had left for each.
Not only was the manuscript always on time, it was invariably
clean. The rule in Japan among well-known authors is an illegi-

ble scrawl. In fact, certain writers are consistently so impossible to read that large publishers retain specialists to decipher a particular author's manuscript when it comes in. Apparently, Mishima did not even have to recopy his work; his editors agree that he almost never revised: the text was completed in his head before he set it down in his neat hand.

But it was not simply in the matter of deadlines and neatness that Mishima departed from the pattern. Save for the fact that he worked all night long and took his breakfast at noon, the routine of his life more resembled that of a banker than a novelist. He drank little and smoked little; from the beginning to the end of his career he refused to patronize the "author bars" where Tokyo's established writers regularly gathered. Once Matsumoto expressed her surprise that he lived what appeared to be such an orderly life. Mishima replied, "Most writers are perfectly normal in the head and just carry on like wild men; I behave normally but I'm sick inside."

Although this was spoken with the familiar donkey-bray of a laugh, Mishima undoubtedly meant it. With *Confessions of a Mask* he had hoped to leave behind the world of blood, and night and death, but it continued to haunt him. At the very least he was feeling increasingly entangled in "the jungle of feelings" he had entered through *Forbidden Colors*.

At the end of 1951, he attempted once again to free himself, not with a book this time but a first journey to the West. A short article he wrote a few weeks before departure suggests that the trip was less a well-earned vacation — he was almost twenty-six and had just published his sixth novel and twenty-second volume — than a determined quest for health:

On the 25 of this month [December] I am going abroad. . . . Until now my work has been too highly sensitive. Perhaps I should say I have indulged my sensitivity too extravagantly until now. On this foreign trip I shall take only little money with me, but hope largely to expend this sensitivity of mine before I return.

Writing about the trip years later Mishima would employ the same metaphor and speak of his determination to "wear down [my] sensitivity like an old shoe." It is a curious goal; undoubtedly he meant by it a desire to render himself "insensitive" to that "morass of feeling" that was pulling him down.

In 1951 it was no easy matter for Japanese nationals to leave Japan for whatever reason. There were still no passports, only travel permits signed by MacArthur himself, and these were next to impossible to get. Fortunately an old friend of Azusa's was head of the publications division of the Asahi Shimbun, and he managed to have Mishima designated a "special correspondent." Even so, he was required to undergo a rigorous physical at St. Luke's Hospital in Tokyo and a long interview at GHQ before his permit was issued. On Christmas Eve 1951 he sailed from Yokohama aboard the S.S. *President Wilson*. Mitsuo Nakamura, the critic who five years earlier had assessed him at minus one hundred and twenty points, saw him off. Waving from the deck as the ship pulled away, Mishima put on a pair of dark glasses, according to Nakamura, to hide his tears.

Mishima called his journal of the trip *Apollo's Glass*; the very first entry, written on shipboard bound for San Francisco, indicates his determination to become a new man:

Sun! Sun! Perfect Sun! I have the feeling none of the unknown lands I am to see can exceed the wonder of this. . . . Today I did not watch the sunset. Having spent the day gazing lovestruck at the sun I had no heart to see her in her ancient, feeble make-up.

In my boyhood I too felt that the sunset was the only justification for the sun's existence. As I bared myself to the sun today I felt throughout my body the joy of release from that oversensitive stubbornness of my youth. . . .

After a day each in San Francisco and Los Angeles, Mishima went to New York for ten days. His guide for some of the time was a Mrs. Kruger of the American Committee for Cultural Freedom (a mutual friend had notified her of Mishima's arrival). She took him to the top of the Empire State Building and to Radio City Music Hall, and tried without success to convert him to socialism. On his own Mishima visited the Museum of Modern Art and saw *Call Me Madam, South Pacific, The Moon Is Blue,* and Strauss's opera *Salomé,* which he admired for pages in his diary. But the city itself seemed to put him off rather than excite him. His conclusion after ten days was that "New York is like Tokyo five hundred years from now."

From New York he went to Rio, where he stayed a month waiting for Carnival to begin at the end of February. His guide was the *Asahi* correspondent, a man named Mogi. Mogi remembers Mishima as very young and pale, extremely polite, free and easy with his money and "a genius at feeling people out and accommodating himself." It was also his impression that the young man was determined to hide his delicacy under robust mannerisms; when Mishima tilted his head back and laughed up at the Brazilian sky, Mogi wondered how so large a laugh could issue from a face so fragile. It was hot, and the heat bothered Mishima; he spent much of the day sleeping in his hotel room. But even at night he often stayed in and worked. Sometimes when he and Mogi were walking together he would excuse himself and go back to write. It seemed to Mogi that "he was working constantly." He also sensed that

111

Mishima was bored after the first week, but when he invited him to the races Mishima declined to go. Neither did he show any interest in food or drink; when they did eat together he invariably ordered tongue stew.

But the biggest surprise was Mishima's "unabashed homosexuality." According to Mogi, he regularly brought to his hotel in the afternoon young boys of seventeen or so, "the sort who hung around in the parks." Since he was open about it, Mogi asked how he managed to meet the boys, and Mishima explained that in "that world" there was an understanding without words. He told Mogi that he was interested in the process of courtship and female psychology but entirely uninterested in "the final act." He demonstrated the truth of this by calling Mogi one afternoon and begging him to come to the hotel to rescue him from a Japanese woman (the wife of a resident Japanese) determined, so he said, to seduce him.

While he waited for Carnival Mishima went to São Paulo for a week. There he was lavishly entertained by the community of Japanese farmers grown rich on coffee. Since 1945 this group had been split in two over the question — incredibly — had Japan won or lost the war! The "victory group," as they were called, insisted from their isolation in Brazil that Imperial Japan had been victorious; it was with this group of rough, wealthy fanatics in particular that Mishima became involved. He wrote articles for their private newspaper during his stay on their plantations, and they vied for his attention.

Carnival began on February 23. In his journal Mishima noted ecstatically, "I danced the three nights away." In fact, according to Mogi, he found the courage to throw himself into the melee only on the final night, but once he had begun he did "relinquish" himself to the frenzy of the dance, half naked like all the others, and seemed to Mogi "happier than at any other time." In his long report on the Carnival he dwells, predictably, on the swirl of bodies, the passion, the number of babies conceived, mentions that Goethe had also been fascinated by the [Roman] Carnival, and concludes: "Through dancing I too knew intoxication. You cannot watch, you must participate in order to become intoxicated."

On March 3, Mishima flew from Rio to Paris and checked into the Hotel Grand, intending to stay one week. The next day on the Champs Élysées a man approached him with an offer of 500 francs for the dollar instead of the official 350. Mishima followed the man to the back room of a café and took out $2,500 in travelers' checks, intending to convert a few hundred. Suddenly a whistle blew, the man indicated there was danger, seized the checks and ran from the room. Mishima followed, but once outside discovered that he was alone. He went back to look for the man but he was nowhere to be found. Mishima reported the theft to the Japanese legation (there was still no embassy) and payment on the checks was stopped. But he had to wait a month to get his money back, and for that month he was penniless in Paris. Fortunately, the legation directed him to a small Japanese restaurant and boardinghouse called Botan-Ya, on l'Avenue Mozart across from the Opéra, where he was able to stay on credit. The only other boarder was the film director Keinosuke Kinoshita. Through Kinoshita, Mishima met and became good friends with the composer Toshiro Mayuzumi, who was living in Paris at the time. Shortly after they met, Mishima asked Mayuzumi to take him to a "bar for pederasts." With Kinoshita they went to a place called the Café Blanche. According to Mayuzumi, all the boys came to him because he spoke French, and Mishima was angry.

113

Not surprisingly under the circumstances, Mishima hated Paris. He spent most of his time in his room writing his first four-act play, *Sunflowers at Night*. When he looked out the window as he wrote, it seemed to him that there were only children and old people in the avenue below. To Mayuzumi he observed, "Paris is a place where one goes directly from child-hood to old age with no youth in between." In his journal he likened the "beauty of Paris" to the "thick makeup of an ugly woman."

On April 18 Mishima finally left Paris and flew to London, where he stayed at the "American-style" Hotel Mt. Royal. During his five days in London he walked in Hyde Park, shopped on Oxford Street, saw *Billy Budd* and *Much Ado about Nothing*, and took a day trip to the town of Guildford in Surrey. What he saw seems to have pleased him, but it is clear from his journal that he was impatient to be on his way; his next destination was Greece, the land in all the world he wanted most to see. He arrived in Athens on April 24 and stayed a week, including a two-day trip to Delphi. To judge from the journal, he found the "land of his dreams" every bit as exciting as he had expected. The exuberance of the first entry never flags: "I am in Greece. I am drunk on supreme happiness. . . . I shall let my pen dance where it will. Today, at last, I saw the Acropolis! I saw the Parthenon! I saw the Temple of Zeus!"

What Mishima wanted from Greece was an antidote to his "romantic" affliction. It was not only the reason, the rule and measure of classicism that he sought; he wanted physical and mental sunlight in place of darkness, radiant surfaces in place of deep interiors, a balance between the intelligence and the body uncomplicated by the "spirit," the conscience, the poetic imagination. Naturally he found all this and more, because he was determined it should be there, in the ruins, in the Greek tragedies he watched performed at the theater of Dionysius, and above all, in the marble statues of youth that testified to the Greeks' belief in "the immortality of beauty," in the statue of Antonius, "the last unbaptized flower of Greece," and in the young charioteer at Delphi, "bashful with victory." As he gazed at the statues in the "copious virulent light," he exulted, "The Greeks believed in the exterior and that was a noble philosophy." And the lesson he learned from what he beheld was the lesson he required, a liberating lesson; that "beauty and ethics were one and the same"; that "creating a beautiful work of art and becoming beautiful oneself were ethically identical." Mishima returned to Japan a "classicist" and declared about his journey, and about Greece in particular, "It seems to have taken something from me, to have cured something in me." He meant of course that "sensitivity" he had set out to spend away extravagantly. Elsewhere he wrote just as sanguinely, "Greece cured my self-hatred and my loneliness and awoke in me a *will to health* in the Nietzschean sense."

Shortly after his return to Japan in May 1952, Mishima enrolled in a course in Greek at his alma mater, Tokyo University. At the same time he began to "date" a college girl, the daughter of a wealthy industrialist. Her name was Eiko, and Mishima met her in July at a high society party in Karuizawa. When they were introduced and he learned that she was a sophomore at the Peers' School, his only comment was that the late founder, General Nogi, would undoubtedly be displeased to know that women were now admitted. Eiko was offended, and surprised, when Mishima called her a week later in Tokyo to ask her out. She was even more surprised, being something of a playgirl and used to easy informality, when he arrived for their first date with flowers *and* perfume and insisted on waiting for her in the vestibule. Mishima and Eiko saw each other more or less regularly until Eiko graduated from the Peers' School in March 1954 (she claims that Mishima wrote her senior thesis on the French Revolution). Unquestionably the relationship was platonic; Eiko implies that Mishima was far too timid to have made advances. Mishima seems to have enjoyed her company particularly because of her willingness to participate in what she calls his "passion for masquerading." For example, he would telephone and ask her to meet him in a plain dress and without makeup in front of the main gate of Tokyo University. At the appointed time he would appear dressed in his old student uniform and inform her that they were going on a student date. He would then take her with him to Greek class, and afterwards to a "drab and dingy" student hangout for tea and "curry rice." At other times he would direct her to dress up to an occasion, asking her beforehand to wear kimono to the Kabuki or "a black dress" to the Comédie-Française.

According to Eiko, Shizue was always in the picture. Mishima would invite Eiko to ballet and Shizue would come too. Afterward he would propose to Eiko that they go dancing and Shizue would comment, "with envy in her voice," "Aren't you a lucky girl." As Eiko tells it she liked and respected Mishima but would never have dreamed of marrying him because of Shizue and his attachment to his mother. What Mishima thought of Eiko is impossible to know; but soon he would begin to consider marriage for complicated reasons of his own and it seems likely that she would have been a candidate had she not married in 1955.

Mishima's social life during these early fifties was already extensive and complex, and would remain that way. To begin with, there was the literary crowd. On his return to Japan in May he had been invited to join a small coterie of writers who called themselves the Potted Tree Society. The members were the critic Mitsuo Nakamura, the cantankerous London-educated novelist Ken'ichi Yoshida (son of the former prime minister), the critic, director, and translator of Shakespeare Kozon Fukuda, Shohei Ooka, a novelist *(Fires on the Plain)* who had established himself as important at the same time as Mishima, and an art historian named Itsuji Yoshikawa. Once a month the group met at one of the members' houses to drink and to talk literature. Beginning in 1958 they also edited a magazine called *Voices*. Mishima belonged to the coterie for ten years. In 1961 he dropped out because of unpleasantness developing between himself and Ken'ichi Yoshida and, for different reasons, Fukuda. Nakamura says he was never really comfortable in the coterie, having been the youngest by ten years, and, in Nakamura's words, "temperamentally incapable of fooling around." In other circles, Mishima was known as a compulsive clown; apparently where literature was concerned he could only be serious.

Another of Mishima's circles was the homosexual crowd he had discovered during the writing of *Forbidden Colors*. These friends, Japanese and foreign, tended to gather for intricate and emotional parties at the home of a wealthy American businessman long a Tokyo resident. Mishima attended regularly until shortly before his marriage in 1958. At that time he also broke off with a young Japanese lover who seems to have been his only long-standing affair.

There were also Mishima's theatrical friends. By 1953 he was saying about plays that they were like "mistresses" (as opposed to wifely novels) and that he needed at least one a

year.* In June of that year the Bungaku-za Theater, one of
five major repertory companies specializing in "modern
drama," produced his first four-act play, *Sunflowers at Night*.
In 1950 and 1952 the same company had produced two of his
one-act "modern Nō plays," his finest dramatic efforts, and
from 1953 on it was principally for the Bungaku-za that
Mishima wrote his contemporary plays. Naturally he became
friends with many of the younger members of the troupe. He
was closest to an actor and then aspiring director named
Hiroshi Akutagawa, the son of the famous literary suicide
Ryunosuke Akutagawa (author of "Rashomon"). There was
also an unknown actor named Takeo Matsuura who was eventually to direct all of Mishima's major plays and who remained
a lifelong friend. Matsuura in particular, in 1953 and 1954,
attempted to initiate Mishima into the art of genuine Tokyo
carousing, and is the first to admit that he did not succeed.
Not only did Mishima remain sober, noting what he observed
of the Tokyo night on the cards he always carried, Matsuura
found it impossible to get drunk in Mishima's company. At
eleven o'clock Mishima invariably excused himself and headed
home to his study. His parting words were always "People who
stay out all night drinking will never amount to anything." As
soon as he had driven out of sight, Matsuura would go back
inside the bar and "start all over again."

Among Mishima's theater friends were also some of the

---

* Beginning in 1953, he did produce one full-length play a year until he
died, not to mention innumerable one-acts and adaptations. Generally he
worked on his plays in a room in the Imperial Hotel—the "Imperial Jail," as
he referred to it in English—on the last three days of two consecutive months.
He began with the curtain line of the last act; once he had it, he produced
the rest with astonishing speed, two acts in three days, a four-act play in six
days. Not surprisingly, in view of his tendency to emphasize curtain lines, he
demanded a theater in which the curtain could be lowered by hand and
therefore quickly.

players in the Kabuki troupe. In December 1953, the Kabuki-za presented Mishima's first Kabuki play, an adaptation of an Akutagawa story called "Hell Screen," about an artist who causes his daughter to be burned alive in a carriage so he can paint a beautiful girl descending into hell. Mishima made the daughter the lead: he wanted to be sure the part would be large enough for the famous Kabuki female impersonator Utaemon, whom he passionately admired. Utaemon did play the part, and Mishima was able to become friendly with him. Throughout the fifties he saw the "prima donna" often, wrote "her" praises frequently, and finally in 1958 edited a lavish photographic retrospective.

By the summer of 1953 Mishima was well on his way to becoming a celebrity. Thus when a thief shouldered his way into the Midorigaoka house in July and got away with "twelve suits" while Mishima hid in terror in a neighbor's house, all six major newspapers carried the story prominently. That same month, he became at twenty-eight the youngest Japanese author to have his "collected works" published (in six volumes). But Mishima's fame, or more properly his notoriety, was not merely due to his writing; he was already developing the distinctive persona which seemed designed expressly to fascinate and antagonize the Japanese. In these early days, before he had hit his stride, his style was a blend of Hollywood cool and Roman drugstore cowboy. He wore loud sport shirts, often alohas, black "pegged" trousers, and pointy black shoes. He wore the shirts open halfway to the waist to expose a chest which for a Japanese was hirsute; around his neck he hung a golden chain and a variety of medallions which he had bought in Italy and Greece. He was never without dark glasses, and, literally to top it off, he affected a crew cut, considered in Japan in 1953 to be "the latest Hollywood fashion." In this

getup Mishima liked to stroll down the Ginza in broad daylight, or late at night, but before his eleven o'clock curfew, to
be seen dancing "rock-a-billy" at Roppongi clubs with young
actresses from the Bungaku-za. The impression being created
by these so far rather mild shenanigans was evident in a caricature which appeared in the *Asahi Shinbun* on June 22, 1953;
Mishima, crew cut and dressed in a snappy suit, sits ostenta-
tiously in the first row of a Greek class. The title reads,
"Creepy and cocky, not easy to like, but a kind of genius."

Mishima's "Greek fever" culminated in his 1954 novel *The
Sound of Waves*, inspired by the Daphnis and Chloe story.
Shinji, the handsome fisher boy, meets Hatsue, a diving girl
newly arrived on the small island — "song island" — and first
love blossoms. In the book's most famous scene, the children
confront each other's nakedness across a bonfire in a cave;
Shinji leaps the fire to Hatsue's side and they exchange a first
kiss, then shyly desist and agree to wait for their wedding
night. There are obstacles in their way, but these Shinji over-
comes, and after a final ordeal in which he swims a stormy
stretch of sea, the lovers are betrothed.

Mishima conceived this sunlit book in the spring of 1953, at
a time when, in his own words, he was "seeing Greece wherever [he] looked." Through Azusa's contacts in the Bureau
of Fisheries, he was able to locate just the island he needed for
a model, a tiny island called Kamijima off the coast of Izu.
Early in the summer, he spent ten days on the island, riding
out with the fishermen at dawn and becoming friends with the
lighthouse keeper. He began writing in the fall, and completed
the novel in April, 1954. Shinchosha published it in June and
immediately it became not only Mishima's best-selling novel
to date but broke all postwar records with a sale of 106,000
hardback copies (in paperback it continues to sell 100,000

copies annually). By July, the major film companies were fighting for the film rights; in August Toho studios rented the entire island and shot the film in three weeks. Released at the end of October, the film, for which Mayuzumi wrote the music, was a smash hit. The following month Mishima was awarded the first Shinchosha prize for the novel.

The Sound of Waves is the only love story Mishima ever wrote that was neither perverted nor sardonic. Except for a passage or two which linger more lovingly on the body of the handsome fisherman than the young girl, the book is unremittingly normal in the most conventional sense; in fact, it is Mishima's most assiduously healthy work. Shinji's world is one of "consummate accord between himself and the opulence of nature that surrounded him." What is more, astonishingly, "he had never once thought about such a thing as dying"! In this he is unique among the entire canon of Mishima heroes.

In later years Mishima often referred to *The Sound of Waves* as "that joke on the public." He even indicated a certain chagrin that it should have done so well, writing in 1963 that its "popular success" had thrown "icy water on [his] Greek fever." But it is unlikely that he was conscious of perpetrating a hoax at the time (as, for example, Erich Segal was likely to have been when he wrote *Love Story*). On the contrary, he was almost certainly in earnest, determined to demonstrate to himself not only that he was capable of creating a world so different from his own but even that he had a place in it. As he wrote several years later, "From about this time I had a desire to turn myself into my own opposite even in real life. Naturally I cannot be certain whether I actually created my own opposite or merely an aspect of myself which until then had been ignored."

The Sound of Waves originated in Mishima's determination to transform himself into "his opposite," to rebuild himself cell by cell not only physically but psychically. It was a fierce determination, so fierce in fact that it drove him to assert repeatedly that the "self-improvement" on which he had embarked was already accomplished, as in the following entry from a 1955 diary:

> I obtained substantial physical health only after becoming an adult. Such people have a different mental set from those who are born healthy. We feel, having become healthy at last, that we have the right to be insensitive about trivial matters, and we train ourselves to be just that way. I . . . developed an indescribable contempt for thinking about death. . . . I allowed my thoughts of death to become vine-entangled, like an old manor house no longer inhabited.

But in less sanguine moments Mishima knew better than anyone that this claim to physical and mental health was unfounded. On his thirtieth birthday, January 14, 1955, he invited two friends to his house for drinks, the critic Takeo Okuno and a young student of Japanese literature named Viglielmo, and told them that he was now too old to die beautifully, that suicide after thirty would be "as unseemly as Dazai's." He then rather horrified his friends by showing them a name card on which he had written his name with different characters pronounced Yu-ki-o Mi-shi-ma but meaning "mysterious-devil-tail devil-bewitched-by-death." "It's eerie when you write it this way," Mishima guffawed. Then abruptly somber, "This is the real way to write my name." According to Okuno, an uncomfortable moment of silence followed.

But moments of truth like these could not alter Mishima's determination to rebuild himself. On his return from Greece he had written that the trip had "cured" him of thinking of his environment as fate. By 1955 his "realization" that "[his] environment was [his] determination" had become the governing principle of his life. Vanished without a trace was the fatalist of the *Confessions* who was so certain "[he] had been handed a full menu of all the troubles in his life while still too young to read it." In his place was a man who could say about Osamu Dazai, in the same 1955 diary, "The defects in his character, a goodly half of them, could have been cured by cold-water massage, mechanical workouts, and a regularized life. . . . To employ something of a paradox, an invalid who does not wish to recover does not qualify as a true invalid." Crystal clear in this is Mishima's sense of himself as an invalid, and his determination to recover. The entry is dated June 1955. In July, he began the weight lifting which was to be his principal physical activity for the rest of his life.

Mishima had been edging up to weight lifting since his return from Europe. In the summer of 1952, he had begun his athletic life with swimming, something he had not attempted since that first traumatic summer on the beach with his mother. He had a hard time learning, for he was badly coordinated; Mayuzumi remembers his "jumping in and sinking to the bottom of the pool like a stone." But he would not give up; by the end of the summer, by dint of sheer will, he had learned to swim. As with other sports he managed to acquire by driving himself without mercy, he was fiercely proud of his swimming once he had mastered it. The novelist Morio Kita tells a funny story about swimming with Mishima in the late fifties. They were at a hotel pool in Tokyo. Mishima dived in and swam for the far end, using the breast stroke that was his pride. Kita dived in after him and, with a crawl, quickly overtook and passed him. At the far end of the pool Kita waited for Mishima to join him. As he tells it, "I expected him to say at least 'you're faster than you look.' But he didn't say a word, he didn't even smile. He got out of the pool without looking at me and went into the bar."

From swimming Mishima proceeded to boxing. In 1953 and 1954 he took lessons once a week at a gym, shadowboxed constantly, and tried to convert the young men in the Bungaku-za to the sport by sending each of them a pair of red boxing trunks. As a boxer he was hopeless; in fact he was taking so cruel a beating at his lessons that his friends began to worry and finally prevailed upon him to give it up. In 1958 he resumed it briefly and once again was roundly beaten by all his sparring partners; possibly he took pleasure in these drubbings. Although he did not box after 1959 he remained actively interested in the sport, sponsoring several fighters in much the spirit that Norman Mailer sponsored José Torres.

Once Mishima began lifting weights in July of 1955 he maintained a regimen of three workouts a week for fifteen years and allowed nothing to interfere. The first thing he did on arrival in a foreign city was to locate the gym nearest his hotel; in Tokyo he put in his time at the Korakuen Gym even when he had a fever or had been up writing around the clock. Not even friends were allowed to interfere; in the summer of 1956 Donald Keene arrived in Tokyo expecting Mishima to meet him at the airport and was met instead by an editor who explained that Mishima-*sensei* had been detained by *body-biru*, that is, "body-build."

Apparently he did not get quick results: three years after he had begun, in 1958, he impressed a weight lifter named Kubo who met him at the time as "too anemic to go on." But gradually his body responded to his demands; judging from a published diary, it was Mishima's personal view that he had come a long way by January 5, 1959:

In the *Shukan Yomiuri* [a weekly magazine] that came out to-day there is a story about the rumors that I have begun *kendo* and a photograph naked from the waist up. I don't know where they got it, but it's a picture taken three years ago, only a week after I'd begun body-building. It is very annoying that people may think of me even now as such a weak and anemic creature. If it is assumed this is the shape I am in now, I will be thought of as an empty boaster. I have a mind to sue for defamation, but in view of the auspicious time of year [i.e., New Year's] I'll forbear.

In 1963 the editors of a new encyclopedia (*Shogakkan*) asked Mishima to pose for a photograph to appear beside the "body-build" entry. Mishima told his friend Kubo that this was one of the happiest moments in his life. He took Kubo with him to the photographer's and asked for his advice on lighting and the proper pose to improve even a little on reality. The problem was that he had concentrated on his arms, chest, and stomach and had neglected his legs, which remained meager, two matchsticks supporting the muscled trunk. In later years he would agree to pose for weight-lifting photographs only from the waist up.

The transformation that came over Mishima as he entered the Korakuen Gym at three or four in the afternoon was wonderful to behold. Somehow he managed to strut and pose, to talk and even to think with the same synapses as the gen-uine muscle men who exercised with him. Naturally they accepted him entirely as one of their own. He was called *sensei*, a term of respect equivalent to "sir," but so was the delivery boy who held the gym record for the bench press.

First he would change into white sweat pants, a thick black leather belt, and a white running shirt. Then as he emerged from the locker room and stepped onto the crowded wooden floor he would strip off his shirt and pause to peer into a mirror, as if he had lost his arms and shoulders and hoped to discover them in the glass. As he examined himself his face would assume a vapid look, the kind you see on Muscle Beach. Satisfied, he moves away from the mirror and lies down on a wooden bench. He is about to lift the dumbbells on the floor when his neighbor completes a sit-up and asks, "Where's your gold chain today, *sensei*." Mishima doesn't miss a beat: "It was a drag, man, kept getting in my way. I never wear it when I'm working on my lats."

Mishima's single-minded dedication to weight lifting is most simply explained by his determination to improve his physical health. In the winter of 1955, Toshiro Mayuzumi and Mishima happened to be staying at the same hotel in Atami. They were working on separate projects, but they ate dinner together and then worked through the night. One night Mayuzumi heard "agonizing groans" coming from Mishima's room next door. He dashed in and found Mishima writhing on the bed with stomach cramps. Mishima pointed to a hypodermic needle on the table and when Mayuzumi handed it to him gave himself an injection. The pain quickly subsided; Mishima explained that he had been "plagued by pain" all his life, that the cramps had been getting worse, and that they were interfering with his work since they regularly occurred at night. He spoke of taking steps to cure himself and then swore Mayuzumi to secrecy. Shortly afterward he began weight lifting.

But there is abundant evidence that Mishima himself was conscious of more as he labored with the barbells over the years than a desire to recover physically, or even a narcissistic exhibitionism, although to be sure that was also an element involved. His conclusion in the long autobiographical essay called *Sun and Steel*, written near the end of his life, was that his labors to transfigure himself had been in fact a quest for what he called "the ultimate verification of existence." As he perceived the process of his life in *Sun and Steel*, the quest had become necessary when "the boy who wrote poetry" discovered that words were no longer an adequate substitute for reality. There came a time, presumably in the mid-fifties, when he began to experience difficulty in feeling that he truly existed, in knowing that he was really alive, and he decided that language (art) was to blame, "eating reality away" before he had a chance to experience it. It was then that he began to seek consciously for something "antithetical to words," and this proved to be muscle, the "language of the flesh."

Like all Mishima's major efforts in self-definition beginning with the *Confessions*, *Sun and Steel* (1968) is too ingenious and schematic to describe what must have been a more ambiguous reality. But there are far earlier indications that he was indeed experiencing trouble feeling alive beginning at this time, and that he did conceive of muscle as a kind of incontestable proof of existence. For example, there is a diary entry dated July 5, 1955, only weeks before he began to lift weights, in which he confesses for the first time to an *emotional numbness* he fears may be schizophrenic:

It's surprising how the external world has ceased to threaten me these days. . . . Can it be that I have tamed the external world? Not a chance. Kretchmer writes: "Schizophrenia advances by stages until it reaches a pinnacle of icy numbness. In the process the patient becomes enwrapped in something hard as ice (or stiff as leather) and gradually all strong feelings weaken and recede." "Stiff as leather" is perfect; how did he know!

There is also the narcissist-actor Osamu in his 1958 novel *Kyoko's House*. Osamu is a narcissist because he can never be certain of his own existence: "For a fleeting proof of his existence he slept with women. Women could be depended on to respond to the fascination of his good looks. But there was something that responded even more faithfully — the mirror." Osamu's constant need to verify his own existence leads him early in the novel to weight lifting! And, for at least a time, as he adds layer after layer of undeniable muscle to his body, it seems that he has solved his problem, albeit the mirror is still indispensable:

In the mirror now, unmistakably, he existed! The disappointed, abandoned youth of a few moments ago was nowhere to be seen. Here was only strong, beautiful muscle, the proof of its existence clear. For what he now beheld was something he had created himself; moreover it *was* himself.

There is hardly any question that Mishima was consciously in touch with the same motive for beginning to lift weights as he later ascribed to the narcissist Osamu. Similarly, Osamu's existential triumph when he looks in the mirror and discovers that he exists unmistakably was a triumph Mishima himself had experienced just one year after beginning to exercise, on a hot festival day in August 1956, when he joined the local merchants in shouldering a portable shrine through the streets. The shine, known as a *mikoshi*, is a wooden structure in tiers, ornately carved and brightly painted and weighing close to two thousand pounds. It takes from forty to sixty young men to carry it by the two long wooden bars which run its length on both sides. When the neighborhood festival parade begins, the youths shoulder the heavy shrine and begin moving through the streets, shouting rhythmically to help keep themselves in step. The shrine moves up and down and sways precariously from side to side; the bearers gradually accelerate until they are weaving down the street almost at a run, a tangle of feet and sweating bodies, shouting at the top of their lungs and somehow just managing to keep the swaying wooden edifice upright above them.

The spectacle of the *mikoshi* seems to have fascinated and terrified Mishima as a child. In fact he concludes the childhood chapter of the *Confessions* with an early memory of a festival day when the neighborhood youth left the street *in a kind of frenzy* and trampled the Hiraoka garden with the *mikoshi* tilting crazily on their shoulders. Recalling the moment as he worked on the *Confessions* in 1949 (Shizue says it happened as he described it), Mishima wrote:

Through it all there was only one vividly clear thing, a thing that both horrified and lacerated me, filling my heart with unaccountable agony. That was the expression on the faces of the young men carrying the shrine — an expression of the most obscene and undisguised intoxication in the world. . . .

In Mishima's imagination this *intoxication* was and continued to be synonymous with the ecstasy of existence. For years he had felt "tragically" excluded from it (though it terrified him), and therefore "tragically" excluded from life itself. Now, after one year of preparation with barbells in a gymnasium, he felt ready to attempt participation. On August 19, 1956, he dressed himself up in loincloth and belly band of newly bleached cotton, snug white trousers that hugged his hips, a festival jacket and uniform headband, and, tying the sleeves of the jacket up and out of the way with a pinkish yellow cord, he joined the young men from the Jiyugaoka merchants' association beneath the great *mikoshi*. The experience was a revelation. In a jubilant, even ecstatic essay written the very next day, "On Intoxication," Mishima explained that he had beheld the same "divine blue sky" the others had beheld, that he had become part of the *mikoshi* and the group, that with the others he had *"drowned in life!"* "At that moment," he would later write, "I participated in the tragedy of all being."

For seven years, since he had sat down to write *Confessions of a Mask*, Mishima had been laboring toward this moment. The photographs taken at the end of the day testify that his joy was real. On that afternoon in August 1956, surrounded by the youth of the Jiyugaoka merchants' association, sweating, exhausted, his newly acquired muscles aching sweetly, Mishima surely felt alive. But the feeling didn't last.

five

1957-1959

In 1956, thirty-one years old, Mishima climbed nearly to the pinnacle of his fame and success. That year he serialized two very different novels simultaneously. One was *The Temple of the Golden Pavilion*, about a Zen Buddhist acolyte who burns his temple to the ground in an attempt to free himself from his obsession with beauty. *The Temple* was a rich and vivid book which contained some of Mishima's strongest scenes and most memorable, if twisted, characters. Moreover, it was an even bigger success than *The Sound of Waves*: two months after publication, when it had already sold 155,000 copies, the publishers released a limited edition of 200 copies which sold for 2,500 yen, $7, an unheard-of price to pay for a novel in those days. The second novel, *Too Much of Spring*, was equally successful. A love story designed to appeal to the ladies, and therefore serialized in a magazine called *Women's Club*, it had its own enormous sale of 150,000 copies. Mishima's play for 1956 was also a smash, by far his most popular play to date, and indeed, ever. It was called *The Hall of the*

Crying Deer after a dance pavilion of that name which the government erected in the 1880s to demonstrate to western diplomats that the Japanese elite was perfectly at home at dance parties *à l'Occidente*. The play was not only set in the Rokumeikan period, as the 1880s were known, the last two acts took place at a great dance in the hall itself. The elaborateness and aristocratic pretentiousness which characterized the period were the perfect materials for Mishima's talent, and he produced a rococo extravaganza of romance and intrigue which ran for months on end, first in Tokyo, then all over Japan, then back in Tokyo again. In September, in a splendid, final touch to an altogether spectacular year, Alfred A. Knopf published the English translation of *The Sound of Waves*, and the "deceptively simple love story" received excellent notices.*

The following spring, Mishima wrote his most popular novel, *A Misstepping of Virtue*, the story of a love affair between a young married woman and a still younger bachelor. Mishima himself considered his tale of adultery a "minor work," and properly so. Nonetheless it was entertaining and very, very deft. From the first line — "One hesitates to begin with an indiscreet topic, but the fact was that while Mrs. Kurakoshi was only twenty-eight, she was a natural genius at sensuality" — Mishima created and sustained a tone of highbrow scandalousness which the Japanese in particular find irresistible. And irresistible it proved to be, to a degree that

---

* The translator Meredith Weatherby was one of a number of army intelligence officers with the occupation who settled in Japan. He came to know Mishima well in the early fifties, during Mishima's Brunswick days. His first translation was not *The Sound of Waves* but *Confessions of a Mask*, which he had completed as early as 1954. *The Sound of Waves* was published first because Knopf was reluctant to introduce Mishima to the West with a "homosexual novel." The *Confessions* were not published until 1958, by New Directions.

exceeded even the publisher's expectations: by the end of the year it had sold 300,000 hardback copies (not to mention a limited edition of 1,000) and the standard Japanese expression for "adulteress" had become "lady misstep" (*yoromeki fujin*). It is no exaggeration to say that Mishima had also become a household word.

In July 1957 Knopf published Donald Keene's translation of *Five Modern Nō Plays*, and at the urging of Harold Strauss, his editor at Knopf, Mishima went to New York to help promote the book (it was Knopf's policy to release Japanese fiction during the off-season, on the assumption it would not attract attention at a busier time). Before he left he put an edge on his English by practicing with tapes in his study, and on the way he stopped at the University of Michigan to warm up with a speech, "The Present State of the Japanese Literary Establishment." In New York early in July, he went the usual round of promotional parties and interviews, often in company with Keene. As he quickly discovered, he was not yet a household word in Manhattan. As he sat down for an interview with Louis Nichols of the *Times*, Nichols glanced at a page of notes and said, "You say you write plays and here you say you write novels. What are you?" Mishima was crushed. Out on the street he turned to Donald Keene and asked, "What do you have to do to get famous in this city?" Keene consoled his friend by assuring him that "Faulkner and Hemingway could walk arm in arm down this street and no one would pay any attention."

But never mind Louis Nichols, the book was being well reviewed, and Mishima was pleased with the attention he was receiving from the American literary crowd. Judging from the diary he kept and later published, he was particularly impressed by a weekend he spent at the Connecticut home of

James Merrill, who took him on a yachting party, and by an evening spent with Alfred A. Knopf himself, at Knopf's estate in Purchase, New York. Describing the August 15 evening, Mishima dwelled on the fine lawns, the trees, the butler, and then confessed his surprise, in spite of a warning he had received about Knopf's outlandish mode of dress, on encountering the old man in a blazer and a pair of shocking pink trousers, looking to him "like the King in an operetta, or a whiskey trademark." After drinks the company of six (Knopf, Knopf's nephew and his wife, the Harold Strausses and Mishima) went for dinner to the nearby Century Country Club, where the "pervasive elegance" of the surroundings moved Mishima to express in his diary a desire that similar clubs would soon be established in Japan: "Golf clubs proliferate like rabbits, but there is no reason why those of us who do not play golf should be left to our own devices." During dinner, Knopf informed Mishima that the company had published only three books on the Nō theater, "Fenellosa's, Lord Waley's, and yours."

August was a good month. Mishima saw Christopher Isherwood, Angus Wilson, Tennessee Williams and their friends. He also saw eight Broadway shows (*West Side Story*, *New Girl in Town*, *Li'l Abner*, *My Fair Lady*, *Most Happy Fella*, *South Pacific*, *Happy Hunting*, *Jamaica*, *Threepenny Opera*) and went several times to the City ballet. Most exciting of all, he signed a contract for what was to be his first Broadway production.

As Mishima had neither a literary nor a theatrical agent (later Audrey Wood, Tennessee Williams's agent, would represent him in the theater, but he never took a literary agent, entrusting his affairs until he died to Harold Strauss), the Knopf edition of *Five Modern Nō Plays* had included a note

134

directing inquiries about production to Donald Keene. Of
those who applied to Keene, Mishima was most impressed by
two young men with no previous experience, Keith Botsford,
a sometime novelist, and Charles Schultz, a former football
star at Princeton who apparently had access to some money.
Botsford's idea was to produce three of the short plays as one,
with transitional passages added to establish continuity. Mishima agreed. Late in August, he sat down in Botsford's apartment above an antique shop on Third Avenue and wrote
passages connecting the Poet in *Sotoba Komachi*, the Genji
figure in *Lady Aoi* and Yoshio in *Hanjo*. Keene translated the
new passages and when Botsford read them he was full of
confidence about the "new play." He and Schultz planned
to open before Christmas; Dolores del Rio would be asked
to play all three female leads.

On August 27, Mishima left on a trip to Puerto Rico, Haiti,
the Dominican Republic, Mexico City and Yucatan, expecting
to find the play in rehearsal when he returned to New York
in early October. All along the way, whenever he could find a
New York Times, he searched it eagerly for an announcement
about the production, and found none. Returning to New
York on October 2, he checked into the Hotel Gladstone on
Park Avenue and called Keene to ask about progress. Keene
had nothing to report; he had had no word from Botsford in
Mishima's absence.

The next three months were a dreary chapter in Mishima's
life. As Keene had realized but could not bring himself to tell
his eager friend, Botsford and Schultz were getting nowhere
except in leading Mishima on. They had asked Dolores del
Rio to play the female lead but she had declined, saying she
was not a good enough actress. They were not having much
success in finding backers. It was the end of October before

they had even come up with a young director they considered right.

Early in November the producers placed a call to open casting in *Show Business*. More than one hundred young actors responded, as Mishima gleefully noted in his diary, "girls so beautiful they would instantly be stars in Japan and one young man in particular who is the spitting image of James Dean." In fact the tryouts were a fiasco, at least partly because Mishima insisted on attending and on interrupting nervous actresses to say "once more with feeling please." Botsford and his associates were furious and told Mishima he was not welcome at auditions. Mishima withdrew to his Park Avenue hotel and nursed his indignation.

Throughout November one mishap followed another; by the end of the month the production was no closer to opening. Meanwhile Mishima, who had expected to be home by early October, was running low on money. On December 2 he decided he could no longer afford the Gladstone Hotel and moved downtown to Greenwich Village. In the first hotel he tried he was shown a room which reminded him of the addict's room in *Man with a Golden Arm* and he left in a huff, "not quite ready to become an addict." He settled on the Hotel Van Rensselaer, where he took a room for $4 a day (he had been paying $16). He also began budgeting his daily expenses; he even learned to use the subways. Donald Keene remembers him suddenly appearing at his apartment near Columbia after a test run on the IRT and proudly announcing that he had come all the way by himself.

But during this final month of his stay in New York, Mishima kept mostly to himself. Wherever he went he was asked first of all when the play was opening, and this was "torture" he could not bear. "And so," he wrote in his diary, "my days of solitary walking began. . . . On some days, when it was raining heavily, I couldn't even leave my shabby hotel room, because I had only one coat with me and I couldn't afford to have it soiled."

When he moved to the Village, Mishima had resolved not to see the producers unless they contacted him. But it became evident they were not going to call, and on December 17 he finally went to see them. From Schultz he learned that Sputnik had brought the market down and made investors cautious ("even the satellite works against me," he wrote in his diary); that somehow or other every female star approached had refused the part: that the situation looked grave. But Mishima only half listened; he was waiting for Botsford to say he was sorry. Botsford did not apologize; and Mishima returned to his hotel room downtown, hurt and furious.

On New Year's Eve, without a word to anyone, he flew to Madrid. "I was tired of being poor," he wrote, "and tired of self-inflicted torture. . . . I changed all my plane tickets to first class and booked myself into the best hotels." He stayed a few days in Madrid, and a few more in Rome, where he consoled himself by buying "numberless ties" on the Via Condotti. He then flew to Japan via Athens, arriving on January 14, in time to attend the closing night of the second Tokyo run of his hit play *The Hall of the Crying Deer*.

Shortly after his return to Japan, Mishima began looking for a bride. His parents had been pressuring him to marry since before he had left for New York. Azusa was impatient for two reasons: Chiyuki had been married for three years and it was not proper that the older son should remain single. More important, he had been hearing rumors that Mishima was homosexual. It is unlikely he took them seriously for even a moment, but they could not be allowed to persist and, he would have reasoned, Mishima's marriage would give them the lie. Almost certainly Shizue knew about Kimitake's homosexuality. But she seems to have been anxious for reasons of her own to have him married. Possibly she hoped that a proper marriage would "cure" him. Not impossibly, she expected that under cover of a proper bride she would be able to indulge her own ardor less circumspectly.

Always deferential to his parents, Mishima had promised before he left for New York to search for a bride in earnest when he returned to Japan, and Azusa held him to his promise. At the end of January he notified Peers' School alumni that Kimitake was looking for suitable candidates. Naturally, the family received a large number of applications (a letter of recommendation stating the girl's pedigree, education and accomplishments, and a photograph). Although any number of applicants had the proper background, Mishima ruled most of them out at once on the basis of their photographs; evidently he had very specific preferences concerning his bride's appearance. But there was one girl who seems to have attracted him strongly. She was a graduate of the Peers' School and, as it turned out, a fan of Mishima's composer friend, Toshiro Mayuzumi. When this was learned, Azusa immediately asked Mayuzumi to approach the girl about marriage (women are not necessarily consulted before they are submitted for candidacy). Mayuzumi summoned the girl and asked if she was interested. She replied she couldn't stand Mishima, that she would rather kill herself than marry such a man. Mayuzumi dutifully conveyed the message to the family, but Mishima was undeterred; he arranged with Mayuzumi for a "chance meeting" with the girl at a Tokyo restaurant called Kettel's. Mayuzumi recalls that Mishima worked on the scenario for the meeting until the last minute and was constantly revising strategic details. Mishima informed him of the final revision the night before the meeting, telephoning late at night to say he thought it "more natural" not to happen into Kettel's alone as planned but in the company of an editor. On the appointed day everything went according to plan. Mayuzumi introduced Mishima, and before the girl could object, plans were made for the entire company to go to dinner and then to the Latin Quarter. The girl immediately saw through the ruse and sat stonily silent. Mayuzumi was "terribly uncomfortable" and the editor broke away at the first opportunity, but Mishima played the evening out gallantly, even to insisting on accompanying the girl to her door in a hired limousine. Needless to say, Mayuzumi did not attempt to make contact again. Incidentally, the young woman's aversion to Mishima was not untypical. In June of 1958, when it so happened that both Mishima and the Crown Prince were married, a weekly magazine polled the nation's young womanhood with the question, "If the Crown Prince and Yukio Mishima were the only men remaining on earth, which would you prefer to marry?" More than half of those who responded said they would prefer to commit suicide! What these young ladies were expressing as much as anything was a physical repugnance: Mishima's by now muscled torso and matchstick legs, his large closely shaven head, the thin, tight, effeminate mouth, the uncomfortable virulence of his physical presence — familiar to all because he was constantly on display — had an unsettling effect on most young women. There were any number of "literature virgins," girls who draped themselves over Mishima's every written word and adored him from afar, the more so because they sensed something unhealthy in his behavior; but Mishima wasn't interested. From the beginning he had made it clear to his parents that he wanted nothing to do with a woman interested in his work.

Sometime in March an old friend of the family brought to his attention a nineteen-year-old college sophomore named Yoko Sugiyama. Yoko's father was Nei Sugiyama, one of Japan's most famous traditional painters, a fact which may have recommended Yoko to Mishima in itself, since he had felt stupid about art all his life, as if it were his cultural Achilles heel. Naturally he also must have found Yoko attractive as a woman, or at least not unattractive. Although it might be expected that he would have preferred boyish women, Yoko Sugiyama was not boyish at all; she was a small woman, but she had an ample body and a full, pretty face which conveys in photographs taken that year a kind of innocence and vulnerability. Certainly Yoko was a pretty young woman by any standards, a young woman who would look well in public and particularly well in company with Mishima (she was, for example, even shorter than he). Unquestionably, this was an important consideration. In an essay called "The Writer and Marriage," which he published in July "to clear up a few simple questions in [his] readers' minds," Mishima wrote that it made no difference to him how badly his wife managed the household, so long as she comported herself in public in a manner appropriate to the wife of a writer: "With regard to her behavior in the outside world I will not be generous with her; the world will be watching."

In the same essay Mishima informed his readers that he had set out to find "a young lady firmly planted, who suited my tastes and who could agree to various difficult stipulations attached to marriage with me." In context, the stipulations seemed to refer to his insistence that his work must always come before all else. But doubtless there were other stipula-

Mishima with his mother, Shizue, in 1925, age seven months

In 1929, age four

Mishima with his grandmother, Natsu, 1930

In 1933, age eight

Mishima with his family on New Year's Day 1942. Left to right: Mishima, Azusa, Mitsuko, Shizue, and Chiyuki

Mishima and his sister, Mitsuko, September 1944

Mishima with his father,
Azusa, on Graduation
Day, September 1944

Mishima with diploma
and silver watch received
from the emperor on
Graduation Day, 1944

Mishima shouldering the portable shrine with the
Jiyugaoka Merchants' Association, 1956

Mishima at work on *The Sound of Waves*, 1954

Mishima with Kabuki female impersonator Utaemon, 1958

Top: Wedding reception at International House, Tokyo, 1958. *Bottom:* Mishima and
Yoko in their new home in Tokyo, 1959

Mishima and Yoko on the Staten Island Ferry, 1960

Mishima and Yoko leaving from the Haneda Airport
on a trip around the world, 1960

Mishima in his dining room, 1966

目標

からだづくり（身体形成）
脚部の筋肉をつくる
脚力を目標にする
男をつくる
（肉体形成）

Mishima working out at Korakuen gym, 1966

Mishima in the snow with sword, February 1969
PHOTO BY TAMOTSU YATO

Mishima posing with samurai sword, 1969

Mishima at the Japan Self-Defense Force boot camp, 1969

Mishima at boot camp mess hall, 1969
PHOTOS BY KEIICHI TOYOIZUMI

Mishima debating at student movement meeting
at the University of Tokyo, 1969

Mishima debating at the University of Tokyo

PHOTOS BY SHINCHOSHA COMPANY

Mishima with members of the Shield Society, 1970.
From left to right: Morita, "Furu-Koga," Ogawa, "Chibi-Koga"

Mishima as Saint Sebastian (after Guido Reni), 1970
PHOTO BY KISHIN SHINOYAMA

Mishima addressing the Japan Self-Defense Force in Tokyo (Ichigaya), 1970

Photo by Yomiuri Shinbun

Mishima addressing the Japan Self-
Defense Force — a close-up

tions as well, concerning his right to privacy. There is no knowing what, if anything, Mishima told Yoko about his homosexuality. The day before his marriage he burned his diaries to date, and this she certainly knew, for she mentioned it later. Moreover, according to a young poet whom Mishima discovered in the mid-sixties and who was close to him until the last year of his life, someone attempted to blackmail him in 1968, threatening to go to Yoko with the full story if he failed to pay a large sum. Mishima refused and left on his second trip to Cambodia and India. When he returned to Japan, Yoko let him know that the blackmailer had made good his threat. The poet claims that Mishima told him what had happened and seemed "angry and upset but not panicked." If the story is true, and there is no reason to doubt the poet, Yoko did know about Mishima's homosexual life. To me she mentioned homosexuality only once. We were discussing the unscrupulousness of the weekly magazines, particularly the "special issues" on Mishima which had appeared just after the Incident. Abruptly, by way of illustration, she said, "A few of them even wrote that Mishima was queer"! There followed an endless silence. Yoko was watching me, waiting for me to nod my assent, which of course I did. At the time I wondered, could it be she didn't know? Later it seemed clear that she was simply informing me there would be no talk of Mishima's homosexuality between us ever.

But of course she must have known, and from the beginning. It is unlikely that Mishima sat her down and spelled out his homosexuality; he was not a man to reveal himself intimately to anyone, certainly not to his wife. "I believe that a writer is a person never understood by his wife, and that is fine with me," he wrote in "The Writer and Marriage." But neither was it like him to trick his bride into marriage. Even if his scruples had permitted this, it was not like him to have risked it. I imagine he made it clear to Yoko that he had a private life of his own which she was not to meddle in and left her to draw her own conclusions. Yoko would have understood: she was inexperienced, perhaps, but not naïve. Very likely Mishima promised her that, whatever he chose to do in his private life, he would permit nothing to reflect dishonorably on the family name, no scandal of any kind. This was a promise he kept.

It is not easy to imagine Yoko's reasons for accepting the "difficult stipulations" which attached to marriage to Mishima. Presumably his fame, his charisma, and his undeniable if disturbing sexuality drew her strongly. There may also be relevance in the fact that the traditionally "Japanese" response to homosexuality is not principally one of abhorrence as it is in the West. In Edo society, an ebullient compound of townsmen and samurai elements which thrived from the seventeenth through the nineteenth centuries and whose values are still discernible in contemporary Japan, the most flamboyant heroes of the pleasure quarters were often famous as bisexual lovers. As a Japanese woman with her particular background — there were geisha on Yoko's mother's side of the family — it seems likely that Yoko Mishima was therefore better equipped to cope with her knowledge of her husband's homosexuality than a western woman would have been.

Mishima's choice of Yoko is easier to understand. He found her attractive, and at least as important, he sensed in her a woman who could learn the part he intended his wife to play. Why he chose to marry at this time — or at any time — is less clear. One decisive factor may have been his mother's health. In March 1958, Shizue was admitted to the hospital for tests and diagnosed as having terminal cancer. A month later the diagnosis was reversed and Shizue came home. It was during this month of March, while she was in the hospital expected to die, that the marriage was arranged between the two families. According to Shizue, Kimitake rushed through the arrangements without even consulting her so that he might give her the assurance that he would be married and have a family before she died.

But filial piety cannot have been the entire explanation. Probably another important factor was Mishima's need to maintain his respectability in the eyes of his public. In Japan a successful citizen, whether he is a banker or a novelist (and Mishima in many ways was more like a banker), is expected to take a wife and raise a family. Mishima was not afraid to shock, even to horrify, the public; he went out of his way to do so in a variety of ways, increasingly after his marriage. But no matter how outrageously he behaved, he was never less than passionately concerned with what the world thought of him: and this concern — call it vanity, call it his essential conventionality — required that he feel anchored in respectability.

For various reasons of their own, Mishima and Yoko settled on one another as marriage partners at once. But in Japan a marriage is arranged between two families rather than individuals, and between the Hiraokas and the Sugiyamas there was trouble. From the beginning, Nei Sugiyama took the attitude that he was favoring the Hiraokas by presenting them his daughter in marriage. Azusa, on his part, more than made up for what he lacked in wealth and fame with aristocratic pretensions based on Natsu's lineage. Besides, his son was the greatest novelist in the land: Azusa made sure the Sugiyamas understood that he was not impressed by the daughter of a nouveau riche painter. Early on, negotiations nearly fell apart when the Sugiyamas demanded that Yoko be permitted to finish college. Azusa would not hear of this; if Yoko married Yukio Mishima she must be Mrs. Yukio Mishima exclusively and not also a student. During the deadlock that resulted, Yoko is said to have gone to her mother in tears to declare that if she could not have Mishima as her husband, she would kill herself. Sugiyama finally yielded and the arrangements were settled. On May 9, Azusa and Mishima visited the Sugiyamas to pay the traditional husband's dowry, a sum negotiated between the families and, in this case, undoubtedly a large one.

The wedding was on May 30. The afternoon reception was held at International House, except for its wonderful garden a spartan institution intended for use primarily by foreign scholars visiting in Japan, but also patronized by that segment of Japanese high society with international, and particularly academic, connections. It was an interesting choice for Mishima's wedding, not at all in his style, since at International House, lavishness, or display of any kind, was impossible. On the other hand, it was and still is very definitely "Peers' School," and it may have been this which attracted Mishima and appealed strongly to his parents.

The party was nearly a disaster: the Hiraokas and the Sugiyamas were not speaking to one another. The man who suffered most was Yasunari Kawabata who, in his ceremonial role as "go-between," was also the official host at the reception. Several of Mishima's friends recall that Kawabata was "beside himself" as he tried to get through the formal introductions of one family to the other.

The next morning, June 1, Mishima and Yoko left Tokyo on a short honeymoon. They went to the hot springs at Hakone, then to Kyoto and Kobe, and from Kobe by boat to Beppu. In Kyoto they visited Dai-ei Studios to watch Kon

Ichikawa filming Mishima's novel *The Golden Pavilion.** Wherever they went, the press was with them; the marriage was a nationwide sensation and Mishima obviously loved the commotion. His diary of the trip is full of entries like the following:

As we walked down the corridor on the second floor, a girl from the beauty parlor [in the hotel] picked up the telephone in the corridor and began informing someone of our every step in a voice so loud we couldn't possibly have missed it. As the elevator doors closed we heard her report, "They've just stepped into the elevator." In our room whenever a girl came to clean up or bring us something she was always accompanied by two or three others who just tagged along for a good look at us on their way out. When a waitress from Room Service appeared and Yoko ordered a cream soda and I ordered one too, the girl said, "You drink the same drink! That's passion!" I was appalled.

On June 15, the newlyweds flew from Beppu back to Tokyo. Waiting for them at the airport, in addition to the press and the usual emissaries from Mishima's several publishers, were Chiyuki and his wife, who had just returned from four years in Rio de Janeiro with the foreign service. The whole family went back to the Midorigaoka house to celebrate the marriage and the reunion.

As Mishima never spoke about his situation at home except in the most casual way, and as Yoko was equally reticent about her life with Mishima, possibly at his insistence, it is hard to know what the marriage was really like. In company the Mishimas always gave the impression of enjoying one another

---

* Mishima was particularly interested in this film because Ichikawa had chosen the young actor Raizo Ichikawa on Mishima's strong recommendation, and Raizo was brilliant. The film *Enjo* was by far the best to be made from a Mishima novel.

genuinely. Yoko never behaved with the diffidence one expects from a Japanese wife even today, nor did Mishima appear to expect it of her. In fact he went out of his way to include her socially in a fashion remarkably un-Japanese. It was not merely that Yoko frequently accompanied him on trips and went with him when he entertained foreign friends who would expect his wife to join the party (many Japanese and most writers cannot bring themselves to make even this concession to foreign expectations). Mishima always drew Yoko into the conversation, solicited and attended her opinion, and in general indicated his respect. Perhaps his public attitude toward his wife was part of his determinedly western pose. But it was always my impression that he took genuine pleasure in Yoko's company. I remember sitting with him in his study late at night discussing work and Mishima suggesting we have a glass of brandy and calling Yoko in to join us. It sounds trivial enough, but I have never seen it happen and can't imagine it could happen with any other Japanese writer.

Naturally the marriage was not as entirely amiable as the Mishimas always made it seem. In general Yoko seems to have closed her eyes to things she was not intended to see, but there were times when she balked. There was a period in the early sixties when Mishima held regular body-building parties at home. He would invite weight-lifter friends from the gym, and the men would drink and talk "body-build" and then strip down to trunks and oil their bodies and pose for a photographer provided by Mishima. Yoko objected. There was no scene, there was never a scene. But according to one of the young weight lifters, the time came when Mishima sheepishly informed his friends that there would be no more such parties. In 1963 Mishima posed in the nude for a photographic study called *Punishment by Roses*. The result was a beautiful though disturbing book which Yoko understandably disliked. There was nothing she could do to stop its publication, but she treated the photographer, Eiko Hosoe, with distinct coldness ever after. In 1965 Yoko precipitated a more serious crisis when she announced to the family that she intended to take up sports car racing. Although Mishima was not what the Japanese ordinarily call a tyrant at home he would not hear of this, since obviously it would suggest that Yoko was not entirely satisfied with her life at home, and since the media could be counted on to make the most of it. Eventually Yoko yielded but not before an innocent bystander had been sacrificed. In 1964 and 1965 the Mishimas often socialized with a young businessman and his wife whose child was in the same kindergarten class at the Peers' School as their daughter. In the summer of 1966 Yoko asked her friends to look into the sports car racing situation for her, and the young couple innocently undertook to find out about license requirements. In August Mishima invited their friends to join them in Shimoda for a week, and one afternoon when they were all sitting on the beach the husband communicated to Yoko what he had learned. Mishima listened to them in silence; that night after dinner he drew the man aside and asked him to leave. He told his dumbstruck friend only that he had violated the family's privacy. The following morning the couple returned to Tokyo and never heard from the Mishimas again.

Probably the most persistent cause of discord in the Mishima house was the antagonism, never resolved, between Yoko and Shizue. In her own quiet, indefatigable way, Shizue was every bit as possessive of Mishima as Natsu had ever been. Very likely she would have found grounds for disliking any woman he had chosen as his wife; certainly for the women he had not chosen she had only praise. Several times she said to me with

a broad smile and a gracious nod of her head that Kimitake's
first girl, presumably "Sonoko," was the best woman he had
known. On another occasion she let slip that the friend who
had introduced Yoko to the family would have made Kimitake
the kind of bride "he deserved." Whenever she mentioned
Yoko, just beneath her politeness she managed to be obliquely
deprecative. She never referred to her daughter-in-law as
"daughter" (*musume*), but always as "the bride" (*yome*), a
choice of words in Japanese which conveys the same chilliness
it would in English.

But if Shizue in her way was as demanding as Natsu, Yoko
was no sheltered girl when she joined the family. She was at
least as assertive and as strong-willed as her mother-in-law,
every bit her match. From the beginning she made it clear that
she was not interested in Mishima's friends from the past and
that they were not welcome in the house. In most Japanese
marriages it is unthinkable that the wife could affect the husband's circle of acquaintances; but it is a fact in Mishima's
case that he did not bring home those of his former friends
whom Yoko disliked, and she disliked most of them. She also
made clear that she would not tolerate interference in their
private lives from Shizue, and generally she seems to have had
her way.

Mishima was caught in the middle, very much as he had
been during his childhood. The difference was that now he was
in a position to ameliorate his situation in a variety of ways
and chose not to. From remarks he dropped to friends it seems
that he was constantly having to mollify Yoko about Shizue,
to plead with her to humor his attentions to his mother. There
is much to suggest that by any conventional standards he remained a mama's boy all his life. For example, during the
eleven years that the family lived together in the house he

built in 1959, one of many small but repeated slights from Yoko's point of view was his practice of stopping in at his parents' annex to chat and wish them good night before he entered the main house. Until the last year of his life, he also maintained the practice of showing Shizue his work in manuscript and asking her opinion. But there is also evidence, stray remarks here and there, that Shizue's demands on his attention were onerous. Doubtless he was ambivalent; what is clear is that his domestic situation placed a very considerable strain on him. Why then, since he was now in a position to improve the situation by separating the two women, did he choose not to? Perhaps he was impelled masochistically to inflict upon himself the same conflict, the same variety of pain, he had suffered as a child.

For the first eleven months of their marriage, the Mishimas lived together with the Hiraoka elders and the tension was severe. In January 1959, Yoko pregnant with their first child, Mishima announced his intention to build a house for the whole family, with a private wing for Azusa and Shizue. Those who knew about the situation at home, Chiyuki in particular, tried to dissuade him, but he would not listen.

Like everything he created, Mishima's house was consummately logical in his own terms. Had he wanted a Japanese house, he explained, he would have copied the famous Katsura detached palace in Kyoto, for surely there could be no finer monument to Japanese architecture. But the simplicity which was Japan's crowning architectural achievement did not allow comfortable living. Since only in the West was comfort the primary consideration in house design, he must have a quintessentially western house, "a house as unlike a Zen temple as any house could possibly be." For Mishima the essence of the West was late baroque, clashing colors, garishness: even the walls of the Parthenon were splashed with color. As he explained to his horrified architect, "I want to sit on rococo furniture wearing Levi's and an aloha shirt; that's my ideal of a life-style."

When the press asked for the proper description they were told "Victorian Colonial," but I have never seen anything like it in England. In flavor it was vaguely Italianate, vaguely Spanish, a two-story white house with a veranda in front overlooking a small garden. In the center of the garden was a sundial of zodiac tiles and a marble statue, not of Dionysius but Apollo. (Mishima once explained to a foreign reporter in English, "This is my despicable symbol of the rational.") Off to one corner was a Venetian loveseat which Mishima had ordered from a prop man at Dai-ei film studios and of which he was very proud. The entrance to the garden was through a wrought-iron gate in a high white wall around the house. In my memory the gate was always kept locked with an enormous padlock which the maid would open when visitors rang.

In the main house there were no Japanese rooms. Just inside there was the traditional Japanese entranceway (*genkan*) where visitors expected to remove their shoes before stepping up onto the wooden floor. But one of the little surprises that awaited guests at Mishima's house was the maid's polite invitation to step up as they were, with their shoes on. (The maid herself stepped out of sandals into slippers, as did the Mishimas when they were home alone.) This had the subtle effect of slightly embarrassing, slightly confusing callers. Visitors, whether dinner guests or editors, were always shown into the first floor room to the right, a combination dining and reception room with a ceiling two stories high. It was a peculiar place, more like a reception hall than a room in the house, except that "reception hall" makes it sound much larger than it was. In fact all the spaces in the house were small (Mishima was a small man, though he never gave that impression) and cluttered. Here the floor was tile squares; there was a Louis XIV table that seated fourteen, a loveseat, a chair and smaller antique table, a small bar, a porcelain writing set, several Renaissance miniatures Mishima had brought home from Italy and, against the far wall, an ivory white staircase with a figured iron banister on which he liked to pose. At the top of these stairs was the living room, somewhat larger than the dining room it overlooked. Here the decor was motley; there was a rather nondescript sofa, chairs from various antique periods, a piano, a brace of brass lamps with smoked-glass bulbs, a Victorian secretary, and a good deal of bric-a-brac. Permanently installed on the sofa was a stuffed lion beginning to unravel, a doll from Mishima's childhood. It was here that the Mishimas served drinks before dinner or gave cocktail parties, a convention Mishima imported from New York and took pleasure in inflicting on Japanese guests.

Until 1965 only these two rooms were open to the public. Then Mishima added a third floor which consisted of a terrace the length of the house looking out toward Tokyo Bay and two perfectly round, dome-ceilinged rooms on both sides of the stairway. These were designed to permit the ladies and the gentlemen to part company for a decorous interval after dinner. The decor was ultramodern: low tables and built-in couches that hugged the curve of the wall, wall-to-wall carpeting, Neptune blue in the gentlemen's salon on the right, scarlet in the ladies' on the left. On display in a niche cut into the wall in the gentlemen's, illuminated by a spotlight from above, was a rare Grecian urn, a gift from Yoko's father.

Through the living room on the second floor, or accessible by another staircase used only by the family, were the bedrooms and Mishima's study. The room in which Mishima worked at least six hours a night every day of his life was remarkably spare. It was a smallish room, perhaps twelve by twelve. Except for the large metal desk heaped with manuscripts, the only furniture was a small table and two chairs where he sometimes sat late at night with editors or, rarely, writer friends. The walls behind his desk and on the right were ceiling-high bookshelves. Here he kept an encyclopedia, atlases, dictionaries, a collection of esoteric reference works such as *One Hundred Finest Luxury Items in the World*, and the dozens of scrapbooks in which he meticulously filed his enormous press. (The bulk of his library of eight thousand titles was shelved in "the stacks" across the hall from the study.) On the door was a full-length mirror. The room was heated (the house had central heating) but not air-conditioned. A small air conditioner had been installed but Mishima found its hum disturbing and removed it: he required silence during the long hours that he worked. The austerity of the study was in striking contrast to the rest of the house, but that was consistent with one of Mishima's cardinal rules, that his work and his life as a family man be strictly separated. He used to tell his friends and family that he became a demon during the hours he spent alone at work but never took the demon from the study — no empty boast in his case.

Azusa and Shizue lived Japanese-style, in a modest Japanese house (*tatami* rooms) at right angles to the main house and within the same surrounding wall. It was not properly a wing, since it did not connect to the main house internally, but an annex, with its own private entrance through a small gate in one corner of the garden wall. Thus the Hiraokas, who had their own small Japanese garden and two maids to do the housework, could live in complete privacy if they chose, isolated from the main house. The opposite was not quite true: the elders' sitting room faced the walk which led from the iron gate to the entrance of the main house. As I discovered, it was possible to visit Azusa and Shizue privately but impossible to get into the main house unobserved by them. On the few occasions when I visited Yoko without informing Azusa that I was coming (something I had been warned against), he was always waiting for me on my way out.

The family moved into the new house on May 9, 1959, and there they remained. During these last eleven years of Mishima's life his routine varied relatively little. Generally he arose at one in the afternoon, read his mail over coffee and, when the weather permitted, sunbathed in the garden for an hour or so. Early in the afternoon, unless he was writing around the clock to keep some impossible deadline, he left the house with his small valise and went either to the gym to lift weights or to practice *kendo* swordsmanship or, later, karate. The late afternoons were generally taken up by meetings with editors or directors, by symposia with critics and other writers which were recorded for publication in literary magazines, by rehearsals, by all the business of his complicated life. Most nights he did not dine at home; unless he was entertaining at the house, which he did lavishly but not frequently, he was rarely back before eleven. He was usually in the study by twelve, never later than one.

Work came first and perhaps mattered most, but Mishima did not neglect his family. He had two children, a daughter Noriko, born in June 1959, and a son Iichiro, born in May 1962, and he was an attentive and seemingly devoted father. A few days every month he set aside for the family; beginning in 1964, he spent August every year with Yoko and the children at the Tokyu Hotel in Shimoda, a seaside resort on the tip of the Izu Peninsula.

In June 1959, a month after the family had moved into the new house and a few days after Yoko had returned from the hospital with his infant daughter Noriko, Mishima completed *Kyoko's House*, a novel he had been steadily at work on for fifteen months, by far the longest period he had ever devoted to a book. The looming importance to him of this novel in particular and the extraordinary exercise of will it took to bring it to completion are apparent in the diary he kept (and serially published) throughout the fifteen months of writing:

March 10, 1958 (Monday)
Clear. The warmth since this afternoon is like honey.
Every day I intend to begin my new *unserialized* novel *Kyoko's House,** but I am afraid to begin. With a thousand pages involved you can't just plan things in your head — since I intend to use the scenery around Harumi beyond Tsukijima I took a cab and went down to look around. I got there at three, just as the drawbridge was being raised. I had a feeling I could use this, so I got out and took notes. . . .
Tonight I tried to begin but couldn't. Tomorrow I'm going to Nara to watch the annual "water drawing" ceremony at the Hall of the Second Month. I'll start when I get back.

March 22 (Saturday)
That heavy, unpleasant feeling that assails me when I begin work on a long novel. To make things worse it was overcast and finally began to rain. At six, Mr. and Mrs. Howes joined me as my

---

* In 1958, serialization was still the rule, and most writers preferred it. For one thing, it permitted an author to construct his book less tightly. It also aided the book's progress by enforcing regular deadlines. And it permitted him to adjust to criticism from the establishment in the course of the writing. Mishima's determination to have this book entirely to himself until it was finished bespoke its importance to him, and, in a way, his confidence: in 1958 and 1959 an unserialized novel a thousand pages long was considered risky even for an established author.

guests at dinner. They are friends of Donald Keene's, recently married, and both have come to Japan to do research. We dined at the Hananoki, snails, quail, and soufflé. Afterward we went to the show at the Nichigeki Music Hall. At home, work was waiting. I hated to come back.

March 23 (Sunday)
I stayed in all day and worked. The book is finally in motion. The happiness I feel when work is going well or when the work is finished is not of this world.

April 11 (Friday)
The first chapter of *Kyoko's House* is still unfinished. The explanation seems to be that I am trying to curtail the showy first chapter like an opera overture which is a fault common to all my novels and begin as inconspicuously as I can, even to understate. Another thing is that until now, like a bad player, I have always flashed too many of my cards in the first chapter, with the result that the development is telegraphed. It's essential to build the introductory chapter as sparely, as simply as possible. All of this goes against the grain of my taste for punch lines and showiness.

August 8 (Friday)
Tonight I felt feverish and light-headed, which was ideal for doing the scene when the boxer trains. A scene like this is hard to write with a clear head. The work went well and by morning I had finally reached page 200 of *Kyoko's House*. Eight hundred pages remain — in short, I'm almost there.

September 18 (Thursday)
Since last night a typhoon has been approaching and at six this morning the electricity went off. But I was determined to oppose the storm, and in a mood combined of oppressive heaviness and exhilaration I brought *Kyoko's House* to page 259 and finished Chapter Three.

So far I've only just managed to finish introducing the central characters. In a manner of speaking I've arrived at the entrance to the gambler's den, but life has been so complicated that it has taken me half a year to get there. My progress has been just half of what I had planned, and although a novel not being serialized is always behind schedule, I must catch up somehow. But I must not feel rushed. I must close my eyes and ears to the frenetic goings-on.

October 20 (Monday)

Ever since I put 300 pages behind me on October 11, work on *Kyoko's House* has progressed sluggishly, partly the effect of a certain sense of relief. But the minute progress slows, relief is replaced by anxiety, which in turn creates impatience and in its own way impedes progress. Thus it is that our work must constantly battle against excuses we make to ourselves.

December 11 (Thursday)

Home at four in the afternoon, I went right to bed in order to catch up on sleep. I woke at ten and began work on *Kyoko*. I'm worried I may not finish Part One before the year is out.

New Year's Day, 1959 (Thursday)

It was my plan to finish Part One of *Kyoko's House*, five hundred pages, by the end of last year. To that end I labored mightily, but as the temple bells tolled the end of the year last night I had managed to finish only 463 pages. I slept for just three hours, took up my pen again at four this morning and wrote through to the end of the fight scene, page 469. I felt quite relieved, and at ten A.M. we all sat down to our New Year's breakfast.

A couple from the Bungaku-za who are to be married in February with us as go-betweens came through the snow for a New Year's visit, and we had dinner together and then drank and danced. They stayed until eleven, but when I tried to call a limousine I found there wasn't a single garage open. So the healthy affianced put on their boots and plunged out into the snow. I went back to work and progressed to page 471.

January 4 (Sunday)

At seven-thirty this morning I finished Part One with 491 pages, slightly fewer than I had planned, and found I was too agitated to sleep. Finally I did fall off and slept until three this afternoon.

January 5 (Monday)

On a New Year's call to Shinchosha's [president] Ryoichi Sato, I also handed him the manuscript for Part One and felt eased of a heavy weight. I consoled myself with the thought that I had, after all, finished Part One *before* the publishers had begun work [for the new year] so it might be said that I was more or less on schedule.

Tonight I begin Part Two.

March 16 (Monday)

Clear. The camellias have finally blossomed.

Body-building at four. Today I added exercises for the triceps. Went to H. Tailors for a suit fitting. At home I wrote like one possessed and at three A.M. on the 17th, I brought *Kyoko's House* to 680 pages and finished Chapter Seven.

Since I moved on to Part Two the book has almost never felt sluggish. Each episode proceeds toward catastrophe, and catastrophe is what I love above all. How to describe the joy of work when it goes this well? It is like saddling this globe of ours, leaping astride, and with one crack of the whip making it gallop through the blackness of the void. The stars all fly by, grazing your cheeks. But enough of foolishness. This is a secret joy that mustn't be told.

April 7 (Tuesday)

Late tonight, after several weeks of slow and inexpressibly lugubrious *rock climbing* I have at last reached 700 pages in *Kyoko's House*. However labored my progress may be it remains more or less constant and it is of course exercise which makes this possible. Were I not able to renew my creaking skeleton five times a week thanks to exercise (coursing blood and sweat) I would long ago have become a corpse in spirit.

May 9 (Saturday)

I slept two hours early this morning and then continued working, bringing *Kyoko* to 790 pages. I had planned to have 800 pages before we moved [into the new house] and then when moving day was postponed to the ninth I had felt certain I could keep to schedule; but here it is the ninth and I am still ten pages behind.

June 16 (Tuesday)

Clear. At four this afternoon, Yoko returned from the hospital with Noriko. What a cheeky little creature she is, smugly moving in as a new member of the family just one month after the house is built and things are finally settling down. I spent the day looking after her.

Since last year I have lived in constant tingling anticipation of three major enterprises in my personal life of 1959. One was the construction of my new house. One was the birth of my first child. One was completing my long novel *Kyoko's House*. Two of these have come to pass at last. One remains.

June 29 (Monday)

For the past week I have been captive to an indescribable anxiety wondering when the completion of *Kyoko's House* would befall me. I have been dreadfully tired, my nerves on edge. It was my intention at least to keep to my schedule of exercise, but when I tried a 150-pound bench press, which should have been nothing for me, I felt a stabbing pain in the back of my head which stayed with me as a headache. After that I developed a headache at once whenever I lifted a barbell above my head and had to leave off depending on exercise for relief. Now there remained no suitable means of refreshing myself available to me, and I was forced to spend every day face to face with this oppressive anxiety like a disease.

For some time the prospect that this endless novel would

finally be completed has been an eery, even an ominous feeling inside me. For a long time completion was like a dream, I even felt such a thing would never be permitted to happen. On the other hand I could picture myself dancing barefoot over the garden on the morning when I finished. I would have fireworks in readiness, I imagined, and on that morning I would send them into the sky one after the other. At the same time I also thought to myself, "You couldn't be that excited about anything."

On the twenty-sixth I felt that my exhaustion had reached its limit, so on Saturday the twenty-seventh and Sunday the twenty-eighth I stayed at home all day, going out only in the early evening for a short walk with my family. I could feel that I was almost finished and I was afraid to go to work. If once I started and my pen plowed feverishly ahead I had no idea how far it would go. But late Sunday night, I finally allowed my pen to go where it would. And at three-thirty this morning I completed *Kyoko's House* in 947 pages. It is more than fifteen months since I began to write on March 17 of last year.

Now I was finished and put my pen down: I didn't feel the pleasure I'd imagined, there was only a forlorn feeling, no pleasure to act on. Fireworks! Exhaustion was all I could feel, pervading me in the form of a blurred, an unfocused anxiety. The feeling of a hangover. As if I were being forced to submerge in bad, murky air.

At four A.M., I got into bed, but exhaustion and excitement kept me awake; idle thoughts kept intruding in my head. Gradually the space between the window curtains whitened. Of course! I would go up on the roof and celebrate the sunrise, give thanks for completion of my book. But when I raised the shutters the morning sky was folded in layers of gray cloud, there was no chance to see the rising sun.

Forced to an alternative I chose a bath, went downstairs to the bathroom, opened the faucets and before the water was fully hot lay down in the bathtub. As I soaked in the lukewarm water I drifted for a long while through my ambivalence, somehow satisfied, somehow unsatisfied.

After my bath I went out to the front gate for the morning paper, sat down on a stone in the garden and read the paper from cover to cover. By the time I really got to sleep it was eight o'clock.

The novel which Mishima labored so single-mindedly to accomplish and which meant so very much to him is an unsettling, even a terrifying, book. To begin with it proclaims from every page his feeling that the identity he appeared to inhabit so substantially and unequivocally, as a famous novelist, playwright, critic, and an eccentric flamboyant with a zest for life, was to Mishima himself nothing more than a collection of masks; that despite triumphant moments such as the summer festival in the streets, he was no more in touch with the vital sense of truly *existing* than he had ever been *since the war's end*. Moreover, *Kyoko's House* reads like an uncannily prophetic scenario. It implants in the reader's mind the disturbing possibility that Mishima foreknew in 1959 precisely the destination he was headed for and even what he would be required to do in order to arrive.

Mishima intended the four young heroes of the book, a businessman, a painter, a boxer, and an actor, to represent facets of himself. Integrating the characters is their shared sense of being confronted by "an unscalable wall." The obstacle represented is an obstacle to participation in life: the question each is forced to seek an answer to is how to exist, how to feel alive.

The businessman's solution is "utter contempt for present reality." He "knows" that what passes for reality is a hoax perpetrated by the present, "a brief respite before the fall." He knows that "sooner or later the world and everything in it will fall" and that the only "true reality" is "the world poised on the brink of destruction." His conviction, which permits him to thrive in present reality by despising it, originates in his (and of course his author's) experience of the war: only then, when the world was truly *on the brink of destruction*, was he able to experience reality as truly real. "Admit it, you love destruction," he tells Kyoko, speaking for himself,

You'll always remember the vast, refreshing radiance of that endless, burnt-out ruin; when you gaze at the city today you see only a memory of the past. When you walk the restored, chilly concrete of a sidewalk, if you can't feel the warmth of embers in the scorched earth beneath your feet, something is missing for you; if you can't see through the glass of a modern building to the dandelions that grew from the chinks in the ruined wall, you're desolate. . . .

Through the businessman nihilist Mishima was expressing his own contempt for postwar reality and confronting the possibility that he might never feel alive and real in it. At the very least he shared the nihilist's conviction that postwar reality was unreal because death and destruction were not immanent in it. In the diary he kept during the writing of *Kyoko's House*, he entered a note which is the basis for the nihilist's view of the world:

A gulf separates the "death" we felt so close to during the war . . . and today's uneventful, peaceful world. Suddenly we were driven from a life in which death was a reality into a world where death is no more than an idea: the sense of reality we enjoyed in a life that was close to death has now been transformed into an idea. Conversely, what was unmistakably fantasy during the War has become the reality of everyday life.

In the boxer, Mishima first expressed the "philosophy of action" that would soon become a mainstay in his new identity as a patriot:

At the very core of his world was action, an effective punch. Thought was the opposite of simplicity, of purity — the opposite of speed. Assuming there was beauty in speed, in simplicity, in power, then all ugliness was represented by thought. To him it was unimaginable that there could be thought as swift as an arrow. How could any thought be faster than the instantaneous explosion of a jab?

So long as the boxer can punch effectively, he knows, without having to think about it, that he is alive. Then he gets into a fight with a hoodlum gang and his right hand is smashed with a baseball bat; when the cast is removed he is no longer able to clench the hand into a fist. Deprived of the possibility of action, the boxer is deprived of his identity. He is "determined as ever not to think," but he knows without thinking that to exist, to know that he exists, he requires "a proper opponent."

Prophetically, in view of Mishima's life, the boxer's solution to this existential crisis is to join a group of right-wing extremists. The scene in which a former classmate persuades him to join is one of several in *Kyoko's House* which now evoke in the reader a chilling sense of déjà vu. The series of clichés which the boxer's friend recites to him, for example, are essentially identical to the cant which Mishima would presently announce as his own position:

"We Japanese must reveal the true form of our imperial land, in which the sovereign and the people are gloriously united. We must become an example of the freedom, the peace, the happiness, and the spiritual enlightenment desired by every nation in the world and every race. It is our heaven-sent mission to stake our lives on our faith in the emperor and to guard the prosperity of our Imperial Throne. Therein resides our greatness, our sublimity —"

162

"What the hell is that?" the boxer said.

"That's ideology. Do you believe it?"

"I don't even understand it."

"Then listen to some more: We will clarify the ideals of empire, uplift the Japanese spirit, sweep communism away, rectify
capitalism, and revise the constitution imposed on us as a de-
feated nation to our lasting humiliation. We will have the traitorous Communist party outlawed, and promote rearmament in
the name of peace, independence, and self-defense. We will over-
overthrow the ruling class acting in concert with the Communist
traitors and providing their spawning ground, and we will establish a new order, a mutual prosperity in which the people shall
thrive."

"What's that all about?"

"That's ideology too."

"And you believe that?"

But the most unsettling moment of the scene is what follows,
the former classmate's admission that his own involvement in
right-wing extremism is merely a personal desire to place himself in touch with what he imagines to be the *rapture of death*:

I wouldn't say I believed it exactly. It's just that phrases like
that give me a *fine feeling*. I feel as if my body can melt into each
phrase as I say it. Probably because phrases like this are closer than
anything to *death*. When I was a cheerleader there were lots of
times when I was singing our fight songs when suddenly I sensed
death and got this fine feeling. You know the way your body
trembles when you've finished a piss you've been holding in —
that's got to be the sensation of *death*.

"You're a pretty heretical rightist."

"You bet I am. But I wouldn't talk like this to anyone but you.
Because I think you and I are alike in this; I think you were discovering the same thing in your boxing."

"I don't think so." As he spoke Shunkichi denied to himself a

163

sensation of pleasure that made him shudder. "How can it not matter whether I believe or not?" he said.

"Because the less a guy believes the more effective he is. Look at me. I know perfectly well I don't believe. I see this ideology outside of myself, and I use it as a tool to obtain an indescribable rapture, to feel that my own death and the death of others is always close to me. That feeling is my qualification as an effective member of the group, as effective as you can be."

There are those in Japan and in the West who will deny with vehemence that Mishima was "a heretical rightist" in the sense prescribed here, but they are wrong: Mishima's patriotism was animated by his quest for precisely the "indescribable rapture" which is equated here with "the sensation of death." Surely he knew it fully as well as the former cheerleader and, by implication, the boxer, who signs a blood oath at the end of the scene (as Mishima was later to do). If there is a false parallel to be drawn it is between boxing and Mishima's art: there were no incidents in Mishima's artistic life of significance commensurate with the boxer's accident. Nonetheless, the nature of the loss of identity which brings the boxer to "swear fidelity to an ideology he does not believe in" is significant. *Kyoko's House* suggests about the relationship between Mishima's art and the final tack of his life that art for Mishima had ceased to function as an adequate verification of existence. As the actor in *Kyoko's House* would have phrased it, art had ceased to be a satisfactory mirror.

The actor's narcissism represents Mishima's perception of his own; Osamu expends so much of his energy on himself because his sense of existing is so tenuous, so very feeble. Like Mishima, he begins lifting weights in hopes of rendering his own existence more palpable to himself, and muscle does help. But the time comes when muscle is no longer an adequate substantiation of existence and disabling doubt returns. Then Osamu makes a new (and final) discovery. It is a hot summer day and he is lying naked on the floor, eyes closed, finding momentary solace in the caresses of his mistress. Suddenly he feels a flash of pain and opens his eyes to discover blood trickling down his side; she has cut him with a razor blade:

Ordinary, everyday attention wasn't enough for him; he had wanted attention so virulent it burned. Mere caresses were not enough, he had needed attention that would corrode him. And until now . . . he had encountered no verification of existence more substantial and certain than this moment of pain. Unquestionably it was pain he had needed.

When he saw the blood trickling down his side Osamu had awakened to the certainty of existence for the first time in his life. Here was his youthful flesh, concern for him so ardent it would not be satisfied short of wounding that flesh, the flow of blood unmistakably his own — here the drama of existence materialized for the first time, blood and pain utterly guaranteed his existence, and with his existence at its center an entire panorama unfolded. . . . The gentle, alluring flow of blood. The blood flowing from his body was an indication of peerless accord between the internal and external. For his beautiful body truly to exist it was not enough that it be merely enrounded by a wall of muscle. What had been lacking, in a word, was blood. . . . Osamu even knew that the pain and blood which had convinced him of existence would eventually function only to annihilate his own. . . .

From that day on, Osamu was bewitched by the concept of lovers' suicide; day and night, the thought never left his mind. Yet the only pain he could imagine was the feather-light touch of a razor blade; and though he understood that it was pain he truly required, this conceptual pain, the minute he brought it to mind, seemed to merge with pleasure. When that happened, death seemed the same as death on stage. . . .

For the blood Osamu envisioned stage blood was adequate; for the agony of death, stage agony sufficed. But his fantasies quickly

165

ran aground; whenever these dreams of the stage revived, the stage which refused to offer him a role, his sense of his own existence weakened and he was again pursued by the idea that real blood must be let. Thus Osamu's concept of lovers' suicide moved back and forth like a pendulum between reality and the stage.

Still, insofar as he had experienced neither of them, death on stage and real death were roughly the same. Sometimes, when he realized that the death he fancied was laced with pleasure only, entirely without pain, Osamu was unable to tell whether he was dreaming of death on stage or the real thing. . . .

Osamu could see as if in recollection the pool of blood on the stage. Presently he would lie there. The pool of tepid blood would soak his beautiful profile. . . . "Before long I'll stop moving. I'll die. I mustn't open my eyes. I mustn't even breathe if I can help it; the slightest breath is visible to the audience. All I have to do is concentrate on some silly thought until the curtain goes down and lie perfectly still. Finally the curtain will fall. Then I can get up."

But the thought that the curtain would not fall, the applause eternally not be heard, returned at once to Osamu's mind. It made him insanely happy. "If the curtain never falls, the play will never end." For any actor, that would be the ideal play.

Of all the troubling passages in *Kyoko's House*, this is the eeriest. In the youth who is a narcissist because he can never be certain that he is real, in the narcissist who discovers in pain a sweet proof of his existence and is therefore also a masochist, in the masochist who anticipates only pleasure in his painful death and who expects from it a consummate verification of his existence, Mishima rendered an unmistakable portrait of himself. The likeness is striking even to Osamu's confusion of death as theater and death as reality: Mishima no less than Osamu was an actor who desperately needed to feel himself the object of "virulent concern" in a drama of existence he imagined would never end. Osamu's confusion of real death and fantasy, the perilous flirtation with actual death in which all of reality was transformed into a stage on which he was to play the central role, was surely a flirtation Mishima himself continued until the moment of his own death.

Osamu does commit double suicide with his mistress. And although the reader learns from references to "newspaper accounts" that it was a bloody death, Mishima does not show us the scene. That is not surprising. Had he allowed the reader access he would have been obliged also to disclose the actor's final thoughts and sensations. Did he obtain the "indescribable rapture" of incontrovertible knowledge of his existence? Did he know (or feel) himself to be the hero of a play never more to end? Mishima does not venture to say. Assuming that such questions were as real to him as they must have been even in 1959, it is not surprising that he lacked the courage to address them. He does, however, comment indirectly on the moment of the actor's death in a letter from the nihilist, presumably the character best qualified to comment because he knows so well the difference between illusion and reality:

All we can know now or ever know is that death must always have been his desire. Death confronted him wearing a variety of masks. One by one he took them off and put them on his own face. When he removed the final mask, death's real face must have been revealed, but we cannot know whether even that was terrifying to him.

Until then his desire for death had made him fervently desire the masks too. With the masks he gradually made himself beautiful. You must realize that a man's determination to become a beautiful person is very different from the same desire in a woman; in a man it is always the desire for *death*. This is as it should be in a youth, but ordinarily the youth himself is ashamed and will not reveal his secret. It is only in a time of war that the secret is publicly revealed.

This returns to the nihilist's conviction that true reality is manifest only in that moment when the world is poised on the brink of destruction, during the war or in that final moment he constantly reassures himself is near at hand. The argument he represents, and which is dramatized most explicitly in the actor, is that death, or the moment before death, is the only reality. Hence to live, to exist, to participate in reality, is to die. The nihilist knows as much, but he is determined to live in opposition to his conviction. The nihilist survives, and so, not surprisingly, does the artist. Thus, while art and nihilism are accessible to the composite hero of *Kyoko's House*, survival is possible. When art and nihilism cease to function as satisfactory substitutes for existence itself, the boxer and the actor within him will have their way.

Kyoko's House was to Mishima's thirties what *Confessions of a Mask* was to his twenties. Both works are an accounting, testimony to an astounding degree of self-knowledge; both works constituted in themselves a process of self-discovery. There is no knowing whether Mishima knew he was predicting his own fate when he wrote *Kyoko's House*. But one thing is certain; the developments of the sixties, the shift to the politics of the Right which culminated in Mishima's "patriotic" suicide, did not suddenly appear. Surely all the elements were there by 1958 and just as certainly Mishima was sensible of them.

SIX

1960-1966

Kyoko's House sold well enough, but the critics received it coldly. Typical of the response from the establishment was a panel discussion which appeared in the magazine *Bungakkai* in December 1959. Not only were the six discussants among the most influential critics, all of them had been extravagant with praise for Mishima in the past. But they were agreed that *Kyoko's House* was "Mishima's first big failure." Although their criticism was various it focused on the social relevance the novel seemed to claim for itself yet somehow lacked:

HIRANO: I find nothing new in this.

ETO: I agree.

HIRANO: There's no significance in having set the period at 1954 and 1955; it's all the same old war nostalgia.

SAEKI: All the characters are just parts of Mishima; all the novel presents is the extraordinarily isolated, internalized world of Mishima himself.

YAMAMOTO: This is his first big failure.

ETO: Balzac would have created a fresco; all Mishima requires is a large mirror.

SAEKI: Initially he may have intended the mirror . . . to reflect the outside world. But all he actually did was to show us an explanation of his own inner world.

ETO: I wonder if he intended to reflect the outside world. I think this is a *trick* of Mishima's: to claim he is going to reflect the outside and actually to show us the inside.

Mishima was extraordinarily sensitive to criticism of work which he took seriously. Generally he hid behind a large, insouciant laugh or an affected contempt for the species known as critic while inwardly he suffered. But there were occasions when he was unable to contain his hurt and vented it like a petulant child. Once a good friend undertook to write an afterword to a collection of his short stories. In order to demonstrate the brilliance of the stories more effectively, the friend mildly criticized other similar works which had not succeeded as well. Mishima was furious; in a curt thank-you note he wrote that an afterword should contain only praise, that it was properly " a photograph and never an X ray."

Although he was silent about *Kyoko's House*, its reception must have been a particularly painful blow. In January 1958, he had complained to an interviewer that certain novels he had "tossed off" had become "best sellers, plays, and even movies" in his absence, though he had no such expectations for them. The complaint was jocular, yet it contained genuine displeasure that a book he did not value should have been so successful. What must have been his chagrin when a novel to which he had given his best for a year and a half was scorned by the critics who mattered most!

One way or the other, Mishima was determined to have the attention he felt he had deserved for *Kyoko's House*; a month after the book was published he decided to star in a gangster movie. Early in November 1959, he told an editor at Kodansha that he wanted to make a film, and asked his friend to approach Dai-ei Studios. When Dai-ei heard the news the company president telephoned Mishima personally to urge him to act on his impulse. Characteristically, Mishima knew precisely the film he would do; he wanted to play a gangster, wear a leather jacket, and die at the end. Dai-ei asked him to read a script which sounded just right, in view of his equestrian skill. It was about a jockey who goes blind but makes a comeback nonetheless(!) and after a final heroic race dies at the finish line. Mishima rejected it and several more before choosing *Tough Guy*. The hero has just finished a jail sentence for having avenged the murder of his father, a gangland boss. The rival gang wants its own vengeance and finally gets it, but in the meantime the hero has a love affair with a beautiful girl and she becomes pregnant. The hero tries to trick her into taking abortion pills and fails. Finally he discovers he loves her and decides to accept the child. Afraid his future bride and child may be harmed on his account, he orders her to stay with her mother in the country until the heat is off. At the train station, realizing he has no gift for the baby, he rushes across the street to a department store to buy a doll. Here the gang catches up. He is shot fatally, stumbles down an up escalator, falls backward, and is carried, clutching the doll, up and out of camera.

In the months before the filming every newspaper and weekly in the land carried exclusive interviews with the soon-to-be star; Mishima seized every opportunity to place himself in the most ludicrous light. He dressed like a movie star in striped shirts and flashy ties, a pinstripe suit, and of course dark glasses. He showed his interviewers "fan letters" which read "Mishima! Have you got the face of a movie star? Take a look in the mirror!" Asked if he had confidence he could play the part, he replied, "Absolutely!" because he had checked and satisfied himself that all the actresses were shorter than he. And more than once he delivered a *coup de théâtre* by unbuttoning his shirt and proudly displaying his chest hair. The media loved it; week after week the headlines hooted: PISTOL IN HAND, HE FLAUNTS THE HAIR ON HIS CHEST; MISHIMA SHOWS US HIS CHEST HAIR; IMPRESSIVELY? MISHIMA PLAYS A HAIRY GUNMAN.

Filming began on February 1, 1960, and took six weeks. The director, Hozo Masumura, is said to have driven Mishima mercilessly. The scenes which brought him the most abuse were those with his beautiful co-star Ayako Wakao: Masumura was determined that the hero should be both tender and gruff, but the tenderness simply wasn't there. So he reshot interminably, working the crew far into the night and making it clear that Mishima was to blame. Finally he threw up his hands and screamed, "You like to slap her so much, go ahead, slap away." In the final version there is scarcely an encounter between Mishima and his lady when he is not slapping her, sometimes "tenderly" on the back but mostly "gruffly" in the face.

Mishima was dead when I saw *Tough Guy* for the first time. It was a strange experience, for I had just surfaced from reading his adolescent fiction, and I could not help superimposing my image of the fragile poet he had been at seventeen on the tough on the screen. What I then saw was bizarre: the lashes were too long; the eyes that narrowed and burned with anger were soft, vulnerable eyes; the snarling mouth was too full, too feminine, the lips too red against the paleness of the face. And the body Mishima hurled around like a sledgehammer was, just beneath the musculature, a frail, unhealthy body, particularly the spindly legs which seemed too meager to support the developed torso. As I watched, the "tough guy" dissolved and there emerged a man with no physical reality at all, a timid, womanish, cerebral man with an inherent loathing for vulgarity and violence and, indeed, physicality of any kind. The man I saw beneath the surface of Mishima's performance was Kimitake Hiraoka; all Mishima's efforts to be a hoodlum, the more determined they became, only revealed Hiraoka the more unmistakably. It was uncomfortable to watch a man laboring to become something so antithetical to himself.

When *Tough Guy* was released at the end of March the critical consensus was that Mishima's performance was "bland," neither arsenic nor gravy. But it is unlikely that Mishima cared what anyone thought, since this was no novel but an escapade, so long as everyone thought something. Besides, he was already deeply involved in another project, directing at the Bungaku-za a production of Oscar Wilde's *Salomé*. He had been fascinated with the play since he had read it first at fifteen, no doubt drawn to it for the same reasons that drew all the decadents to this fatal, tainted beauty. But the Wilde version in particular, with its pervasive doomsday atmosphere, might have been written for him expressly. All through March he worked feverishly on the production; he even designed the sets and costumes. *Salomé* opened on April 5 and was accounted a success.

The spring and early summer of 1960 were a time of violent political confrontation. The issue was the renewal of the Japan-U.S. Security Treaty of 1952 (*Anpo*). Not only the leftist opposition but also the press and public opinion were opposed to the treaty (which authorized the continuance of U.S. military bases in Japan in return for U.S. protection against Japan's hypothetical enemies) on the sensible grounds that it harnessed Japan to whatever military action in Asia the United States might see fit to take. The administration, however, anxious as always to comply with American desires, was determined it should be renewed for a period of ten years. Beginning in April (as *Salomé* opened) tens of thousands of students and workers mobilized by the socialists staged massive "petition demonstrations" which led inevitably to clashes with police and right-wing extremists. In the worst of these, on June 16, a thousand demonstrators were wounded, and a nineteen-year-old coed at Tokyo University was killed. The next day a socialist MP was stabbed while collecting signatures in front of the Diet. On the evening of June 18, three hundred thousand demonstrators surrounded Prime Minister Kishi's house to demand that the treaty be repealed. Kishi did not appear. At midnight, the treaty was "automatically renewed."

The security treaty was an issue which elicited violent feelings pro or con from nearly everyone. Mishima's response, however, suggests that in 1960 he was unburdened by any political consciousness whatsoever. In a brief essay called "One Political Opinion," he describes watching the prime minister's besieged residence from the roof of the Press Club, seeing the torches flicker and hearing the shouts, and wondering what it was about Kishi that made the crowd hate him so. "It is not that he is a former war criminal, or a Machiavelli, or even that he is an American lackey," he decides. "They hate him because he is a little, little nihilist. . . . He believes in nothing, and though he may think he has convictions, the mob knows intuitively that he is unable to believe in his political principles." In the next breath, Mishima acknowledges that "I am also a nihilist." But, "fortunately, I am a novelist and not a politician." The "political opinion" he then advances ironically is that it would be wise in future to select as head of state "a realist" rather than a nihilist like the present prime minister or himself.

These are not the words of a man with political convictions. Yet by 1968 Mishima was promising his friends that he would "die with sword in hand" in the battle with the Left at the next renewal of the security treaty in 1970. By 1968, that is, he had become (or at least was sounding very much like) an ultranationalist. What enabled (or drove) the confessed nihilist in this short space of years to acquire faith?

The beginnings of an answer are to be found in a forty-page story called "Patriotism" which Mishima wrote late in the summer of 1960. The story was inspired by the Army Rebellion of 1936, which Mishima would invest with increasing symbolic importance as his own very special brand of patriotism evolved. At dawn on the snowy morning of February 26, 1936, twenty-one young officers in the Imperial Army attempted to overthrow a government they considered traitorous. Leading 1350 foot soldiers, they managed to occupy in just a few hours a strategic square mile of Tokyo south of the palace and to assassinate in their homes three of the six key figures on their list. Then, from their firmly entrenched position they demanded a reform cabinet dedicated to a "Showa Restoration," by which they meant principally restoring to the emperor himself supreme command of the armed forces.

The insurgents had strong sympathizers in the highest echelons of the military command, the civilian government, and even the Imperial House itself in the person of the emperor's brother, Prince Chichibu. And they might well have succeeded had it not been for Emperor Hirohito himself, who, when he learned of the uprising, demanded angrily that the officers who had risen in his name be punished as "mutineers" for having executed his ministers and involved his troops in insurgency. For two days his counselors urged him not to treat these officers of the Imperial Army as rebels, but he would not listen. On the afternoon of February 28, at Hirohito's insistence, a reluctant division surrounded the occupied zone and made ready to attack. The rebel ringleaders declared they would put an end to the uprising and commit *seppuku* if an imperial messenger was sent to command them to die in the emperor's name. The high command urged Hirohito to comply with this request and thereby avoid a battle between fellow army officers. Hirohito refused, declaring that the "mutineers" were no longer his subjects and did not deserve the honor of an imperial messenger. When no messenger appeared, the rebels said they would fight, even against imperial forces, and leave it to posterity to judge their sincerity. On the evening of February 28, before they were arrested following a brief battle, they turned toward the palace and with tears in their eyes sang the Imperial Anthem, "Kimi-ga-yo." Two did commit ritual suicide; the others were executed.

The hero of "Patriotism" is a handsome young lieutenant in the Imperial Guard whose comrades have kept him ignorant of the plot out of compassion for his recent marriage. Early on the morning of the twenty-sixth the Lieutenant is summoned to the palace by an emergency bugle and is gone for two days. When he returns on the evening of the twenty-seventh he tells his young wife Reiko that he has resolved to kill himself rather than join an attack in the morning against his fellow officers, who have been branded rebels. Reiko expresses her desire to join her husband in death; the Lieutenant agrees. He purifies himself in a bath. The couple makes love a final time. Then, as Reiko looks on, the lieutenant disembowels himself. Reiko kisses her dead husband goodbye, sits in front of his body, and drives a dagger through her throat.

In an afterword, Mishima described "Patriotism" as "neither a comedy nor a tragedy, but a tale of bliss." A reader unfamiliar with Mishima, however, would have difficulty locating the bliss he asserts, particularly in the long and loving description of the lieutenant's *seppuku*, which is the climax of the tale:

Despite the effort he had put into the blow himself, the lieutenant had the impression that someone else had struck his side agonizingly with a rod of iron. For a second or so his head reeled and he had no idea what had happened. The five or six inches of naked point vanished completely into his flesh. . . .

He returned to consciousness. The blade had certainly pierced the wall of his stomach, he thought. It was difficult to breathe, his chest pounded, and in some deep distant region which he could hardly believe was a part of himself, a fearful excruciating pain came welling up as if the ground had opened to disgorge a boiling stream of molten lava. The pain came suddenly nearer, with terrifying speed. . . .

So this was *seppuku!* he thought. It was as if the sky had fallen on his head and the world was reeling drunkenly. His will power and courage, which had seemed so robust before he made the incision, had now dwindled to something like a single hairlike thread of steel, and he was assailed by the uneasy feeling that he must advance along this thread, clinging to it with desperation. His clenched fist had grown moist. Looking down he saw that both his hand and the cloth about the blade were drenched in blood. His loincloth too was dyed a deep red. It struck him as incredible that, in this terrible agony, visible things could still be seen and existing things existed still. . . .

The pain spread slowly outward from the inner depths until the whole stomach reverberated. It was like the wild clanging of a bell. Or like a thousand bells which jangled simultaneously at every breath and every throb of his pulse, rocking his whole being. The lieutenant could no longer stop himself from moaning. But by now the blade had cut its way through to below the

177

navel, and when he noticed this he felt a sense of satisfaction, and a renewal of courage. . . .

By the time the lieutenant had at last drawn the sword across to the right side of his stomach the blade was already cutting shallow and had revealed its naked tip, slippery with blood and fat. Suddenly stricken by a fit of vomiting, the lieutenant cried out hoarsely.

The vomiting made the fierce pain fiercer still, and the stomach, which had thus far remained firm and compact, now abruptly heaved, opening wide its wound, and the entrails burst through, as if the wound too were vomiting. Seemingly ignorant of their master's suffering, the entrails gave an impression of health and almost disagreeable vitality as they slipped smoothly out and spilled over into the crotch. The lieutenant's head drooped, his shoulders heaved, his eyes opened to narrow slits, and a thin trickle of saliva dribbled from his mouth. . . .

And so on. To the end, when the lieutenant finally administers himself the *coup de grâce* by driving his blade through his throat, he is aware of terrible pain only. Nor does the solemn narrator ever hint that there is more to this than meets the reader's eye. If there is bliss in this death — and unquestionably for Mishima there is, though the lieutenant is not made privy to it — then it must be the bliss of excruciating pain.

But that was nothing new. Since the day Mishima had been aroused sexually for the first time by a painting of Saint Sebastian's martyrdom, youthful, martyred, and painful death had been a prospect of bliss. Neither was there anything new in the explicit connection established in "Patriotism" between erotic desire and death:

Was it death he was now waiting for? Or a wild ecstasy of the senses? The two seemed to overlap, almost as if the object of this bodily desire were death itself. . . . As their tongues explored one another's mouths . . . they could feel their senses being fired to the red heat of steel by the agonies of death as yet nowhere pre-figured. The pain they could not feel yet, the distant pain of death, had refined their awareness of pleasure.

But there is also a new element in "Patriotism," something beginning to crystallize. "On a rare night such as this one," Mishima wrote in his afterword, "the love of man and wife reaches the zenith of purity and intoxication, and an agonizing death by one's own sword becomes a soldier's act of supreme sincerity, equal in every way to honorable death on the bat-tlefield." The implication is that death must be more than merely agonizing if it is to be the means to erotic bliss: it must also be a soldier's death, "equal to honorable death on the battlefield." This in turn implies the necessity of some profound disturbance such as the February Rebellion in the absence of an actual state of war. It is here, in this search for a battlefield, that Mishima's interest in terrorism originates.

"Patriotism" suggests that Mishima's imagination is be-ginning to resolve a means of acquiring the death he desires and has always desired. Given that "rare night" on which all the requisites for bliss are within reach, what is it that enables the lieutenant actually "to seize the supreme moment in life"? His *patriotism*. And what is that? It is what Mishima soon would begin to equate with what he called "the essence of the Japanese spirit" and to define as *fanatic* (his choice of words) devotion to ideals which transcend rationality. This very spe-cial notion of patriotism is therefore very like if not identical to religious faith.

The lieutenant is a *devout* patriot. His actions both as a soldier and a husband have all the austerity, measure, and high solemnity of a Shinto prayer. And the basis for all his actions, the fundament of his moral world, is his devotion to the emperor, at once god and high priest of Shinto:

On the shelf below the stairway, alongside the tablet from the Great Ise Shrine, were installed photographs of their Imperial Majesties, and every morning before leaving for duty the lieutenant would stand here with his wife and together they would deeply bow. The offering water was renewed each morning, and the sacred sprig of *sakaki* was always green and fresh. Their lives were lived beneath the solemn protection of the gods and were imbued with an intense pleasure which set every fiber of their being atremble.

The solemnity which pervades the story and is the expression of the lieutenant's devoutness is unremitting, even in those delirious moments when he and his wife are making love: "Even in bed these two were frighteningly and awesomely serious. At the very height of frenzied passion their hearts were serious, serious to a point of solemnity." In another man this would seem an impossible contradiction. But the lieutenant's devoutness (patriotism) is so fundamentally a part of himself that it is indistinguishable from erotic desire; indeed, patriotism and erotic desire are identical:

The lieutenant was confident there had been no impurity in that joy they had experienced when resolving upon death. They had both sensed at that moment — though not, of course, in any clear and conscious way — that the proper pleasure they shared in private was once again sanctified by the Supreme Imperative and the authority of the gods, and of a complete and unassailable morality. On looking into one another's eyes and discovering there proper death, they had felt themselves safe once more within impenetrable steel walls, armored in Beauty and Righteousness. Thus, so far from seeing any contradiction between his physical desire and the sincerity of his patriotism, the lieutenant was even able to consider the two as parts of the same thing.

If patriotism and erotic desire are identical, and if the object of erotic desire is death, then patriotism is also a desire for death. But it is more than simply desire; it is at the same time a means of obtaining death. For the obvious difference between a devout patriot and a mere romantic is that the patriot, provided he is also a warrior, has the physical wherewithal to fulfill his desire. All he requires are the proper circumstances, "that rare night when . . . agonizing death by *seppuku* becomes a soldier's act. . . ."

The seeds of "Patriotism" are contained in *Kyoko's House*. But there is a crucial difference between the boxer and the lieutenant. The boxer's evolution into a right-wing activist is presented ironically: he knows, if not in a fully conscious way, that the faith he professes is only a means to obtaining an "indescribable rapture" very like death. But the lieutenant's faith is airtight, proof against the slightest irony. The drama of "Patriotism" is played against a scroll which hangs in the decorational altar in the couple's room. The two Chinese characters on the scroll mean roughly "sincerity" but carry the additional connotation of the samurai's utter faith in his lord, in this case, the emperor. "Patriotism" is sincere: Mishima was careful to seal his story against whatever impulses to irony in himself might have prevented him from identifying completely with the lieutenant's devout world. When he wrote in the opening lines "The last moments of this heroic and dedicated couple were such as to make the gods themselves weep," he believed it. At least he desperately wanted to believe.

"Patriotism" is the earliest indication that Mishima's quest for death was leading him to Shinto mysticism and emperor worship. Before long his newly found faith in the emperor would become the basis of a nationalism, and a politicized Mishima would emerge. But just beneath the surface of the politics was the old desire for death. There is nothing unusual about a man who has never required faith abruptly embracing religion when he learns that he must die. But surely the reverse is extraordinary: the "patriotism" Mishima began to formulate in the summer of 1960 was in essence his attempt to acquire faith in order to die.

"Patriotism" appeared in the January 1961 issue of the *Shosetsu Chuo Koron*. That same month, the twenty-five-year-old novelist Kenzaburo Oe published in another magazine a portrait of a fascist as a young man called "Seventeen," which was every bit as sardonic as "Patriotism" was solemn. In fact "Seventeen" was a brilliant and vicious attack on precisely the values that "Patriotism" exalted. The seventeen-year-old hero is a paranoid, convinced that people need only see "the pallor of his face and the cloudiness of his eyes" to perceive that he is a "chronic masturbator." The thought fills him with homicidal rage; he wants to "kill them, everyone of them, with a machine gun." But he cannot stop masturbating, because he needs the "sense of power" he experiences on ejaculation. The rest of the time he feels impotent in the face of "others" and of "eternity." When he hears for the first time in physics class about "infinity" and "a world of nothingness" he loses consciousness, soiling himself as he crumples to the floor. And he is sickened with fear at the thought of death, of having to endure nothingness "eternally a zero." One day a friend takes him to hear a rightist ranting from a soapbox. Until then he has always wanted to be on the Left, "because it felt better." But as he listens he understands suddenly that the "enmity and hatred he required to hold his own against the

world" can come only from the Right. He joins the Imperial
Way Party. When he puts on the party uniform he feels
"armored in the Right" and knows that "[his] mushy, weak,
easily injured and unsightly insides" are no longer being observed by the *others*. Now he begins to study the Imperial
Institution, and in a book called *The Emperor as an Absolute*
he finds the clue he has been searching for: "In fealty there
can be no individuality." The young fascist understands at
once: the emperor has "commanded [him] to cast away his
individuality." He does so, and knows "bliss." Vanished entirely is his sense of himself as powerless, ludicrous, contradic-
tory, and out of place. He exults, masturbating: "Even if I do
die, I will never perish. Because I am nothing more than one
young leaf on one branch of a giant eternal tree called His
Majesty the Emperor. I will not perish eternally! My fear of
death has been conquered. Ah, Your Majesty, you are my god,
my sun, my eternity. In you, by you, oh, I have truly begun to
live!"

The shocking coincidence of "Patriotism" and "Seventeen"
was very likely a coincidence with an explanation. On October
12, 1960, the chairman of the Socialist party, Inejiro Asanuma,
was assassinated by a young rightist named Yamaguchi.
Asanuma was delivering a speech when Yamaguchi charged
headlong down the aisle of the auditorium, leaped up onto the
speaker's platform, and ran him through with a short sword,
the traditional weapon of the Japanese terrorist. A news
cameraman happened to record the assassination on film (very
much like the Zapruder film of President Kennedy's assassination in its impact on the Japanese) and subsequently it was
witnessed by the whole world. There is little question that Oe
had Asanuma's assassin in mind when he wrote "Seventeen."
And it is not unlikely that Mishima was "inspired" by the

same incident. Certainly terrorism was beginning to exert a special fascination over him at just this time. And this incident in particular was exciting to him because the assassin conformed to his idea of the hero by hanging himself in jail, thus demonstrating his "sincerity." In 1968, when asked at a teach-in for his opinion of Yamaguchi, Mishima replied: "He was splendid. As you know, he took his own life afterward. In dying that way he was being faithful to the letter of Japanese tradition."

The Asanuma assassination was not the only indication that leftist opposition to the security treaty had reinvigorated the extreme Right. Kenzaburo Oe, for example, paid for "Seventeen" with nearly a year of isolation: the threats against his life kept him in his house and his friends away. And just one month after "Patriotism" and "Seventeen" had appeared there was yet another instance of rightist terrorism, an attempted assassination of the president of Chuo Koron Publishers. This time, perhaps ironically, it was Mishima's turn to suffer.

The Shimanaka Incident, as it came to be known, was provoked by a twelve-page story called "An Account of an Elegant Dream," which was published in the December 1960 issue of *Chuo Koron* magazine. The author, a singular man named Shichiro Fukazawa, was principally a guitarist and only incidentally a writer. In 1955, with encouragement from the director of a musical review in which he was appearing, Fukazawa had written a beautiful "folk tale" about the mountain to which young peasants carried their aging mothers to die and had won the first Chuo Koron Literary Prize for New Writers, hence his special relationship to that publisher. In the ensuing years he had maintained his double career as musician and novelist, and by 1960 he had a considerable reputation. In the story which caused so much trouble, the dreamer-narrator is transported to the Imperial Palace where he enthusiastically witnesses the execution of the Crown Prince and Princess Michiko at the hands of an angry populace (a revolution is in progress) and then in an inner courtyard comes upon the "decapitated bodies" of the emperor and empress. There is no question that Fukazawa was radical in his sympathies. But considering the hysterical fury it elicited, his story was astonishingly benign, even childlike. The single line on which outrage focused, quoted repeatedly, was "the severed head of the Crown Prince left his body and rolled along the ground bumpety-bump-bump."

Shortly after the story appeared the publisher was visited by seven representatives of rightist organizations who demanded that he apologize in the three major newspapers and that Fukazawa be "expelled" from Japan. Threats continued during December and January; the Great Japan Patriotic party hired helicopters to scatter leaflets demanding that the Chuo Koron be "tried by the people and sentenced to death." On January 31, the party held a hate rally which was attended by over a thousand young fascists. Then, on the night of February 1, 1961, the inevitable happened. A young man named Komori — he was seventeen! — broke into the home of Chuo Koron president Shimanaka, found him not at home, stabbed the family maid to death, and seriously wounded Shimanaka's wife.* The incident was particularly terrifying because the Asanuma assassination was still so vivid in memory. Shimanaka immediately announced at a press conference that Chuo Koron had been wrong to publish Fukazawa's story and added

---

* Mishima condemned Komori for his attack on women. In 1968 he told a student audience: "Komori of the Chuo Koron Incident was bad business. The worst thing is attacking women and children. One of the splendid things about the young officers in the February 26 Rebellion was that they didn't harm any women or children."

that he had "reprimanded" the editor of the magazine and removed him from his post. The police, responding to demands from the Opposition that the police commissioner resign and that emergency measures be taken to quell rightist violence, began an immediate crackdown: arrests were made, rightist groups placed under surveillance, and bodyguards assigned to public figures considered likely targets.

On November 1, Mishima had left the country with Yoko on a trip around the world, the "real honeymoon" he had promised her as soon as *Kyoko's House* should be finished.* When he returned to Japan on January 20, he learned of a widespread rumor that he was responsible for Fukazawa's story appearing in *Chuo Koron* because he had strongly recommended it to the editor. He denied this vehemently in print, declaring it was ridiculous to suppose that an established writer like Fukazawa, who was, moreover, the winner of the Chuo Koron Literary Prize, would require anyone to recommend his story to that publisher's magazine. He ended the brief disclaimer saying that "certain people" — meaning Shimanaka — were allowing the rumor to persist in hopes of saddling him with responsibility properly their own; it is a fact that Chuo Koron never publicly stated that Mishima had not recommended the Fukazawa story. Whatever the truth may have been — and it is not inconceivable that Mishima could have appreciated the story despite its irreverence — there was ample basis for the rumor, given the fanatics who spread it, in his association with the Chuo Koron and his well-publicized

---

* They began in New York, where in December Mishima finally had the opportunity to see two of his "modern Nō plays" performed in English, at a single matinee performance at the Theater de Lys. He very much enjoyed one of the plays, *Lady Akane (Ao no ue)*, in which Anne Mitchum played the lead. The other, *Hanjo*, bored him; he dozed twice during the performance. From New York the Mishimas toured Europe, then visited the pyramids, and stopped in Hong Kong on their way home.

friendship with Fukazawa himself. Beginning in 1956, the year after Fukazawa had won it, Mishima had served annually as one of three judges awarding the Chuo Koron Prize. And in 1960, when he had decided during the filming of *Tough Guy* that he would also like to sing the theme song, it was Fukazawa he had asked to set his words to music and to accompany him on the guitar. News of this collaboration had been carried in all the weeklies.

The rumor persisted, and beginning in the last week of January Mishima received repeated threats against his life and his family. Then came the Shimanaka Incident. For several nights afterward Mishima patrolled his garden himself, Japanese sword in hand. Then the police assigned him a "bodyguard," who lived in the house and accompanied him wherever he went for the rest of February and half of March. Outwardly Mishima made a joke of the "cop" who was always just around the corner or standing out on the veranda while the Mishimas dined. And Azusa, in his inimitable way, insists that his son did enjoy the episode. But the rest of the family agree that Mishima was "shocked and terrified." His brother Chiyuki is emphatic about this. Chiyuki even attributes, at least partly, Mishima's "swing to the Right" to his determination to overcome the "profound fear of the Right" he experienced at this time. This seems farfetched, although unquestionably Mishima did possess what amounted to a masochistic impulse toward "self-improvement." More likely the lasting effect of these weeks of terror is to be read in his refusal to associate with what he called the "established Right." Time and time again, particularly after 1966, central figures of the Right offered Mishima support which he refused.

But, however frightening this encounter with reality may have been, terrorism — more properly, Mishima's notion of terrorism — retained its excitement in his imagination. The most immediate evidence of this was his major play for 1961, written in the summer and performed in November on the twenty-fifth anniversary of the Bungaku-za. *One Day Too Late* takes place sixteen years after the February Rebellion. The hero, then the minister of finance, has narrowly escaped assassination on that snowy dawn, and in escaping has lost an opportunity which will not present itself again (the very opportunity the lieutenant in "Patriotism" seized). Ever since, the minister has survived on the "desolation of his spirit," a "living corpse" continuously rehearsing in memory that "moment of supreme glory." Every year on the anniversary of his escape, he is visited at the villa where he lives in retirement by his former chief maid and head butler, who join him in toasting the incident with French wine and pâté de foie gras. The action of the play is essentially an attempt by the minister and his former maid to recreate the tension of that night and its glorious possibilities without the aid of the young rebels and their blazing guns. Inevitably, they fail. And the play implies that their failure is due to the engulfing and apparently unassailable peace of the postwar age. In a private, undramatic sense, peace is the villain of the play. It was no accident that Mishima specified the time in his stage directions as "1952, in other words, the year the Japan-U.S. Peace Treaty went into effect."

Kyoko's House is evidence that Mishima was holding the postwar peace responsible for his difficulty in feeling alive as early as 1958. In "Patriotism" and *One Day Too Late* he represented terrorism as a "blissful" or a "glorious" alternative to peace. It was only a matter of time before he began to complain of peace in person instead of through a character in a novel. He first sounded the lament that was to be a leitmotif of his final years in August 1962, on the seventeenth anniversary of the surrender. His one-page article was called "These Seventeen Years of *Warlessness*" (the coinage is Mishima's):

I can remember watching a movie during the war that had been made in peacetime and sighing at the sight of the Ginza all lit up with neon lights. But when I later found myself in an age of more neon than had ever been dreamed of, all I could think of was how easy it had been to live in a wartorn world and how painfully difficult it was to live in a world of peace. How arbitrary we are!

When I imagine the three hundred years of Tokugawa peace and how tedious that must have been I am embarrassed as a Japanese to complain of boredom after a mere seventeen years. . . . But during that three hundred years the samurai [warrior] class, for all its corruption and overindulgence in sexual pleasure, maintained an artificial consciousness of peril which it seems to have employed as spiritual hygiene. But today, *bushido* is *passé*. . . .

Bushido, the "way of the warrior," demanded that the warrior bear the prospect of his own death ever before him, even that he seize the first opportunity to die: when Mishima spoke of a "consciousness of peril," he had in mind the consciousness of death. And in declaring that the only solution to the lifelessness of peace was the consciousness of death, the sense of proximity to at least the possibility of death, he was in effect reaffirming a fascination from which he had labored to free himself for fifteen years. In fact he was reaffirming precisely the death-hungry romantic in himself he had been at such pains to exorcize since the writing of *Confessions of a Mask*. His conscious efforts to place himself in touch with that romantic once again are evident in a stunning autobiographical essay he serialized from January to May 1963, "My Literary Wanderings." He began the essay nostalgically with the war

189

years and ended with the return from Greece, cured of "self-hatred and loneliness" and with an awakened "will to health." But as always there was a punch line:

Today I no longer believe from the bottom of my heart in that ideal known as classicism which I embraced so passionately at twenty-six. . . . And I have already begun to feel that youth and the flowering of youth are foolishness, of little value. Which is not to say that I look forward to old age with any pleasure. What remains then is the concept of death, present, momentary, instant to instant death. It seems likely that to me this is the only truly enticing, truly vivid, truly erotic concept. And in just that sense it seems likely that I am inherently and therefore incurably afflicted with the disease called romanticism. For all I know, that twenty-six-year-old, that classicist who felt about himself that he was as close as possible to life, was a phony.

In the same five months it took him to diagnose himself as an incurable romantic, Mishima also wrote a novel called *The Sailor Who Fell from Grace with the Sea*, which was so quintessentially "romantic" in the Mishima manner it might have been intended as proof that his diagnosis was correct.* The sailor has long cherished the very dream that animates all of Mishima's adolescent writing; he dreams of "glory knifing toward him like a shark from some great distance in the darkly heaping sea," of a "glittering special-order destiny no ordinary man would be permitted." Familiarly, the "special destiny" he awaits merges in his imagination with visions of erotic death:

* The Japanese title *Gogo no eikō* pivots untranslatably on a homonym (*eikō*) for "glory" and "towing," and means *Glory (Towing) in the Afternoon*. When I was unable to come up with anything in English better than *Glory Is a Drag* I went to Mishima for help. Mishima remarked that it would be nice to have a long title in the manner of *À la Recherche* . . . , paused, then rattled off a dozen titles which I jotted down in English. When I read them back, Mishima chose *The Sailor*.

For Ryuji the kiss was death, the very death in love he had always dreamed of. The softness of her lips, her mouth so crimson in the darkness he could see it with closed eyes, so infinitely moist, a tepid coral sea, her restless tongue quivering like sea grass . . . in the dark rapture of all this was something directly linked to death. He was perfectly aware he would leave her in a day, yet he was ready to die happily for her sake. Death roused inside him, stirred.

But the sailor does not leave the beautiful widow he has met in Yokohama. Instead he turns his back on the sea, symbol and agency of his quest for glory and death. And in punishment for this betrayal of his dreams he is coolly vivisected by a gang of precocious thirteen-year-olds that includes the widow's son. Into the mouths of these avenging angels Mishima puts a good deal of sophistry about dismantling existence and restoring it to the proper state of chaos. But their real importance is that they contribute one final essential element to the adolescent fantasy world to which Mishima returned with this novel. That element is blood. In the words of the "chief": "We must have blood. Human blood! If we don't get it this empty world will go pale and shrivel up. We must drain that sailor's fresh lifeblood and transfuse it to the dying universe, the dying sky, the dying forests, and the drawn, dying land."

The Sailor was Mishima's first unserialized novel since *Kyoko's House* and this time he was determined to make a success of it. During the writing he went frequently to Yokohama to sketch the ships in port, the park where the sailor and the widow meet, the swank shopping district where the widow has her shop. He seemed excited about the book, pleased to have another opportunity not to serialize, and confident of success. But when it was published in September 1963 it received a lukewarm reception from the critics and a modest sale (for a Mishima novel) of fifty thousand copies. Mishima was very disappointed. He went to Kodansha, the publisher who had commissioned the book, thanked his editors for the opportunity, and then apologized for having failed to produce a best seller.

The Sailor's reception was only one indication that Mishima's popularity had declined sharply since its peak in the late fifties. His major novel for the previous year, an excited rumination on the possibility of global annihilation called *Beautiful Star* (probably inspired by the development that year of the hydrogen bomb), had sold fewer copies than any book he had ever written, a paltry twenty thousand. His serious effort for 1964, *Silk and Insight,* was similarly a dud. The trouble seems to have been that he was losing the college and fresh-out-of-college audience to writers like Shintaro Ishiwara, Kobo Abe, and Kenzaburo Oe. His "minor works" however, whose primary readers were housewives, retained their popularity; by 1964, with his name on 150 volumes (including reprints and anthologies), Mishima was earning close to $75,000 a year in royalties. But he was not attracting the audience he wanted, and the knowledge hurt him.

Not only because of the decline in his popularity, the first half of the 1960s was a canyon in Mishima's life. There was the Shimanaka Incident in February 1961. The very next month a former ambassador on whose life he had modeled his 1960 novel *After the Banquet* sued for invasion of privacy, Japan's first privacy suit. At the end of the year Mishima withdrew from the Potted Tree Society.* Nineteen sixty-two was

* In November Mishima told Mitsuo Nakamura that he wanted to withdraw from the society, explaining that he could no longer bear, in Nakamura's words, "a certain person." Almost certainly the person was the eccentric, acidulous, London-educated author Ken'ichi Yoshida. In his cups one night at the monthly meeting just after *Kyoko's House* had appeared, Yoshida is said

a gray, inconclusive year which ended with the resounding failure of *Beautiful Star*. In the fall of 1963 the Bungaku-za objected to "derogatory references to mainland China" in his new play *The Harp of Happiness*, which was already in rehearsal; Mishima reclaimed the play in a fury, and in a scathing open letter dissociated from the theatrical company for which he had written all his major plays for ten years. A few months later, in a tangentially related incident, he broke off with yet another old friend, Toshiro Mayuzumi.* In Septem-

---

to have muttered, in Mishima's presence, "If he can't do any better than this we ought to expel him from the group." At about the same time, according to Shohei Ooka, Yoshida gravely offended Mishima in another way, at Mishima's housewarming, by guessing aloud the price of each piece of furniture with mock admiration.

* In January 1963, Mishima and Mayuzumi had contracted to write an opera for the 1964 spring season of Tokyo's newest and most luxurious independent theater, the Nissei Gekijo. In April, Mishima showed Mayuzumi a synopsis, called "Minoko" after the heroine, which he promised to develop into a three-act libretto on two nights in August he had already set aside. On August 30, Mayuzumi and Mishima met at eleven P.M. at the room in the Imperial Hotel Mishima always reserved for working on his plays. First Mishima ordered "thick steaks" for both of them. When he had eaten he took a bath. As Mayuzumi tells the story, he came back into the living room naked except for a towel around his middle, sat down at the desk, and proceeded to produce page after page of dialogue as fast as his pen could move, handing each page to Mayuzumi as he finished it. By three A.M. the first act was finished; Mishima sang it himself from beginning to end, making up his own tunes. At dawn he had completed two acts, and told Mayuzumi he would finish the third by himself the following night since now he knew what Mayuzumi wanted.

A week later Mayuzumi received the finished libretto and set to work on the score. *Minoko* was scheduled to premiere in April; Keita Asari, who was to direct, had said he would need two months of rehearsal. Therefore the opera had to be completed by the end of January. But the end of January came and Mayuzumi was only halfway through the second act. He promised to finish by the end of February, giving Asari a full month to rehearse, but this was Asari's first opera and he refused. In the meantime Mishima had taken *The Harp of Happiness* away from the Bungaku-za and had arranged for it to be performed at the Nissei theater in May. Mayuzumi now proposed that *The Harp* be moved up one month to April to give him an extra month with *Minoko*. When Mishima learned this, he canceled production plans for *Minoko* and terminated his friendship with Mayuzumi. "I did not think he was the kind of man to renege on a promise," he wrote in a weekly magazine; Mayuzumi ber 1964, after three years of litigation, he lost a final appeal in the *After the Banquet* privacy suit. There was little money involved, but the humiliation was considerable.

It was probably no accident that this bitter, lonely period was also the most flamboyantly social, the time when Mishima acquired his reputation as one of Japan's lavish hosts. For example, there was the annual Christmas party (on December 22) held for the first time in 1962 and for the last in 1965, when Mishima entered a new (and final) phase of his life. It was, of course, a Mishima touch to have a Christmas party at all, since Christmas is not customarily celebrated in the Japanese home; it was even more like him to invite the guests as couples, a practice which had not even begun to catch on outside of diplomatic circles. Although the guest list varied considerably from year to year, there were certain regulars who survived Mishima's fluctuations during this unstable period in his life. These included his closest publisher friends, Nitta and Kawashima (the Kodansha editor who "produced" his two biggest hits, *Too Much of Spring* and *A Misstepping of Virtue*); a critic named Okuno who was a tireless Mishima enthusiast; novelist Morio Kita; Takeo Matsuura, the director who left the Bungaku-za with Mishima; Takehiko Shibusawa, an authority on Sade and the marquis's translator in Japan; a matinee idol with Peers' School background, Jiro Tamiya; Mishima's beautiful co-star from *Tough Guy*, Ayako Wakao; "fighting" Harada, the bantamweight world champion; Tatsumi Hijikata, an avant-garde dancer; and, after 1963, two Mishima discoveries, the young poet Mutsuo Takahashi and

---

did not hear from him again. Like others who found themselves the sudden object of Mishima's displeasure, Mayuzumi felt strongly that Mishima was being oversevere. But, like others, he also had to admit that Mishima was just as severe with himself: he had never failed to meet a deadline.

the postermaker, now well-known in America, Tadanori Yokoo. But the guests were not writers and celebrities exclusively; Mishima always invited a banker or two who went back
to his Peers' School days and some friends from the PTA at
the Peers' School kindergarten where his daughter Noriko
was enrolled. One such couple was the clothier and his wife
who were constant companions of the Mishimas until Yoko's
interest in sports car racing resulted in their unwitting fall
from Mishima's esteem. The less distinguished guests (including Yoko's sister and her husband and one or two of
Yoko's former classmates) tended to group together downstairs leaving the round rooms on the third floor to the stars.

The party began at seven with caviar and champagne served
by waiters in white gloves in the living room on the second
floor. The "buffet supper" was set out in the parlor below;
there was always smoked turkey and roast beef and, for dessert, baked Alaska. After dinner, coffee and brandy and Cuban
cigars were served upstairs in the round rooms. Yoko was a
faultless hostess; Mishima, who wore a white tuxedo, always
seemed to grow manic as the evening progressed; one minute
he would be singing "Jeanie with the Light Brown Hair" in
English alongside the piano, the next minute he would be
growling and arching his back on the floor in an imitation of
a dog treeing a cat, or calling loudly for tequila, salt, and
lemons and challenging his translator to see who could better
imitate Marlon Brando drinking tequila in *One-eyed Jacks*.
The only thing remotely Japanese about the parties was that
they broke up early, before midnight: everyone knew Mishima
had work to do.

To the Christmas parties foreigners were not generally invited, but there were a number of dinners every year at which
most of the guests were foreign. Unlike other Japanese authors

of his importance, Mishima always bent over backwards to accommodate the foreign community in Tokyo. Whereas writers like Tanizaki or Kawabata took a certain pleasure in loftily refusing to see a reporter for an interview, Mishima was known to all the major papers and magazines as a "friend of the bureau." When the senior editors of Time-Life visited Japan, for example, it was Mishima who introduced the grateful Tokyo bureau to the solid gold baths at Atami by the sea, and Mishima who volunteered to host "an evening with Japanese writers and intellectuals." Similarly, when the cultural officer in any of half a dozen major western embassies wanted to meet some Japanese personality or another, he knew he could count on Mishima to arrange a meeting, usually with a dinner party. Naturally Mishima was rewarded for his pains: when he needed an introduction to the Thai court he got one from the U.S. embassy; *Life* and the *New York Times* carried several feature articles about him and faithfully reviewed all his books; when he wanted to visit Korea incognito to observe military maneuvers there the *Newsweek* bureau chief arranged it for him — and so on. But it was not primarily his ambition that motivated him, although, to be sure, he was passionately concerned with his reputation in the West; it was his particular brand of dandyism, which required him to feel not merely at home but at his best in smart western circles. Mishima loved hobnobbing with the right foreigners: when the British embassy invited him to a reception for Dame Margot Fonteyn, and he was able to wear his tuxedo and present Dame Margot with a dozen cattleya orchids, he felt more than repaid for whatever pains he may have taken to be accommodating.

When he entertained foreigners at his home, Mishima's chief pleasure was in overwhelming them with the *western* elegance he was able to provide. Before the guests even arrived they were apt to be impressed if not overwhelmed by the engraved Tiffany invitations. And the food, which Yoko prepared herself, was always extravagant and remarkably good. Alone in the house Mishima liked nothing so much as *cha-zuke*, Japanese tea over rice and seaweed. But a typical dinner at the Mishimas was *escargots* (served with special silver picks Mishima brought home from Paris), vichyssoise and quail in raspberry sauce. Salad was served as a separate course and often as not was dandelion leaves. As the exotic greens were being served Mishima liked to exclaim with a loud laugh that most Japanese wouldn't dream of eating such "horse fodder." Yoko's specialty for dessert, learned from the head chef at the Dai-Ichi Hotel, were crêpes suzette flambantes. At the end of such a meal over which, for example, the Swedish ambassador and his wife had just met Tennessee Williams and Harold Clurman, as Yoko ignited the Grand Marnier, a look of limitless satisfaction would suffuse Mishima's face.

In fact, although no one watching him across that candlelit table could have guessed it, the truth seems to be that Mishima was feeling increasingly isolated from the world around him by an icy numbness that was spreading. "In those years," he would soon write about himself in 1963 and 1964, "I practiced *kendo** with a passion and was able to discover some

---

* *Kendo* (the "way" of the sword) is the grueling Japanese equivalent to western fencing. The "sword" is actually a bamboo pole fitted with a guard, which is grasped in both hands. The "kendoist," armored in leather skirts, vest, gloves, and helmet, violently attacks his opponent, seeking to break through his defenses to score hits on any of three target areas: the wrist, the flank, the brow. The techniques, derived from those used with the heavy, razor-sharp Japanese sword, surely the most lethal sword ever developed, are closer to those of saber than foil.

Mishima began *kendo* in January 1959, during the writing of *Kyoko's House*, and by 1968 had ascended in proficiency all the way to the fifth rank, no mean accomplishment. Some maintain that he would never have been

little sense and pleasure in being alive only in the violent, fanatic shouts of the kendoist and the hiss of the bamboo sword." This suggests what was almost certainly the truth, that he had reached a point where he was able to feel truly alive only when he turned away from reality and relinquished himself to his now principal fantasy, the agonies of a warrior's death by the Japanese sword. Evidence of the spell being cast by this dominating fantasy was his decision in January 1965 to play the lieutenant in a film version of "Patriotism," and thus for the first time to enact the fantasy, albeit on the stage.

Only a few people knew the film was being made, and although I was not among them, I seem to have had a hand in the secret preparations. On January 26, 1965, I received this letter:

I hope this finds you well. It appears that you came to the gym to work out only twice, and that worries me a little. Once you take up body-building you must go three times a week for the first half-year or nothing will come of it.

I am very grateful for *The Sailor*. I imagine you have completed it by now — Strauss seems to be craning his neck in eagerness.

Now — I am truly sorry to bother you with a favor at this busy time, but recently I found it necessary to write up a commentary in English on my short story "Yukoku" ("Patriotism"). I am thinking of calling it in English "The Rite of Love and Death." Please let me know your feelings about the feasibility of this title.

I realize that my English commentary is scarcely English at all; but it was at least my intention to do the preface in the past tense and the numbered episodes in the present. Would you be

---

awarded the fifth rank had he not been Yukio Mishima; others say that he was indeed of fifth-rank skill but that his style was "sly and cowardly" rather than "bold and beautiful." But all agree that given his bad coordination it was a remarkable testimony to the force of his will that he was able to become as good as he was.

so good as somehow to correct this awful, awful, awful English? I have in mind a fairly conventional reader. I would be most grateful if you would red-pencil this as boldly as you like and send it back to me. You would be doing me a great favor indeed if you could also put me in touch with someone, perhaps a friend, who could translate your corrected English into French and German.

Please drop over to the house sometime soon again. Best regards to your wife.

In haste, Yukio Mishima

Mishima's "English commentary" was remarkably good despite his apologies. I corrected it slightly and asked a friend at the Swiss Embassy to prepare French and German translations. It was more than a year before I realized that I had been working on subtitles for foreign versions of "The Rite of Love and Death."

As Mishima's choice of English titles declares, his singular notion of "patriotism" was even clearer in the film than in the original story. In order to enhance the ritual quality, he used a Nō stage draped in white as the only set. His performance was designed to turn the lieutenant into a robot; what he wanted was "merely a soldier, merely a man who sacrifices himself for a great cause." To reduce the hero's individuality even further, he wore his soldier's cap down over his eyes, as if it were a Nō mask. There was no dialogue; brief descriptions of each episode unrolled across the screen on a handwritten scroll (Mishima did the calligraphy). The only sound track, intended to integrate the episodes and at the conclusion, as Mishima hoped, to elevate the film to an entirely different dimension wherein "death and beauty would be united," was the "Liebestod" from *Tristan und Isolde*, a choice of which he was very proud.

Early in January, Mishima asked two friends to help him,

Masaki Domoto, an avant-garde director and specialist in the
Nō, and a producer at Dai-ei Studios named Fujii. On January 20 he read the script aloud to his friends and proudly
demonstrated that the "Liebestod" was a perfect fit. In February, he spent weeks tracking down an old artisan who had
made the caps which the young officers in the February
Rebellion actually had worn. He ordered an authentic cap
and, elsewhere, an authentic Imperial Guard uniform. Meanwhile he was interviewing girls to play the lieutenant's wife.
Late in February, he finally chose an aspiring actress who had
appeared briefly in several Dai-ei films. Interviewed in the
lobby of the New Japan Hotel, where the Mishimas were
staying while the third floor was being added to their house,
the girl apparently did not recognize Mishima; as the story
goes, she told her mother when she got home that night that
she had received the part from "a gangster type who seemed
important." On March 10, Mishima went to England for two
weeks to participate in a cultural conference; in London he
bought the china figurines which the lieutenant's wife leaves
as mementos to her friends both in the story and the film. Back
in Tokyo on the twenty-eighth, he prepared the subtitle scrolls
(in English and French as well as Japanese!). There was one
day of rehearsal on April 12, on a Nō stage Domoto arranged
to use, and camera tests on the thirteenth. The shooting took
the two frantic days — there were 170 cuts — of April 15 and
16. The film was completed one week later at the Aoi Studios
when the "Liebestod" was recorded.

One reason Mishima made *The Rite of Love and Death* in
secret was that he intended from the beginning to show the
film abroad before releasing it in Japan. He was determined to
have "a foreign reaction first" because he knew that Japanese
critics would view the film as "just another Mishima prank."

With help from the president of Dai-ei and Madame Kawakita, the formidable lady who brought French cinema to Japan, he arranged to show his film for the first time at the cinematheque in Paris in September 1965. Naturally he was present at the private screening at the Palais de Chaillot when an audience two-thirds French and one-third Japanese cheered the twenty-eight-minute film. Mishima was jubilant; he invited half a dozen of the French critics back to his hotel for champagne.

In Japan, the film remained a secret until it was shown at the Tours Film Festival in January 1966. Earlier in the month it had been one of forty films chosen for the competition from among three hundred entries. At Tours it created a sensation thanks to several ladies in the audience who fainted during the *seppuku* scene. There was no way of keeping this from the Japanese press, which now began to clamor for the film, particularly after the announcement the following day that it had placed second for the Grand Prix. Throughout February and March the weeklies were busy with speculation about Mishima's *Rite* (known in Japan only as *Patriotism*), and when it was finally released in April it immediately established a box-office record for a short film. Some Japanese fainted too.

All told, Mishima spent nearly half a year on *The Rite of Love and Death*. Apparently he seems to have felt he could afford the time at this moment in his life because he was consciously resting up before beginning work on the cycle of four novels he would call *The Sea of Fertility*. Since 1963 he had been talking with Hiroshi Nitta about writing something very long that would be his major statement. In March 1965 he had announced to the press that he was about to begin a work "three thousand pages long" that would take him "six years to write" (five years later, when he completed the tetralogy several months before he died, it was twenty-eight hundred pages long). By this time he had arranged with Shincho-sha to begin serialization of the first novel in the cycle, *Spring Snow*, in September. He began work in June 1965 and finished on November 25, 1966. He immediately began the second volume, *Runaway Horses*, and completed it on May 23, 1967. On July 1 he started volume three, *The Temple of Dawn*, and the following year the final volume, *The Decay of the Angel*, which he finished three months before his death. It is easy to forget that through all that was to happen in the five years to come he was continuously at work on the four novels he considered his most important.

In September 1965, Mishima took a trip around the world with Yoko that had to do partly with *The Sea of Fertility*. One of the reincarnations of the hero of *Spring Snow* was to be a Thai princess; Mishima had arranged through friends at the American Embassy for an introduction to the Thai court. Bangkok was therefore the final destination. But first he went to New York to help promote *The Sailor Who Fell from Grace with the Sea*. The next stop was Paris, and the excitement of watching his film premiere. Nor was that all; Gallimard was preparing to publish *After the Banquet* and entertained the Mishimas lavishly, as did the Rothschilds. Mishima's pleasure floods a letter he wrote home to his parents:

I was relieved to hear that you are both well. In spite of all my worrying, Paris has been a great success. The night we arrived the Rothschilds took us to dinner at the Tour d'Argent; the next day I was guest of honor at a lunch with critics; the day after at dinner with more critics, and this time Madame Malraux was there. I've also had an invitation from Gallimard himself, and too many interviews to mention; and on Saturday I'm being taken out to the Rothschild's country villa. Their Paris house is like a palace — I've stepped into a world of Paris high society which until now I've only known through films and novels. And not as a tourist, either, but as a central figure.

From Paris the Mishimas went to Stockholm. Mishima had no business there; no doubt he simply wanted to have a look at the place where the Nobel laureate was awarded. Before leaving Japan he had heard a rumor that he had been "nominated" for the prize. On September 25, the Japanese press picked it up. According to the evening *Asahi Shimbun* on that day, a "reliable source" in Stockholm had indicated that Mishima, along with ninety other writers, was a "strong candidate" for the Nobel Prize. Then, on October 15, by which time Mishima was in Bangkok, the papers carried a dispatch from Stockholm which declared, "according to a source close to the academy," that Yukio Mishima and the late Junichiro Tanizaki were definitely among "the final candidates." The next day the academy announced that the sixty-year-old Russian novelist Mikhail Sholokhov had won.

Unquestionably, though he never said so to anyone, Mishima was disappointed. Just as certainly he was even more deeply disappointed in 1967 when he allowed himself to be tantalized once again by a rumor he knew was meaningless (as his publisher friends repeatedly told him, there are no "nominations" for the Nobel Prize). No doubt he couldn't help it: he wanted the prize desperately. From the end of 1966, when he first declared himself "an exponent of 'expel-the-foreigner-ism' from the cultural point of view," his need for recognition from the West became increasingly a contradiction; yet he continued to desire the prize avidly, as if in spite of himself.

Early in February 1965, Mishima told me explicitly he

wanted the prize and moreover asked me to help him get it. I had just finished translating *The Sailor*, and Harold Strauss had reported from New York that I had done "an outstanding job." Mishima was very pleased; he read Strauss's letter to me on the phone, and suggested we go out to celebrate. I met him at Hamasaku, a Japanese-style restaurant on the Ginza patronized by the literary establishment. We ate at the wooden counter and drank a lot of *sake*. Mishima was in high spirits and naturally so was I. He thanked me for the translation; I expressed my relief at having lived up to his expectations. Abruptly serious, he then told me he considered us "an unbeatable team" and asked me for a promise, not only to translate his next novel but to become his official translator and help him win the Nobel Prize. I agreed deliriously, and we shook hands. Then I went home to read the book I had just obligated myself to translate.

Silk and Insight (1964) was the portrait of a middle-aged owner of a textile mill who is compelled to meddle in the lives of his young employees and finally drives them to rebel against him with a strike. Mishima had told me he had written into the novel all his feelings as a father of two children (later he told the critic Takeshi Muramatsu that the betrayed hero represented the emperor), but I found it empty of genuine feeling. Furthermore, the writing was jugular, a gorgeous example of what Japanese critics were calling "Mishima-beauty." To render it in English would have been an enormous labor; even before I had finished that first reading I knew I would never find the enthusiasm I would need to sustain me through the translation.

I should have gone straight to Mishima and told him what I felt; I lacked the nerve. And so I waited, and in New York Harold Strauss waited too. The truth was that Knopf was no

more anxious to publish *Silk and Insight* than I was to translate it. But Strauss was in an awkward position. He had already
turned down *Beautiful Star* on the grounds that it was an
essay rather than a novel. And in return for the complicated
option clause in the contract which gave Knopf the English
rights to everything Mishima wrote, Strauss felt obliged to
establish what he called a "continuity of publishing." He was
therefore prepared to go ahead with *Silk and Insight* if
Mishima insisted. In a long letter dated May 14, 1965, he
urged me to "take the same position":

It amounts to a respect for Mishima's wishes, but some hesi-
tancy about translating this novel. In the long run I think it will
be very much worth your while to become Mishima's official
translator. This would involve you in an implied commitment to
translate whatever he and I agree is to be the next book, but it
also gives you the prior right to translate anything Mishima does.
You know that book publishing is a jackpot game, but some first-
rate European publishers such as Bonnier of Sweden think that
Mishima will win the Nobel Prize some day. This will mean a lot
to all of us, including you as his translator.

I wasn't convinced. Particularly because in the meantime I
had discovered Kenzaburo Oe's 1964 novel, *A Personal Matter*,
and wanted to translate it. I wrote Strauss that I had decided
not to do *Silk and Insight*, that I hoped to translate novels
rather than authors, and that I expected there would be opportunities to do other Mishima novels in the future. But telling
Strauss was one thing, telling Mishima another. During the
summer of 1965 I saw him only once, at a buffet dinner he
gave for foreign friends late in July. In August he took the
whole family south to the beach at Shimoda. In September he
and Yoko left the country. In October I received a long letter

from him, written from the Rama Hotel in Bangkok. Since
the tone is so distinctively Mishima's, it deserves translation in
full:

I hope this finds you well.

I suppose you have seen most of the reviews of *The Sailor*.
It was unfortunate that the newspaper strike prevented the Sunday *Times* from coming out, since the book review section had
a review and an interview. This is the second book of mine to
appear in the middle of a newspaper strike; the first was *After
the Banquet*. And yet newspaper strikes in New York are considered rare — what a disheartening coincidence.

The reviews seem to be extremely good, but sales are the same
as usual. As far as New Yorkers are concerned, all that has happened is that a quality publisher has published another quality
book, nothing to get very excited about.

After New York I exhausted myself in Paris, Stockholm, and
Hamburg and didn't even have the energy to write letters. But
swimming in the pool every day here in Bangkok has entirely
reinvigorated me. It appears that after all I am best suited to the
tropics. I just can't take the northern countries, and wine doesn't
agree with me — I don't care if I never see another bottle.

In Paris, the famous woman critic at Gallimard, Dominique
Aury, had read *The Sailor* and kept exclaiming to me, "It's a
marvelous translation; it's marvelous English." Thanks to your
translation two or three people have even told me they thought
The Sailor was my best novel. I've read a lot of the reviews, but
the one in the English *Yomiuri* is the most extravagant in its
praise, and that makes it the best. Like a woman being told
"You're the most beautiful person in the world.". . .

In New York I worked very hard at promoting the book. I got
up early every morning and raced to some radio station or other
to be machine-gunned with questions in my still-sleepy head. In
all, I did six radio interviews. The most ridiculous was for Voice
of America; a *nisei* woman asked me, "Has a Japanese-language
version of the novel gone on sale in Japan too?" I'm afraid my
mouth dropped open at that one. And since the VOA interview

was the only one in Japanese, I know I didn't misunderstand. Another day I went all the way to Westchester to have lunch at a women's club and answer asinine questions about Tokyo taxi drivers. At lunch one lady read me a letter from her son who was studying literature at college, and reeled off names like Dostoevsky's *Crime and Punishment*, etc.; but when she came to Andre Gide she said "Geed? Guide? I've never heard of this one"!

In New York, Oe was staying in the same hotel and we had lunch together and spent a pleasant afternoon saying bad things about Japanese novelists. I took him to a favorite shop on Park Avenue and he bought a large rhinoceros made of leather, worrying all the time that his wife would be angry at him for it. But it was a purchase that seemed just like Oe.

Of all the places I toured, Hamburg struck me as having a marvelous flavor, for all that it is in the north. I went out alone for a cruise around the harbor and saw a large Japanese ship just coming into port. The sight stirred me so that I waved my handkerchief with all my might. But since I was wearing dark glasses there was no response.

Regards to your wife. I'll have more details when I see you in Tokyo.

The letter was dated October 18, two days after the Nobel Prize had been awarded to Sholokhov. At the time it didn't occur to me that there might be any connection (and for all I know it was entirely a coincidence), but it was plain to see that Mishima had written the letter to please me and that was quite enough to fill me with guilt. I resolved that I would see him as soon as he returned and tell him the entire truth. The entire truth was that I had contracted to translate Oe's novel *A Personal Matter*, and was already at work on the manuscript.

I went to see Mishima in the middle of November. He was waiting for me upstairs in the gentlemen's round room. The maid wheeled brandies into the room on a bronze cart and left us alone. We chatted briefly about his trip and I must have communicated my nervousness: before I had a chance to begin my confession he beckoned me outside to the balcony and thrust a pair of binoculars into my hand. He had a pair for himself, too, and although the mistiness of night prevented us from seeing more than a few yards down the street, we kept our eyes to the lenses throughout our conversation, as though we were transmitting through the binoculars across a vast distance.

"I reread *Silk and Insight*," I began, and in truth I had read it twice, "and I don't think I want to translate it."

"You changed your mind about the book?"

"The style seemed so rich, I don't think I could make it work in English."

"I've never changed my mind about a book once I've read it."

"Oh —"

"But you're wise not to try something you're not confident about. I'm glad you told me."

This much of our conversation is, I think, verbatim. The rest I remember only in essence. We stepped back inside and had a drink. I said, meaning it, that I hoped there would be other opportunities to translate Mishima. Mishima assured me nothing would please him more. He repeated how gratified he was that I had been honest with him. Honesty was the key to friendship. And he saw no reason why we shouldn't continue to be friends. Certainly he hoped we would; someday he would show me an entry in his diary, written shortly after we had met two years earlier, in which he described his relief at having encountered a translator he genuinely liked. . . .

I left Mishima's house that night feeling forgiven and even justified. I had been guilty of indecisiveness and, yes, dishonesty: I should have had the courage to inform him at once that I did not want to translate his book. On the other hand, he had extracted a commitment from me when I was giddy with my own accomplishment and with his reliance on me. But none of that mattered now; we had reached an agreement.

I never heard from him again. Six months later, in May 1966, just before I left Japan for several years, I saw him one final time. A good friend whom I had met through him gave a going-away party and Mishima came. He stayed briefly. On his way out he came over and very politely wished me a safe trip across the ocean.

I still don't understand very fully what was behind Mishima's adamant repudiation, but one thing seems certain now (although I was too bitter to see it at the time): I had hurt him badly. It was not only that I had rejected him (from his point of view), I had rejected him for Kenzaburo Oe, the one younger writer in Japan whom he recognized as a rival. Not long after our last meeting he told a group of writers that I was "a hoodlum" who had been "seduced by the Left," suggesting that Oe was very much part of what he was feeling about me.

Inasmuch as Mishima remained friends with certain foreigners until his death (Donald Keene principally, and, for example, the English journalist Scott-Stokes), there is no reason to suspect there was anything xenophobic in his attitude toward me. It is true, however, that his "ultranationalism" was surfacing rapidly just at this time. At the end of his October letter to me from Bangkok he had mentioned the "stirring" sight of a Japanese freighter he had seen docking at Hamburg; and he began his annual New Year's Day newspaper article for 1966 with the same freighter moving him "proudly" to wave a white handkerchief. In April, the freighter appeared again in a long article exhorting the Japanese to stop praising or condemning Japan according to what they saw "in a western mirror." Then in June he wrote a richly poetic story-essay called "The Voice of the Hero Spirits," which was like a beacon illuminating the direction his "patriotism" would take.

The story is presented as the record of a terrifying séance at which the spirits of the young officers of the February Rebellion and the kamikaze pilots of World War II bitterly reproach the emperor for having "betrayed" them by declining to be a god. In their view this betrayal was responsible for the spiritual decadence of postwar Japan. The refrain constantly on their lips, *Why did the emperor become a man!*, thus bespeaks both personal and patriotic grief.

The hero's lament was based on two historical facts. One was Emperor Hirohito's refusal to sanction the February uprising in his name. For the young officers in Mishima's fantasy, this was proof that he had chosen not to be a god, since the "national polity," in which the "sovereign and his subjects are one," was founded on the impossibility of "unrequited love" for the sovereign. The other fact was Hirohito's "human proclamation" of January 1946, in which he declared at the urging of his prime minister (and pressure from GHQ), that his divinity was "an imaginary and harmful notion." In so declaring, the spirits of the kamikaze pilots lament, he rendered their own deaths meaningless and pitiful:

But if we ourselves are living gods, His Majesty above all must be a god. High on the ladder of the gods His Majesty must shine for us. For in his divinity is the source of our imperishability, of the glory of our death, the one and only thread connecting us with history. . . .
Brave soldiers died because a god has commanded them to go to war; and not six months after so fierce a battle had stopped

instantly because a god had declared the fighting at an end, His Majesty announced, "Verily, we are a mortal man." Scarcely a year after we had fired ourselves like bullets at an enemy ship for our emperor who was a god. . . . *Why did the emperor become a man!"*

"The Voice of the Hero Spirits" was Mishima's first work to be widely interpreted as political (the Communist Party paper *Red Flag* condemned it for being cast in "the rhetoric of the Right"; the extreme Right was even angrier about Mishima's criticism of the Showa emperor). And to be sure it has strong political overtones. Yet, like all Mishima's "political writing," it is so unmistakably a private fantasy generated by private needs that it is difficult to take the political implications seriously. Consider the long poem in which the spirits recite the consequences of the "smiling full-bellied peace" which has Japan in its grip (not a good poem, but to Mishima an important one: later he would recite it on a record). The striking thing about the catalogue is how unpolitical it is, how very private:

> Strength is decried, the body disdained
> Pleasure has lost its substance
> Joy and grief alike vanish in an instant
> Purity is marketed, dissipation enfeebled
> Feeling is dulled, sharpness blunted
> Virulent and manly spirits have fled the earth. . . .

This adds up to what Mishima summarized elsewhere simply as the "tediousness" or "insipidness" of peace due to the absence of a "sense of peril." But in the closing lines he gets down to what he really misses: "Running blood is sullied and clogged with peace / The gushing river of blood has dried up."

Another striking example is the young officers' evocation of

211

the scene that would have occurred if only the emperor had deigned to be a god by accepting their love:

Imagine it. There is a hill. The snow has stopped but the sky is gray under low-hanging clouds. From off in the distance, as if the snow had sprouted wings and was swooping down upon us, there gallops a single white horse bearing a man who is a god.

The white horse neighs, tosses his head, breath steaming in the air, and gallops to us through the snow. We salute with our swords. Looking up into that august face we see fierce determination there and know our hearts have been understood. He speaks:

"We have understood your resolve. Your allegiance pleases us. From this day forward we shall govern this land in person, as you wish. So die peacefully — you must die at once!"

Unhesitatingly we open our jackets, shout "Long live His Imperial Majesty" as if to tear apart the snowy sky, then drive our bloodied swords deep into our sides.

Thus the blood of the evil counselors we have slaughtered mingles with our own pure blood and with it is purified at the emperor's feet.

We feel no pain. This is the death of bliss. Yet as we move the sword lodged so firmly in our flesh we hear the sobbing behind us of our men who have followed us into battle.

It is then that we are visited by an instant of unearthly bliss. Our generalissimo descends from his white horse and stands on the snow dyed scarlet with our young blood. At his feet lie our bodies now about to die. As we move toward death our majesty salutes us.

As consciousness slips away we gather our strength and, straightening our heads, look up at the august face. It shines in a single ray of light that has pierced the low clouds. And on the verge of death we behold a miracle.

Imagine it.

On those majestic cheeks, tears shed for our death.

In the light piercing the clouds, a trickle of tears.

A god moved to tears by our sincerity.

Truly it is as bliss that death descends upon us. . . .

212

There is scarcely any likelihood the young leaders of the February Rebellion actually cherished such a dream. Needless to say, Mishima did, and just as certainly his interest in the young rebels and the kamikaze squads is to be located in these visions of blood and death and glory which their exploits ignited in his imagination. Not that "The Voice of the Hero Spirits" was without political implications Mishima fully intended; on the contrary, the importance of this nearly hysterical fantasy is that it points so clearly toward something like a political position. In deploring the "spiritual hollowness" of the postwar age the heroes are attacking postwar democracy. And in holding the emperor responsible for the decline Mishima implies that the solution to the baleful state of peace into which Japan has fallen must be an imperial restoration. Yet just beneath the surface of the politics was the crying need for death, "the only erotic concept."

However different they may have been in class and consciousness, the young officers and the kamikaze pilots were alike in being martyrs to the imperial cause. And even as he wrote "The Voice of the Hero Spirits" Mishima was preparing to celebrate yet another group of imperial martyrs, known as the League of the Divine Wind. This was a band of samurai who were horrified by the new government's westernization of sacred institutions following the Meiji Restoration in 1868. As a group they refused to have anything to do with the West; they would pick up paper money only with chopsticks, and when they could not avoid walking beneath the newly erected telegraph lines, they covered their heads with white fans. Finally, unable to countenance what to them was at once misgovernment and sacrilege, they consulted the will of the Shinto gods through a special rite and received divine sanction to "cut down the unworthy ministers by striking in darkness with the sword." They knew they had no chance of overthrowing the local government, which commanded forces outnumbering their own ten to one; they knew they would be sacrificing their lives in accordance with the will of the gods for the emperor. And that is what they did. At the end of one day of battle, those of the ringleaders who were still alive gathered on a hill — doubtless the same hill in Mishima's imagination as the one to which he brought the leaders of the February Rebellion — and committed *seppuku.*

In the summer of 1966 Mishima researched the 1874 uprising in preparation for using the martyrs as model heroes in the second volume of *The Sea of Fertility* (*Runaway Horses*). Their significance to him, as he explained it to the apostate Marxist Fusao Hayashi in August 1966, was that

the league conducted a pure experiment, primitive and fanatic, in the Japanese spirit. . . . Naturally it was doomed to fail: westernization was the only political course Japan could have taken at that time. It was an experiment bound to fail, but not before it revealed purity and orthodoxy and the substance, call it the core, of what we mean when we speak of Japan and the Japanese.

So fanatic devotion to the emperor which led to martyrdom in the imperial cause was not merely heroic; Mishima was now perceiving such martyrdom as the very essence of Japaneseness. In other words, he was now able to view a martyr's death by *seppuku* as the ultimate nationalism; conversely, becoming an ultimate nationalist, a transformation he would now precipitately attempt, meant dying a martyr's death.

Obviously martyrdom is impossible without faith: beginning with "The Voice of the Hero Spirits," which he later claimed he wrote "involuntarily as though possessed," Mishima was engaged in a largely conscious effort — ultimately successful — to become a believer. The earliest visible evidence of his attempt to acquire faith is a brief article called "My Last Words," published in July 1966, one month after "Hero Spirits." He began by claiming to have discovered in a small box that had been sitting on a shelf for twenty years the "last words" he had written in 1945 when he had received his draft notice. Then he quoted the document:

Last Words — Kimitake Hiraoka (My Real Name)

Humbly I thank for their benevolence
My Honorable Father
My Honorable Mother
My esteemed mentor Shimizu-*sensei*
And those other *sensei* who so kindly instructed me at the Peers' School and Tokyo Imperial University:
    I will not easily forget the friendship of my classmates and seniors at the Peers' School. I pray their future will bring them honor.
    I want my younger sister Mitsuko and my younger brother Chiyuki to do all they can in their brother's stead to care for our honorable father and mother.
    I trust that Chiyuki, following his elder brother, will hasten to become a brave warrior in the Imperial Army, ready to die in His Majesty's defense.
Long Live His Majesty the Emperor!

As he read these "last words" after so many years, Mishima was puzzled by their simplicity. "Naturally, I would have had to be careful not to write anything impolitic since the will might have been discovered before my death. . . . And certainly at twenty I understood that form alone was sufficient to satisfy a mere formality. Neither is there any question that the careful banality of the style concealed my dandyism. Still, for all that, it was just too conventional." But then as he considered the "will" further he began to suspect it was as simple as it was because it contained the truth:

> It would be easy to say that these "last words" were entirely false. A young man who had already published a volume of stories cannot have had so simple, so straight a psychology. Yet to say that they are entirely lies rings false in another way. Not true, but not entirely false either. Then where was the *truth?* Clearly I didn't believe what these words said at the time I wrote them. Just as clearly I didn't possess a *truth* of my own, a standpoint from which to determine that everything I wrote was false. Then the truth involved must have been intrinsic to the will itself.

There is nothing very compelling about the logic of this. Assuming the will was real, it is more likely to have been so conventional for reasons Mishima himself suggests and then discards. But neither the authenticity of the will nor the logic matters; what counts is the conclusion Mishima manages to draw, however tentatively:

> Is it not possible, I wonder, that a giant hand was at work, gripping a hand even as cynical and self-conscious as my own and moving it swiftly up and down the page? Is it not possible that something — neither the authority of the state nor militarism — had infiltrated my spirit and taken form there, that another spirit of a different dimension had come to abide even in me?

Thus Mishima reads proof in his "last words" that the sacred spell of the nation was upon him during the war years. Naturally, where faith has been possible it is possible again: he would now begin to devote a large measure of his enormous energy to placing himself back in the grip of that "giant, invisible hand."

216

seven

1967-1969

In December 1966, Fusao Hayashi introduced Mishima to two young men who had a decisive catalytic effect on him. Their names were Bandai and Nakatsuji and they styled themselves "neonationalists." They believed in Japan, in the Japanese "folk," and in the emperor; they had grave reservations about postwar democracy. Recently they had pooled their resources to found a magazine called *Controversy Journal* (*Ronso* journal). It was about this, specifically, that Hayashi had suggested they see Mishima. The magazine was in financial trouble and they went to ask if he would help.

Mishima was smitten. He volunteered to donate articles to the journal and to persuade others to do the same. He even promised the young men a good meal any time for the asking. Later, in an article he wrote for the journal called "On Youth," he would describe this first meeting as "an event which produced a revolutionary change in [him]":

It is a date I will not forget, December 19, 1966, a dark rainy winter afternoon. . . . As I listened to him [Bandai] describe in

217

his halting way the difficulties experienced by a group of youth who belonged to no political party but were resolved to cure Japan of her ills and who had sworn unity, something stirred in me. . . .

The earliest intimations of what that "something" was appeared in two short articles Mishima published on New Year's Day 1967 and probably wrote in the flush of his first meeting with the boys. One was an apology for the western style in which he lived called "Faith in Japan." It was only natural, he began, that people should doubt a man who championed Japan and yet "had been to the West seven times, had many Westerners for friends, lived in a purely western house without a single tatami room, loved western food, considered a western toilet best, and never wore a kimono all the year round." But who, in this day and age, lives in purely Japanese style? In one corner of the Japanese room there will be a television set, in the kitchen, a washing machine:

And for people who live thus to find fault with me is like wax in the eye laughing at wax in the ear. I cannot believe that the Japan which persists in this compromising stylistic confusion is really Japan. Nor is it possible that the Japanese who created the Nō and Kabuki with their magnificent stylistic integrity can have been the forefathers of Japanese who think nothing of sitting in a chair and watching television in kimono.

Rather than be a party to this "ugly syncretic Japanism," Mishima has opted for a western style of life which at least permits "stylistic integrity." He concludes, however, "My true life as a writer is the pure Japan of the Japanese language I use every night in my study. Compared to this, nothing else is of any importance."

218

Perhaps when he wrote of "stylistic integrity" Mishima had forgotten what he had told his architect eight years earlier, that the life-style he wanted was "to sit in a rococo chair in Levi's and an aloha shirt." In any event, "Faith in Japan" was a lame and a silly argument whose only interest was the new apologetic impulse it revealed. The second article was more dramatic; it was called "A New Year's Dilemma":

It will be at least five years until I can complete this major work [*The Sea of Fertility*] and by that time I will be forty-seven. In other words, by the time this work is completed I will have to resign myself to the eternal impossibility of a gorgeous, heroic end. To give up becoming a hero or to abandon my masterpiece — this decision is drawing near and the prospect fills me with anxiety.

I can hear people now: "But you are a writer, and for a writer the most important thing is to accomplish good work. You speak of becoming a 'hero' — if you complete your work successfully you may become a literary hero."

But as far as I am concerned it is an abuse of language to speak of a literary hero. A hero is a concept to be found only at the opposite pole of literature. . . . As always, the glory that draws me is the glory of the hero, not the writer.

I can hear people reply: "But you are dwelling in the past. Attempts to become the kind of active hero you speak of are futile after thirty at the latest and you are forty-five. Why not stop playing the old maid who hides behind thick makeup, give up life and action and concentrate on literature?"

Yet I am still as strong and energetic as a young man, at forty-two still just young enough to become a hero. Takamori Saigo [another nineteenth-century fanatic who committed *seppuku*] died a hero's death at fifty. . . . If I act now I am still in time. On the other hand there is important work. . . ."

Mishima would not again be so explicit about his need to die a hero's death. And this was the first time he so sharply

opposed the pen and the sword, literature and action. In fact
it was never the case, despite his protests, that the "glory of
the writer" held no attraction for him. But it was certainly true
that he had been discovering that the pen alone could not
satisfy him, that his need for an alternative to what he experienced as the lifelessness of peace, an alternative symbolized for
him by the sword, had been building implacably inside him.
Then, providentially, there appeared two young men determined to fight. It is not surprising that Mishima chose to see
Bandai and Nakatsuji as fierce young warriors eager for death,
or that he attributed his "newly achieved readiness" to die to
inspiration from them:

> Until that meeting I had no such readiness. I had felt at times,
> like Saigo, that "I wanted to die," but I had assumed the feeling
> was merely the nihilism that besets a writer. . . . Until that time
> I had been arrogantly confident there was nothing to be learned
> from youth. But now I realize if anything can make me firm in
> readiness and give me courage where there is none, it will be their
> influence.

In fact, Bandai and Nakatsuji considered themselves writers,
social critics. They had no taste for battle, certainly no appetite for death. Presently this would estrange them from
Mishima, but not before they had introduced him to other
young men who were keen to do actual battle.

On April 9, 1967, Mishima "enlisted" secretly in the Army
Self-Defense Force (ASDF) and subjected himself to forty-six
days of basic training. He had been trying to get in for over a
year, but apparently the ASDF was reluctant to accommodate
itself to civilian fantasies even when the civilian was Yukio
Mishima; in December his request had been turned down
"indefinitely." After the new year, with encouragement from

his new friends at *Controversy Journal,* he tried again, and this time he succeeded, how is not clear. There is a man called Kanemaro Izawa who introduces himself as an "education specialist." When Mishima was about to publish "The Voice of the Hero Spirits," he anticipated that his criticism of the Imperial House would anger the extreme Right and asked Izawa to smooth things over in sensitive quarters. Subsequently he relied heavily on Izawa as a buffer between himself and the Right and as a source of information about the police. Izawa claims that he had a hand in applying pressure in the proper places. Others say that the decisive role was played by one of the gray eminences on the far Right, Seigen Tanaka. Several of Mishima's associates knew of his plan and tried to dissuade him. An editor at Shinchosha warned him that he would become "a ridiculous figure" if he "enlisted." Mishima laughed, then informed Shinchosha he would have no further dealings with the man.

Mishima was enlisted as "Hiraoka," without rank (Izawa claims he tried to get in as a second lieutenant). He began with a week at Officers Training School in Kurume, on the island of Kyushu. From Kurume he went to the Infantry Boot Camp at the foot of Mount Fuji for a month. He spent two final weeks running up and down mountains with the ranger division, and, at nearby Narashino, hurling himself off a thirty-foot jump tower with fledgling paratroops. Mishima was forty-two, his fellow volunteers in their high teens. Yet he managed to keep pace day after day, driving himself as only he could. Secretly he suffered stomach cramps and diarrhea. But the physical punishment very likely added to his pleasure, if for no other reason than that it helped him feel like one of the men.*

---

* In an interview with a magazine reporter (who was actually himself), Mishima was careful to defend himself in advance against the charge that he was "merely in search of masochistic pleasure":

Later he proudly reported being made to run ten extra laps with full backpack just like anyone else when he failed to pass inspection because of a tarnished button. In the boyish letters he wrote home to his parents, it is clear that playing soldier agreed with him:

It was an inexpressible thrill to take a rifle in my hands for the first time in more than twenty years. Although I was praised for catching on so quickly, this was actually old hat to me. People say the war generation feels nostalgic even for military drill and I know what they mean now. The day begins at six with reveille, muster, cold water massage, and a two-mile run. I scrape my plate clean at every meal. And I sleep like a baby on my iron bed wrapped in an army blanket. I am sure that getting away from writing for a while will be good for me and the writing. My only complaint is that I'm not allowed off the base because I have to remain incognito. . . . Strange as it may seem, I am about forty percent cut out to be a soldier.

Mishima's professed reason for enlisting was concern about national defense. The problem originated in Article Nine of the postwar constitution, which declared that "the Japanese people forever renounce war as a sovereign right of the Nation" and that "land, sea, and air forces, as well as other war potential, will never be maintained." In Mishima's view, the "renunciation" clause meant that the Japan Self-Defense Force, created under the Self-Defense Act of 1954, could never develop into an effective fighting force. The constitution must therefore be revised to permit the JSDF to assume its rightful

---

MISHIMA: You must be joking. You won't find anyone whose daily schedule is as severe as mine. If anything, the schedule I keep ordinarily is even more complicated and grueling than what I experienced in training. What did make me very happy is that my stoicism was counted as a virtue whereas in the literary world it's considered an aberration.

place as a "national army." He was also interested in the JSDF
as a metaphor, at once a victim and a living example of the hy-
pocrisy of postwar society: here was an army pledged to defending a constitution which forbade its existence, an army
obliged to refer to tanks as "special vehicles" because Japan
had renounced its "war potential."

But patriotic concern was only part of the picture. Privately
Mishima enlisted as a conscious first step in becoming a warrior, a samurai. His decision therefore signified his conclusion
that the dilemma he had posed on New Year's Day was not a
dilemma after all, that he could have both his literary masterpiece and a heroic death. For in Mishima's scheme of things,
preparing to become a samurai meant preparing for death. As
he put it: "The samurai's profession is the business of death.
No matter how peaceful the age in which he lives, death is the
basis of all his action. The moment he fears and avoids death
he is no longer a samurai." Mishima wasn't making this up; he
was merely paraphrasing a famous treatise on *bushido* written
in the first years of the eighteenth century:

> Know that the essence of *bushido* is to die. This means that
> the samurai when faced with a choice between life and death
> chooses death. It is as simple as that. To say that death which
> achieves nothing is death in vain — dog's death as it is called —
> is the kind of calculating *bushido* practiced in the Kyoto area. . . .
> So long as you have chosen death it does not matter whether you
> have died "in vain" — death cannot be to your discredit.

The passage is from the *Hagakure* (*In the Shadow of the
Leaves*); the author was a former samurai turned monk named
Jocho Yamamoto. In 1699, when the lord of Saga Fief died,
Jocho was prevented from committing *seppuku* and following
his lord in death by a new statute prohibiting that traditional

act of samurai allegiance. Apparently unable to sustain the blow to his sense of honor, he renounced his worldly life and retired as a monk to a hut "in the shadow of the leaves" where he dictated the *Hagakure* to a retainer and died in his sleep at sixty-one. In September 1967, Mishima *dictated* a book-length commentary on the *Hagakure*. He seems to have identified with Jocho, which is not surprising; for the monk's disgust with peace was identical with his own. In his introduction to the text, he wrote that the *Hagakure* was the only book he had read during the war that he still kept at his bedside. He called it "an anecdote to peace," "a key to freedom," and, strikingly, "proof that such a thing exists as orthodox madness." In fact the *Hagakure* was considered a kind of heresy in its time because of its extraordinary emphasis on death. Expectably, Mishima tapped the tradition of *bushido* at the spot where death ran richest in it.

Having taken a first step toward becoming a warrior, Mishima proposed to the student group at *Controversy Journal* in October 1967 that it was time to take political action. He meant the creation of a civilian army to be modeled on the territorial armies of Europe. Its purpose would be to aid the ASDF should it be obliged to combat "indirect aggression" from the Left. Twice a year, for a month at a time, student and office worker volunteers would be accepted into the ASDF for military training. They would return to their schools and offices prepared to lead twenty men in a time of emergency. Periodically they would receive a refresher course. The immediate objective was a group of twenty to thirty students who could be trained to form an officer corps. In March 1968, when Japanese universities were on spring vacation, Mishima personally would lead his first group for a month of training at the ASDF camp. The army was to be called, prosaically enough, the Japan National Guard. Mishima wrote a fight song in three verses and had it set to music.

On February 26, 1968, in the one-room office of the *Controversy Journal* in a small building on the Ginza, Mishima and eleven students signed a blood oath. The idea was Mishima's, one small part of a fantasy about blood and death and soldier heroes that he had been nourishing since childhood. The "document" no longer exists; shortly before his death Mishima remembered it and had it stolen from the new offices of the journal and destroyed. According to one of the signers, it read, "We swear in the spirit of true men of Yamato to rise up with sword in hand against any threat to the culture and historical continuity of our Fatherland."

Two weeks later, Mishima led twenty-three students through a month of ASDF boot camp. Bandai and Nakatsuji were there. But the student captain was a senior at Waseda University named Hiroshi Mochimaru. For most of his college career, Mochimaru had been a central figure in the reactionary student organization called Japan Students' League (Nichigakudō). Since the spring of 1967, he had also been the managing editor of *Controversy Journal*, and hoped for a career as a "neonationalist" critic. Unlike the co-founders of the journal, Mochimaru was enthusiastic about Mishima's war games, and already had begun to replace Bandai and Nakatsuji in his esteem. Nearly half of the students in this "first enlistment" belonged to the Waseda chapter of the Japan Students' League and had been brought along by Mochimaru. The group slept and ate with the ASDF regulars but drilled separately: in addition to the physical training given any boot camp private, Mishima had arranged for classes in tactics, ordinarily a part of officers' training. For the first two weeks, Mishima lived and drilled with the students. Then he went home for ten days to write, rejoining them at the end of the month.

Mochimaru was engaged, and his fiancée was apprehensive about his involvement with Mishima and the army. At his request Mishima wrote her a reassuring note from boot camp. The writing was gentle, not only in the language but even the hand. It read, in part:

Our task is a curious, uncertain one. On the surface it is harsh, but to me it seems a task very like a poem. There is nothing so important to us as purity. Here at this military camp, as if in a laboratory flask, we are conducting an experiment in purity, with an eye to the uncertain future. I hope you will understand.

"An experiment in purity." A year and a half earlier Mishima had used the very words to characterize the fanatic exploits of the League of the Divine Wind. There is hardly room for doubt that he was beginning to conceive of himself and his small band as similar martyrs to the imperial cause.

The experiment was accounted a success. The drill instructors had greeted the students skeptically, but as they shook hands and said goodbye it is said that they wept together. "Except for movies and plays," Mishima wrote, "this was the first time since the end of the war that I saw real men's tears."

Even so, before the month was over he had abandoned his original plan for a national guard. One reason was that discussions with men in the ASDF indicated there was neither sympathy nor matériel sufficient to make a second army feasible. But the decisive factor was financial. For months Mishima had been soliciting help from leading figures in finance. But those few who were interested in a national guard also wanted a voice in its political affiliation, and Mishima was determined there should be no strings attached. He concluded that to insure the army's freedom from any political party or organization, it would have to be only as large a force as he could maintain personally. The figure he settled on was one hundred men. He was of course aware that as the leader of a corps of one hundred men he would be a centurion, an idea he must have fancied.

Late in April, Mishima and eleven of his young comrades drove out of the city in a rented Volkswagen bus. Their purpose was to celebrate the first wearing of the handsome winter uniforms Mishima had ordered (the Japanese designer had worked on de Gaulle's uniform). At the temple they changed into the new uniforms and posed beneath some cherry trees in full blossom. Mishima had brought along a press photographer he had sworn to secrecy to take the pictures. Standing there beneath the blossoms, with Mochimaru on his right hand and the others grouped around him, Mishima looks like a man who has found what he has always wanted.

In July, Mishima took a second group of twenty-three students to the Mount Fuji camp for a month of training. This time he stayed with them the whole month, in a room of his own. At night he wrote, and at six every morning he led his group on the two-mile run that began their day. Several of the first "enlistees" were back to help, including Mochimaru, who returned as student captain. This time, officers at the camp had instructions to make Mishima and his cadets feel at home; the Self-Defense Force had decided it could hope for no better public relations man than Yukio Mishima.

In October, Mishima permitted rumors to entice him for the third time to expect the Nobel Prize. The year before he had been in India with Yoko when the Japanese press had carried a UPI release from Stockholm announcing that he was "definitely among the four most likely candidates," the others being Neruda, Malraux, and Beckett. The *Mainichi Shimbun* had sent a reporter named Tokuoka (one of the two newsmen Mishima would alert on the day he died) all the way to India to be with Mishima just in case; Mishima had taken the precaution of packing a tuxedo. But Samuel Beckett had won. This time everyone was saying the prize was "earmarked" for a Japanese author, who was certain to be either Tanizaki, Kawabata, or Mishima. On October 17, Mishima spent the evening waiting for the announcement to come over the telex at the Publishers Club. Hiroshi Nitta was there at his request, as was his friend Munekatsu Date, a reporter from Japan National Broadcasting to whom Mishima had promised the television scoop (and the other newsman to be alerted on the day of his death). At 7:30 P.M. Mishima emerged from the telex room and informed his friends "It's Kawabata-*sensei*." The first thing he did was phone Kawabata at his home in Kamakura and congratulate him. Then, while his friends looked on, he wrote a formal congratulation, "On the Occasion of Kawabata's Winning the Nobel Prize" for publication the following morning in the *Mainichi*. Nitta recalls watching in amazement at the speed with which Mishima composed the beautifully finished little essay. It began with lines he might have dedicated to himself as he wrote them:

The awarding of the Nobel Laureate to Yasunari Kawabata is an honor to Japan and to Japanese literature. There is no happiness greater than this. Kawabata has preserved in his own work the most fragile and the most elegantly mysterious traditions of Japanese literature; and at the same time he has walked the dangerous edges of this country which has recklessly flung itself into modernization. This tightrope walk of the spirit is ever enfolded by Kawabata's fine and gentle style; his despair at modern times has always blended into the quietude of classical beauty. . . .

From the Publishers Club Mishima went home to change from a sport shirt into a dark suit; then he and Yoko drove to Kamakura with Date to pay their respects. Date says that Mishima seemed "agitated" during the fifty-minute drive. At one point he said, to no one in particular, "It'll be at least ten years before they award another laureate to Japan."

There are people close to Mishima who consider his disappointment about the Nobel Prize an important factor in his decision to end his life. Unquestionably he was bitterly disappointed, although he never breathed a word or otherwise betrayed what he was really feeling (particularly about having lost the prize to Kawabata). But it is unlikely that his disappointment can have been decisive at this late date: by the fall of 1968, with his private army more than forty strong and himself committed publicly to defending the emperor with his life, he was already well on his way toward a hero's death. When he remarked in the car that the prize would not come again to Japan for ten years, he must have known that he would not survive long enough to be in the running again.

At a formal meeting on November 3, 1968 (Culture Day), the forty students who had completed a month of military training voted on names for their small army. Mishima's suggestion won. It was Tate no Kai (Shield Society). On November 4, Mishima called a press conference with Mochimaru and a few others in uniform and announced the formal founding of the society. From the outset the press was derisive, referring to the group as "Captain Mishima's Toy Army." In March and again in July of 1969, Mishima led groups of students to the Mount Fuji training camp for a month of training. In

March of 1970, there was a fifth and final "enlistment." At that time the society attained its full complement of a hundred soldiers.

Roughly fifty students a year applied to the Shield Society. They came from colleges of all kinds including Keio, Waseda, and even Tokyo University, and they tended to be rural youth, or at least not from Tokyo. During the first year (1969), applicants were screened by Mochimaru and his followers, in the second year by Masakatsu Morita, the student who was to die with Mishima. Those who passed were taken to Mishima either at a restaurant or his home for a personal interview. The society was looking for students unaffiliated with formal political organizations who had "the proper regard" for the emperor and the spirit and physical vigor to fight for what they believed. The only other formal requirement was successful completion of a month of basic training at the Self-Defense Force Camp. There was also a military "refresher course" lasting ten days which was required six months after the initial "enlistment." Members were not paid; but they were issued a winter uniform, cap, battle fatigues, and combat boots. After April 1969 there was also a summer uniform.

Except in March and July, when the cadets were at boot camp, the society met once a month at the Ichigaya Kaikan, a public hall adjacent to and owned by the Ichigaya headquarters of the Self-Defense Forces. Mishima began the meeting with quick comments on current events and lengthier explications of his own political essays. There followed half an hour of political discussion. There was no attempt to unify opinion; factions within the society disagreed about even such basic issues as the proper role of the emperor and constitutional reform. At twelve-thirty the cadets lunched on the unprepossessing dish known in Japanese as curry rice, although it is rarely prepared with curry (Mishima's choice of menu was an indication of the determined frugality that was his policy in his identity as warrior leader). After lunch, there was an hour of military drill on the roof before the meeting adjourned.

Where Mishima was concerned, the monthly meetings were largely duty; real pleasure came during the months of training at the Mount Fuji camp. The nature of that pleasure is clear in his description of an evening in the barracks during the July 1969 "enlistment," when he listened to one of the cadets playing the Japanese flute used in court music and Nō dances. The cadet came to Mishima's room after supper with four of his comrades, took the flute from its brocade bag, and began to play. Watching him, Mishima observed, "It is said that Alcibiades declined to play the flute lest he mar the beautiful shape of his lips, but the Japanese flute appeared to pose no such danger." The piece the boy performed was an accompaniment to the exploits of a Chinese prince, Lan Ling, who was of so gentle an aspect he was obliged to wear a fierce mask when he led his troops into battle! Listening to the ancient keening of the flute played by a young man preparing himself for battle, Mishima heard and felt the marriage of delicacy and fierceness that was for him the essence of the Japanese warrior, and the essence of his dream.

The Shield Society was a "standby" army. The command "Go!" would not be heard until what Mishima liked to call "the final, desperate battle." Theoretically this would be a battle to protect the person of the emperor against "any political force which ultimately denies the emperor." The society was pledged to defend the emperor with its life.

Assuming the cadets required a rationale for this commitment, with its pronounced emphasis on the readiness to die, they had one as elaborately evolved as they could have wished in the several volumes of "political" essays Mishima wrote during the last two and a half years of his life. Frequently he said of his political writing that it was prose "of the sword and not of the pen" and had "nothing to do" with literature. Yet even here he maintained the literary distinction between major and minor works. The major essays, such as "The Defense of Culture" ("Bunka boei-ron"), were abstract, richly elaborated, and immensely difficult. There were also minor essays in which he argued the same position more colorfully and in a vocabulary any college graduate could read. These included "Essays for the Young Samurai" and "Introductions to the Philosophy of Action," which appeared serially over a period of two years in the magazine *Pocket Punch Oh!* Naturally the completed series were published as books which brought in extra revenue Mishima needed to maintain the society.

The theoretical basis for all that followed was "The Defense of Culture," a long, impossible essay drafted at boot camp during the first "enlistment" and published in July 1968. Very roughly, it argued: that the Japanese were Japanese by virtue of Japanese culture; that the emperor was the sole "source and guarantor" of total Japanese culture; that defending the emperor was therefore tantamount to defending culture and the ultimate form of self-defense. The surface of the syllogism was simple enough; the difficulty lay in the pivotal, second premise, that the emperor was the source of Japanese culture. Mishima's explanation hinged on the concept of *miyabi*, a value or quality in classical Japanese esthetics which is generally defined as the "courtly elegance" identified with court poetry. In Mishima's singular definition, *miyabi* was "the essence of court culture *and* the people's longing for that essence." Just as court poetry was the source of all subsequent Japanese literature, he argued, so *miyabi* was the source of all subsequent esthetic values (such as *yugen, hana, wabi* and *sabi*). Therefore all popular culture (culture outside the court) must be *the imitation of miyabi,* the people aspiring to the elegance of the court. Since "courtly elegance" without an emperor was an absurdity, it followed that the emperor was the source of *miyabi.* "Hence" the emperor as "source of Japanese culture."*

* Naturally this argument elicited angry charges of cultural elitism, to which Mishima responded in various ways. Sometimes he had recourse to a kind of righteous indignation, as in the following exchange at a teach-in at Ibaragi College, October 1968:

STUDENT F: To say as you do that culture developed together with the emperor implies that culture is the special possession of one very limited group. In Japanese history that period when the emperor was in control was a time when a great many people lived almost like slaves. In my opinion the culture that belonged merely to the privileged class is just nonsense. If culture like that is a tradition, then that tradition should be destroyed.

MISHIMA: Culture cannot be understood in Marxist terms of history as class struggle. . . . All philosophies fail when it comes to theories of literature and art. Those of you who have read Kant know this, but when the *Critique of Pure Reason* tries to handle the question of beauty it tumbles as if it had slipped on a banana peel. The same happens to Hegel when he tries to organize culture into a system. If ever there was a Marxist who understood culture it was Trotsky. Trotsky maintained that government had to be a dictatorship of the proletariat, but that culture could be bourgeois. As a result, it was only during the brief time that Trotsky was in power that the Soviet produced anything deserving the name of culture. That's when you got Mayakovsky's poetry. . . . Unlike Hitler, Trotsky didn't label all previous European culture decadent and urban, and he eagerly imported new art from Europe. Then Trotsky was purged—by people like you.

At other times he was less defensive, more or less admitting that he was an elitist:

Only the emperor has continued to function as preserver of court culture (*miyabi*) on the one hand, and at the same time has constantly managed to interact with the essence of the Japanese people [folk]. In my view, without the emperor the Japanese people can have no ultimate *identification.* Naturally it would be possible to write a cultural history which excluded court culture, or, for that matter, a popular cultural history. However, such thoughts as these easily transform themselves

233

Having established the crucial necessity of defending the person of the emperor, Mishima defined His Majesty's principal enemy as "any totalitarian system on the left or the right." The logic was simple: since totalitarianism consisted in a monopoly on *totality* it must violate the *totality* of culture of which the emperor was the sole source and guarantor. Communism, therefore (Mishima saw no immediate likelihood of totalitarianism on the right), was logically the ultimate opponent of the "total" or "cultural emperor."

The severe inadequacy of this as a basis for political action is that Mishima had been at pains to demonstrate in the same essay that the "cultural emperor" he was now committed to defending with his life no longer existed. In fact he never made clear just who the "cultural emperor" ever was, but he seems to have had in mind the sovereign and high priest, amorous lover, fierce warrior, and fine poet who galloped on his white steed, half man, half god, across Japan's earliest mythology. In "The Defense of Culture" he represented such an emperor not as myth but as a reality, palpable and splendid, until as recently as the promulgation of the Meiji Constitution in 1889. According to Mishima, the constitution transformed the cultural emperor into a merely political emperor by imposing upon him the "pseudopolitical system called western constitutional monarchy." The postwar constitution had further violated His Majesty's totality by declaring him "the *symbol* of the State and of the unity of the people. . . ."

But if the "cultural emperor" existed no longer, and if the "cultural emperor" had been the only guarantee of "total

---

into a kind of abnormal passion that strives to deprive culture of its highest refinement, beauty, and nobility. And what one finally arrives at are Madame Mao's Peking Opera Reforms and Mao's view that "culture a peasant cannot understand is not culture."

Japanese culture," then the *totality* of Japanese culture must have been violated already. Mishima himself had argued persuasively that it had, that the "tinniness" of postwar culture, "like the sound of a *koto* with half its strings broken," was the result of a surgical separation of the chrysanthemum and the sword.* If, however, the totality of culture had been violated, then Mishima's basis for opposing totalitarianism (communism), that it threatened that totality, was absurd.

Mishima was perfectly aware of the contradiction, and tried to resolve it with another. In order to restore to the emperor his former, essential "totality," he concluded it would be necessary to return to the emperor's hands the right of supreme command which had been his under the Meiji constitution:

> Since the ultimate source of the honor of the chrysanthemum and the sword is the emperor, military honor must also proceed from the [cultural] emperor. Supreme command must be restored to him; needless to say he must accept a military guard of honor [since 1967, Mishima had been complaining of Hirohito's postwar policy of refusing an honor guard on formal occasions of state] and battalion flags must be delivered by him directly. . . . It is urgent that the emperor and the army be linked with bonds of honor. . . . Naturally, the restoration of supreme command and other rights of sovereignty must result in the revival not of a political but a cultural emperor.

* Total Japanese culture, he wrote, included not only the chrysanthemum, those "harmless" objects which can be exhibited peacefully, but equally the sword, culture as "action and styles of action," including the martial arts, *bushido* and even (or perhaps particularly) terrorism. But postwar cultural policy, beginning with Occupation directives against revenge plays in the Kabuki theater and gangster movies, had been a continuous and successful attempt to "sever the eternal circularity of the chrysanthemum and the sword," and to retain only those safe elements — "culture as assets to be shared by humanity" — which were useful in the development of civilian morality.

235

But how might a connection between the emperor and the army create a "cultural emperor" when, according to Mishima's own reading of Meiji history, the cultural emperor is replaced by a political emperor the moment such a connection is established? In his conclusion Mishima not only committed himself to the defense of an institution which did not exist, he advocated establishing that institution by means irreconcilable with his own logic.

The minute "The Defense of Culture" appeared in July 1968, it was passionately attacked by the literary Left. Some critics took it seriously as an avowal of cultural elitism and militarism. Hideo Odagiri, for example, retracted an earlier remark that Mishima's "poison was mild," asserting that now Mishima had taken his place among other "dangerous thinkers" on the far Right heading straight for fascism. Others, notably Bunzo Hashikawa, concentrated on tearing the argument apart. In a long essay called "The Logic of Beauty and the Logic of Politics," Hashikawa exposed the contradictions, and pointed out that the conclusion Mishima would have drawn had he chosen to follow his own argument was that "the logic of the modern state and of the emperor as overseer of beauty were essentially irreconcilable." In his "rebuttal," Mishima dodged the attack with his customary adroitness. He admitted that Hashikawa had uncovered illogicality. "However, as any good detective knows," he wrote, "when a suspect begins contradicting himself and trying to hide the contradictions, he is beginning to tell the truth."

But there is unambiguous evidence that Mishima was not telling the truth in any of his "political" writing, certainly not the whole truth. Most dramatically, there is the book-length essay *Sun and Steel* which he completed just at the time he was posing beneath the cherry trees with his young lieutenants.

In *Sun and Steel*, Mishima accounted for his actions past and future more persuasively than anywhere else, and in a context that had nothing to do with the constitution, the emperor, or anything social. The context was his knowledge that he would obtain the incontrovertible "proof of existence" he required to feel alive and real only in the moment of death:

. . . let us picture a single, healthy apple. This apple was not called into existence by words, nor is it possible that the core should be completely visible from the outside. . . . Thus at the heart of the apple, shut up within the flesh of the fruit, lurks the core in its wan darkness, tremblingly anxious to find some way to reassure itself that it is a perfect apple. The apple certainly exists, but to the core this existence as yet seems inadequate; if words cannot endorse it, then the only way to endorse it is with the eyes. Indeed, for the core, the only sure mode of existence is to exist and to see at the same time. There is only one method of solving this contradiction. It is for a knife to be plunged deep into the apple so that it is split open and the core is exposed to the light. . . . Yet then the existence of the cut apple falls to pieces; the core of the apple sacrifices existence for the sake of seeing.

When I realized that the perfect sense of existence that disintegrated the next moment could only be endorsed by muscle, and not by words, I was already personally enduring the fate of the apple. Admittedly I could see my own muscles in the mirror. Yet seeing alone was not enough to bring me into contact with the roots of my sense of existence, an immeasurable distance remained between me and the euphoric sense of true being. . . . In other words, the self-awareness that I staked on muscles could not be satisfied with the darkness of the pallid flesh pressing about it as an endorsement of existence, but, like the blind core of the apple, was driven to crave certain proof of its existence so fiercely that it was bound, sooner or later, to destroy that existence. . . . That, precisely, is when the knife of the foe must come cutting into the flesh of the apple — or rather, of my own flesh. Blood flows, existence is destroyed, and the shattered senses give existence as a whole its first endorsement, closing the logical gap between seeing and existing. And this is death.

Having demonstrated that death is the "ultimate endorsement" he requires to know that he exists, Mishima ponders how to achieve it in this piping time of peace, and is led back to reflections on his adolescence. As a youth, his imagination clamored for death incessantly. And, he reasons, "if the psychological life of that excessively decadent youth had happened to be backed up by the strength and the will to fight, it would have constituted a perfect analogy with the life of a warrior." And so it is, in the context of *this* logic, that in April 1967 he contrives to enter the Self-Defense Force in order to prepare himself as a warrior. He hypothesizes that the process should make possible the recovery of time, taking him back to the moment when he longed for death as an adolescent. Possibly it will even permit the recovery of "that beautiful death which had earlier eluded me."

But six weeks of playing soldier turns out to be just that, a game and nothing more. Certainly time has not been reversed: the war this army trains for is a hypothetical war. Mishima laments:

How ironic it was! At a period when the futureless cup of catastrophe had been brimming over I had not been given the qualifications for drinking from it. I had gone away and when, after long training, I had returned armed with those qualifications in fullest measure, it was to find the cup drained, its bottom coldly visible, and myself past forty.

Peace has bereft Mishima of what he now chooses to call "the spirit's consciousness of the End." He means that special excitement he tasted as he watched Tokyo burn in 1945 and sensed the fiery apocalypse near at hand. He wonders how to recapture that excitement. And he reads the answer he seeks in the "wills" scrawled by the kamikaze pilots before they took off to die. He perceives these men as true heroes, physically equipped to embrace death as a reality, and acutely conscious of the End. And he marvels that their language is entirely fine-sounding clichés such as "All lives to the Fatherland," language designed in striking contrast to his own, to "demand the strict elimination of individuality." If it is possible to become a hero by eliminating individuality from language, he "reasons" — obviously the pilots' language was a symptom of their fanatic determination to die and not its source, but Mishima single-mindedly ignores the obvious — then eliminating individuality from action should produce the same result. It is only a short step to the conclusion Mishima reaches at the end of *Sun and Steel*, that becoming a hero by eliminating individuality will be possible only by membership in the group:

Only through the group, I realized — through sharing the suffering of the group — could the body reach that height of existence that the individual alone could never attain. And for the body to reach that level at which the divine might be glimpsed, a dissolution of individuality was necessary. The tragic quality of the group was also necessary, the quality that constantly raised the group out of the abandon and torpor into which it was prone to lapse, leading it to an ever-mounting shared suffering and so to death, which was the ultimate suffering. The group must be open to death — which meant, of course, that it must be a community of warriors.

On the last page of *Sun and Steel* Mishima is running in the dim light of early morning, part of a group. Although he does not say so, it is the Shield Society. As he breasts the cold air he knows that "we were united in seeking glory and death; it was not merely my personal quest. The pounding of the heart communicated itself to the group; we shared the same swift pulse." The pounding of the heart — the dance of existence toward death which has beckoned Mishima and repelled him since he was a boy of twelve. Now, at last, through the agency of the group, he knows that he will be able to take up the fatal step. *Sun and Steel* concludes: "The group had come to represent for me a bridge that once crossed left no means of return."

Surely *Sun and Steel* was closer to the essential truth, firmly rooted as it was in the earliest drives and needs of Mishima's erotic life, than all the political talk: surely Mishima's band of warriors was essentially an access to heroic death. Does that mean that his "patriotism" was merely an excuse for a group which in turn was simply a means to a private end? Who is to say? Perhaps Mishima was able to believe in both rationales, both the private and the social, just as he had managed to animate them both with equal passion. But such dexterity is hard to imagine. And there is much to suggest that the erotic context is the fundamental one. For example, though no one but Mishima could have written *Sun and Steel*, there is not the slightest hint of the patriot in its pages. Yet, the political writing is suffused with the "death esthetic" which originated in Mishima's adolescence and is exhumed in *Sun and Steel*. There are examples beyond counting, both in the writing and in public debate. Consider the following exchange, from a teach-in at Waseda University in October 1968:

STUDENT 0: I wonder about your reasons for opposing communism. I have the feeling you're mostly afraid that your own superior talents wouldn't have adequate outlet in a communist society. . . .

MISHIMA: . . . In the beginning, I was an art supremacist. I believed that all I had to do was defend the castle of art. But that isn't sufficient for a man to maintain his spirit. That may be all right for a "living cultural treasure" who paints lacquer boxes or makes beautiful pottery. But there was something inside me that couldn't be satisfied with art alone. It occurred to me that what I needed was action with which to move my spirit. What could I do to get my spirit moving? I realized I would have to move my body first. So I moved my body, but just moving your body is madness, although plenty of people do it at Go-Go clubs and the like. . . . For every action, there must be a reaction. And where does that reaction come from? It comes from your opponent. Without an opponent, there's no point to action. Well, I was very much in need of an opponent and I settled on communism. It's not as if Communists had attacked my children or set my house on fire. I have very little reason really. I simply chose communism as an opponent, because I needed an opponent to provoke me to action.

In the political context, a remark like this can only be construed as either facetiousness or nonsense. In the context of *Sun and Steel*, where it belongs, it makes perfect sense. A more striking example is the "Counterrevolutionary Manifesto" that Mishima wrote in February 1969 when his cadets asked him to summarize the society's position in a single document. It was a credo in five articles that declared opposition to "all plans and all actions, be they violent or nonviolent, which attempt to establish a connection between communism and the government." For the most part, it was conventionally political and might have been written by any ultranationalist. But two of the articles seemed out of place and entirely without logic, at least political logic:

2. We consider ourselves the final preservers, the ultimate representatives and the essence of the Japanese culture, history, and traditions to be defended. . . . The kamikaze squads based

241

their action on the principle that they were the personification of
history, that the essence of history was manifest in them, that
they . . . were the End, the last ones. . . . Effectivity is not a
concern.

5. The battle must be fought once only and must be to the
death. . . . We are the embodiment of Japanese beauty.

The former cadets I spoke with were not able to account for
these passages satisfactorily. They were not clear in what sense
they were "the personification of history," nor did they consider themselves necessarily "the End, the last ones." None
could explain the tactical necessity of the battle being fought
"once only" and "to the death," except to say that action must
not allow for any compromise. And when asked what "they"
meant by "the embodiment of Japanese beauty," they merely
shook their heads.

Had Mishima's cadets been familiar with his literature as
well as his politics they would have understood much more.
They would have recalled the sixteen-year-old author of "A
Forest in Full Flower" who conceived of himself as the privileged "heir" to beauty which he was equating even then with
the "ecstasy of death." And they would have recognized the
more developed fantasies of the nineteen-year-old in 1944 who
considered the morning star his personal emblem because it
"invested him with the power of the End," who was convinced
that he was the "final heir to the tradition of Japanese beauty,"
even "beauty's kamikaze squad." They would have perceived,
in short, that Mishima's political position was designed to
bring him into proximity with precisely that death as supreme
beauty that he had so longed for as an adolescent. They then
would have gained a new perspective on why the future did not
matter, why "considerations of effectivity were secondary." At
the very least, had they read *Confessions of a Mask* if nothing

else, they would have understood that Mishima's emphasis on self-sacrifice was very different from their own. But the Shield Society did not read Mishima literature. In fact no one in the society had any familiarity with Mishima's "prose of the pen," which included *Sun and Steel*. It was even a policy of Mishima's that "literary youth," and particularly his admirers, would not make suitable warriors.

This calls into doubt Mishima's claim that he and the cadets were "united in seeking death and glory," that it was "not merely [his] personal quest." I do not believe he abused the society consciously. I am confident, for example, that he did not use it as a kitchen garden from which to pick young lovers for himself; almost certainly he had had his fill of Wildean pleasure with young men, and was now intoxicated by the more Spartan camaraderie the society afforded. Still, it seems certain that his "patriotism" was of a different quality than the cadets', unimaginably more complex, and that he was acutely conscious of the difference.

It is hard to imagine what Mishima really thought of the young men to whom he devoted so much time during the last two years of his life. Often he complained that it was "exhausting" to be with them because they were "so serious," "so naïve," "so very straight." Yet those who knew him well agree that the society made him a new man, happier than ever before. Until now, he had always been the fastidious famous author who demanded and received of everyone strict observance of proprieties; suddenly he was surrounded by young men who refused to obey the rules. They telephoned at all hours, obliging him to arrange for an answering service at night so that he could work in peace. Not satisfied with the phone, they visited the house whenever they had an impulse to talk with their leader. Eventually Mishima rented the lower floor of a coffee shop on the Ginza called Salon de Claire and awaited their pleasure every Wednesday afternoon from three to five; but the late-night visits continued. Like any children, the students were satisfied with nothing less than a hundred percent of Mishima's attention; Mishima (very much like any father) grumblingly gave in. In the process he seems to have loosened up; almost everyone I spoke to, from weight-lifting friends to Hiroshi Nitta, described him as "more affectionate."

Still, it is difficult to understand a man as complex as Mishima devoting so much time to young men who were so simple — unless their simplicity was what made the cadets so important to him. Judging by their characterizations of Mishima — "naïve," "boyish," "someone who enjoyed the same things we did and liked to laugh a lot" — it seems that in their company he managed to operate on a level he could not otherwise have obtained. Perhaps he can be said to have "used" the society to keep himself simple and easily moved, free of the self-consciousness, the logic, the skepticism, and the fear which threatened to keep him from fatal action. As one of the cadets innocently informed me, "Mishima-*sensei* climbed down the ladder of reason to be with us."

The hero's death Mishima certainly had in mind when he founded the society was not the death by *seppuku* he finally achieved. The word constantly on his lips from the middle of 1968 to the end of 1969 was rather *kirijini*, the second form of violent death the warrior code urged samurai to choose when the choice of life or death presented itself. Literally, *kirijini* means to die with sword in hand, to go down fighting. It connotes specifically a small band of vassals, outnumbered, who charge an enemy in defense of their lord in full knowledge that they will be overwhelmed. In the fantasy Mishima entertained until late in 1969 and regularly discussed at society meetings, the Left would initiate violence in the form of mass demonstrations too large for the police to handle. The prime minister would be obliged to mobilize the Self-Defense Force to keep the peace. During the interval of chaos while the police were being overpowered and before the Self-Defense Force mobilized, the society would defend the emperor with its collective life: *kirijini.* There was also a second, more exciting, version, in which the society would spearhead an attack on the Diet together with the ASDF. When the Diet had been occupied, the ASDF would demand revision of the war renunciation clause in the constitution and restoration of supreme command to the emperor. Since the society was to lead (and thus inspire) the attack on the Diet, casualties would be high: *kirijini.*

In the late 1960s anyone looking for a fight on the Left or the Right had an eye on May 1970, when the U.S.-Japan Security Treaty would come up again for renewal. The Left had vowed that the treaty would not be renewed in 1970. The Right spoke worriedly of a coalition between the heretofore irreconcilable Socialist and Communist parties, of a general strike, even of an attempt to overthrow the government. That was Mishima's cue. In 1960, his only response to the huge demonstrations (which had convinced many less complicated patriots on the Right that it was time for action) had been the snide suggestion that a realist rather than a nihilist be selected to lead the country. Now his voice was heavy with concern and responsibility, as if he had assumed command of the forces that would protect the nation and the emperor from the Left in 1970. As he told the former president of Japan's West Point, Seido Inoki, in January 1969, "I'm worried about self-hypnosis. If they keep talking about 1970 they'll have to do something or lose face. When you think of the chaos they were able to create on Anti-War Day you just can't be optimistic about how the fire may spread or how the people may sympathize."

The Anti-War Day demonstrations of October 21, 1968, had resulted in hundreds of wounded and arrests. Mishima was on the scene, disguised as a reporter from the magazine *Sunday Mainichi*. His concern was to observe whether there had been "escalation in the weapons the Left had available." He followed the largely student mob down the main street of the Shinjuku district, rushing back and forth to observe outbreaks of violence which he described on his notecards, all the way to the prime minister's residence, which was surrounded at just past noon. Hoping for a better view, he dashed across the street to the headquarters of the Foreign Office where his brother, Chiyuki, had his office. Chiyuki was just sitting down to lunch in the cafeteria on the top floor of the building when Mishima rushed in. He wore a storm jacket, boots, riot helmet, and press armband. He was also equipped with a *bentō*, a box lunch of cold rice garnished with a bit of fish or meat and a few pickles. Chiyuki was embarrassed by his brother's getup and by what he describes as his "boyish excitement with the action in the street below." He urged Mishima to take off his jacket and helmet, but Mishima remained as he was, face pressed to the window. When the waiter came, Mishima waved him away and opened his *bentō*. Chiyuki had never seen Mishima show anything but contempt for a lunch of cold rice. Now he was eating with gusto and exclaiming loudly, his eyes on the prime minister's residence below, that "[he] liked this better than any food." As Chiyuki put it, "He was like a child with a new toy, which was the riots and the outfit and even the cold rice."

In Chiyuki's view, all of Mishima's political involvement during the last years of his life was a kind of game-playing. "He was playing war, that's all, which had a special excitement for him because he hadn't been allowed to do it as a child." He recalled Mishima coming to him for an explanation of the newly ratified Nonproliferation Treaty. Chiyuki began a critique, but the minute he suggested that Japan would not be affected adversely, Mishima seemed to lose interest and changed the subject. It was Chiyuki's impression that his brother did not care to know too much about any of the issues, lest he lose grounds for opposing them. "The principle at work," he explained, "was *tous comprendre, c'est tous pardonner.*"

Whether Mishima was limiting his understanding of political issues and events consciously or not, the fact is that his "views" bore little relation to the political reality he was assessing. As a matter of fact, his views were a kind of madness, nonsense at best, at other times ugly and dangerous. Robert Kennedy's assassination in June 1968, for example, elicited a tirade against condemning assassination out of hand. What had to be considered was the "voltage" of the act, the tension of the confrontation of two ideologies, one intent on destroying the other! "You passionately denounce assassination because you feel it isn't right to kill," he told a student audience at a teach-in at Hitostubashi University in June 1968. "To my mind, that kind of thinking is the fault of the so-called humanistic education you've received since the war. You're not able to deal with the problem of murder objectively . . . I think about the deed, the actual act. And there are assassinations of high quality, and assassinations of low quality. . . ." His response to the Russian invasion of Czechoslovakia that same summer was principally contempt for the Czech leaders for having failed to sacrifice their lives in the defense of their country. And it was in accordance with this same bias — "the battle must be fought only once and must be to the death" —

247

that he appraised the major domestic crisis of 1968, the student revolution. The most violent battle took place at the University of Tokyo. It began in March 1968, when the medical school went on strike. In November, the president of the university resigned; shortly afterward, the radical core of the Zengaku-ren, calling itself the Zenkyoto (United Front), occupied Yasuda Hall in the center of the campus. There were hostages involved, and tension built steadily until, on January 19, 1969, eighty-five hundred riot squad police armed to the teeth stormed the building and drove the students out. Mishima had observed the confrontation with admiration for the determination of the students. But when Yasuda Hall fell without a single student death, he was disgusted. "Observe and remember," he told his cadets, "when the final moment came, there was not one of them who believed in what he stood for sufficiently to hurl himself out of a window or fall on a sword." Here, as always, his emphasis was on self-destruction.

In May, the United Student Front challenged Mishima to a debate on its home ground, the Komaba campus of the University of Tokyo, and he accepted. It took courage: these same students had already demonstrated they were capable of taking hostages. When the word got out that he had accepted the challenge, Mishima was offered police protection, which he declined; he also forbade the Shield Society to accompany him. On the day of the debate, he appeared at the entrance to the auditorium alone. He wore slacks and a black knit shirt. His only protection was the traditional *haramaki*, a long length of cotton cloth wound tightly around the stomach to deflect the thrust of an assassin's blade. Inside two thousand students were listening to a preliminary talk. At the entrance was a poster announcing the debate, with a caricature of Mishima as a "modern gorilla." As he stood there outside the door, he must have tasted that "sense of peril" he maintained was so important to survival in a time of peace.

The two-and-a-half-hour debate itself was a kind of anti-climax. Not that tension was lacking; a number of students resisted Mishima's charisma and remained abusive throughout. But the majority seemed to respect him in spite of themselves. It became clear almost at once that the audience was not entirely hostile as expected when the first questioner involuntarily addressed Mishima as *sensei* and then quickly paused in embarrassment to justify himself: "I've just used the word *sensei* without thinking and that's slightly problematical [laughter]. However, it does seem to me that Mishima-san deserves being called *sensei* more than those 'instructors' we have wandering around here at Tokyo University these days, so I'd like to be forgiven for having used *sensei*." The appeal was greeted by applause.

Since the student movement was capable of "logic" no less arbitrary than Mishima's own, much of the long debate was impenetrable. The most interesting moments were Mishima's attempts to convert the movement. The emperor, he maintained, was precisely the symbol and source of the revolutionary energy the students were seeking, in fact, the only possible source of a real Japanese revolution. He did not mean the present emperor, of course, but the emperor of antiquity, the emperor as cultural concept. "If only you would speak the emperor's name," he told the movement in the most quoted line of the debate, "I would gladly join hands with you; but since you refuse to do that, I say kill. It's that simple."

Naturally the students were not persuaded that the emperor was anything but a symbol of exploitation and reaction; essentially the debate ended in a deadlock, both sides agreeing they were "logical enemies." Mishima's most telling statement came very near the end, when the strain of the afternoon had tired him and he saw he was making no headway about the emperor. Abruptly he asked the audience to listen to a "personal feeling":

I grew up during the war as you know, and I've seen the emperor sitting up on a stand like this for three hours without moving one inch, three hours like a figure of wood without budging, at our graduation ceremony. And I received a watch from that emperor, I have that kind of personal feeling of gratitude toward him. I didn't intend to talk about this, and I don't want to talk about it [laughter] but there are things like this in personal history, and there's no way that I can deny this in myself; he was splendid, you know, the emperor was magnificent on that day.

Mishima never mentioned this again but surely there was truth in it. No matter how skeptical and withdrawn a nineteen-year-old he may have been in February 1944, he could not have been immune to the sense of honor and awe which must have accompanied the silver watch he received from Hirohito's hands. Not that this accounts for the devotion to the emperor he developed later. But it does suggest that the emperor was not something he had simply conjured out of air when he began to look for a value for which to sacrifice his life.

In June, Shinchosha published Mishima's confrontation with the student movement and it became a small best seller. Mishima gave the Zenkyoto rights to half the royalties. Later he wrote, "They probably used the money to buy helmets and Molotov cocktails. I bought summer uniforms for the Shield Society. All concerned are satisfied."

Mishima was at pains to maintain a balance between his art and his army lest, as he put it, "the Shield Society be reduced to an artist's pastime or I turn into a politician"; there is no question that he succeeded, at least during the first year. His major literary enterprise during 1969 and 1970 was *The Sea of Fertility*. At this he worked steadily through all else that happened, "weighing each word carefully on a scale like a pharmacist." Originally he had intended not to publish the cycle of novels until it was completed, but in February 1969, possibly because the critics were paying so little attention to the installments, he authorized Shinchosha to release Volumes One and Two, *Spring Snow* and *Runaway Horses*. Since July 1968, he had been at work on the heavily Buddhistic third volume, *The Temple of Dawn*. In addition, he produced his annual serial novel for 1969, a book of popular essays, *Introductions to the Philosophy of Action*, his first and only ballet (*Miranda*) and two three-act plays which he wrote for the new theater company he had just formed with the director Takeo Matsuura. *The Terrace of the Leper King* was inspired by a legend he had first encountered on his trip to Cambodia in 1965, about a handsome young king who was afflicted with leprosy after having begun the construction of a Buddhist temple, and who gradually rotted to death as the temple was brought to completion. Not surprisingly, Mishima, who had long savored the romantic dream of the artist perishing and in perishing becoming his own masterpiece, interpreted the legend as "a metaphor for the life of an artist who transfuses a work of art with his entire existence and then perishes." Apparently he was so excited by the story, and by the statue of the handsome king he saw at the ruins of Angkor Tom, that he drafted the play in a single night. As he worked he was conscious that in wedding the loathsome and the resplendent he was placing himself squarely in the tradition of late European romanticism; in his notes about the play he even cited the "wonderful precedent" of Villiers de L'Isle-Adam's *Count Portland*, in which "nobility and leprosy" were also united. The production

251

in July 1969 at the Imperial Theater was lavish, culminating in the Temple of Baillon materializing as shimmering pieces of silver in front of the audience's eyes.

Mishima's second play for the 1969 season was *My Friend Hitler*. This of course was a sensational title, and Mishima played the sensation for all it was worth, even to posing for a poster complete with swastikas and some copy he wrote himself which read: "An evil hymn to the dangerous hero Hitler, from the dangerous thinker Mishima." Based on the Roehm Incident of 1934, the play was Mishima's version of how Hitler managed in twenty-four hours to destroy potential threats to himself on both the Left and the Right. At the end of the last act, when the industrialist Gustav Krupp congratulates Hitler for having "cut the Left and in the same motion swung back and cut the Right," Hitler brings down the curtain with the line, "Of course; politics must take the middle road." Mishima's ironic point is that totalitarianism often hides in the beginning behind the mask of middle-of-the-road liberalism. Thus the play can be interpreted on one level as a warning. Nonetheless, Mishima could not hide a certain admiration for Adolf's adroitness. In his program notes for the production he admitted it:

All kinds of people have asked me "Do you like Hitler that much?" but just because I wrote a play about the man doesn't mean I have to like him. In all honesty I am fascinated with Hitler but if I had to say whether I liked or disliked him I would have to say disliked. Hitler was a political genius, but not a hero. He was comprehensively lacking in the briskness and brightness indispensable to a hero. Hitler was dark as the twentieth century itself.*

* In a letter to his friend Fumihiko Azuma dated August 20, 1943, Mishima had written, "I feel one hundred times more sympathetic to Mussolini than to Hitler."

In addition to everything else, Mishima also found time in July 1969 to play the terrorist in a hit film called *The Assassins*. One of the stars, Shintaro Katsu (known to a small but ardent group of American admirers as Zato Ichi, The Blind Swordsman), was shrewd enough to sense that Mishima would not be able to resist the role of Shinbei Tanaka of the Satsuma clan, who in the course of the film (and history) dispatched more than a dozen victims with his sword and then suddenly and inexplicably committed *seppuku*. Katsu asked the producer Fujii to approach Mishima and Mishima immediately agreed. The film was made at Dai-ei Studios in Kyoto in July; this time Mishima was entirely at his ease, able to enjoy the role and the other stars. When the film was released in September, the evening *Asahi* remarked that Mishima moved very well, like a real assassin, but that his "gentle features and intellectual eyes" gave him away in close-ups.

On November 3, 1969 (Culture Day again), Mishima's dual worlds of art and action converged in the Japanese National Theater. On the main stage he was directing a dress rehearsal of his first four-act Kabuki play, *The Moon Like a Drawn Bow*. Upstairs on the roof, the Shield Society, now eighty-five strong, was presenting an anniversary dress parade for an invited crowd of a hundred foreigners and Japanese. All afternoon Mishima moved back and forth between these two dimensions in his life; one minute he was delivering a welcome speech in English, the next he was rushing into the theater, unbuttoning his white uniform jacket as he moved, to watch a final run-through of the *seppuku* scene.

The Moon Like a Drawn Bow was Mishima's dramatization of a nineteenth-century romance by the great popular novelist Bakin Takizawa. The complex plot had always discouraged attempts at dramatization, but Mishima had succeeded in reassembling the tale on a manageable scale around scenes that excited him, in particular a bloody battle in the snow (reminiseent of the snowy dawn of February 26, 1936) and the climactic *seppuku* by the hero. He had written the play with his usual dazzling speed, in three sessions in June, July and August (he was at work on it during the filming of *The Assassins*.) Naturally he had used classical Kabuki language; he had even linked the episodes with a recitative in traditional *joruri* style, a feat no other contemporary writer would have attempted. In August the *gidayū* (reciter) Enzo Tsuruzawa of the Bunraku Theater came to the Tokyu Hotel in Shimoda as Mishima's guest to compose the samisen accompaniment and the melody for the recitative.

Rehearsals began in September. On the first day, Mishima did something no Kabuki director had ever done; he asked his all-star cast to listen to a three-hour tape of himself reading all the parts. Later there was public talk about how pleased the troupe was to work for the first time under so firm a directorial hand; in fact considerable tension developed between Mishima and the stars. According to his assistant director, one indica-tion of this was that Mishima never went backstage in all the time he was working at the National Theater because "backstage the actors rule."

Mishima insisted on the final word about not only per-formances but also sets, costumes, and lighting effects; he even designed the official poster he wanted and gave it to his young friend Tadanori Yokoo to execute. The finished poster (which Yokoo finally produced at the last possible minute) in pinks and oranges is a good indication of the kind of Kabuki Mishima was after. He wanted rococo Kabuki, garish Kabuki, vulgar, grotesque, and perhaps, above all, gory Kabuki. On November 3, he stopped the dress rehearsal in the middle of the *seppuku* scene to insist that more blood must be used and that the blood must "glisten." This was the scene he was proudest of; during the run he frequently invited friends to the theater after dinner, just in time to watch it. Everyone agrees that the gore was sickeningly real. About the production in general the feeling seems to have been that it was dazzling in its way but hollow. In the words of a sympathetic critic, "A failure, but an impressive one."

The parade on the roof was to celebrate the society's first anniversary.* After the parade and drill, the cadets changed out of winter uniforms into new summer whites for a lavish buffet reception on the balcony floor. Mishima made a speech in English and Japanese thanking the guests for helping them celebrate. The guest list, which had been drawn up in consultation with Nitta and Date, included writers, celebrities, and Japanese and foreign journalists deemed likely to be sympathetic. No politicians were invited. Most of the invitations were accepted. Those who declined (for example, the novelist Shumon Miura and his novelist wife Ayako Sono), did not hear from Mishima again.

Although the extravaganza on the roof was accounted a success, Mishima cannot have been entirely happy as he stood like a ramrod in the reviewing stand saluting his cadets, for the students who originally had "inspired" him to found the society were not among them. Late in August, the entire *Controversy Journal* group had walked out. The first to go had been Nakatsuji, the co-founder. On several occasions he had

---

* How Mishima managed to use the roof of the National Theater as a parade ground for his private army remains a mystery. He was on the Board of Directors of the theater, but ultimately permission must have come from the Office of Cultural Affairs within the Ministry of Education. Other board members were outraged when they learned what had happened: it is unlikely the roof will ever be used again for a private party.

solicited money for the journal in Mishima's name without permission and Mishima seems to have decided that he was dishonest. The final blowup occurred when Mishima learned that Nakatsuji had approached Seigen Tanaka for a contribution. Tanaka, president of a large construction firm and said to be one of the two or three most powerful figures on the far Right, had taken a liking to Mishima in 1967 when Mishima had approached him about financial help with the Japan National Guard he was planning at the time. They had met frequently to discuss the need to strengthen Japan's defenses against the communist threat (one of Tanaka's many eccentricities was having been secretary to the Communist party at the age of twenty) and they seemed to enjoy one another's company. Then Tanaka called Mishima's publisher Shinchosha and announced that Mishima had promised to write his biography. Mishima, who had promised nothing of the kind, angrily dissociated from Tanaka. Moreover, it was well known that Tanaka subsequently had contributed large sums to the radical student Left, saying he admired their "spunk." Now Mishima was furious at Nakatsuji for having spoken to Tanaka; he ordered him to "pack a rucksack on [his] back and go home to the country." Nakatsuji withdrew, taking with him several others who were close to the journal.

A week later, Mishima received an even crueler blow to his pride when his right hand, Mochimaru, announced that he was leaving too. After Nakatsuji's "betrayal," Mishima had asked Mochimaru to leave the journal and devote himself entirely to the Shield Society. He had also opposed Mochimaru's forthcoming marriage. Inasmuch as the society never knew when it might have to join battle for the final time, the leaders in particular must not weaken their readiness to die with marital or any other bonds. Mishima alluded to the young officers of the

February 1936 Rebellion who had sworn celibacy for just that reason. He went so far as to point out to a somewhat dumb-founded Mochimaru that the young lieutenant's exclusion from glory in "Patriotism" was partially a consequence of having broken his celibacy vow! Mochimaru, who seems to have considered himself ultimately a critic and not a warrior, decided he could not meet Mishima's demands. He told Mishima so, and Mishima yielded about the marriage and even promised to support Mochimaru and his wife in an apartment if he would remain. Mochimaru said no. According to Takeshi Muramatsu, Mishima's grief was "abnormal, as if he had been bereaved."

It was September now, and invitations to the parade had been mailed. Mishima considered canceling it and even spoke briefly about disbanding the society. Instead, he appointed another student captain, a quiet, solid, twenty-five-year-old senior at Waseda University named Masakatsu Morita. Morita had been brought into the society by Mochimaru in July 1968, in the second "enlistment." Previously he had been active in the Japan Students' League where Mochimaru had known him. Unlike Mochimaru, Morita had no literary pretensions. Apparently he had no pretensions of any kind: the words invariably used to describe him were "pure" and "simple." Orphaned at an early age and raised by an elder brother who was a junior high school teacher, Morita had always revered the emperor: in high school he had attacked a classmate with his fists when the student had called the emperor a "tax thief." Morita was more than ready to die for the emperor, he seemed eager. Students who knew him in the society say he spoke of death with a kind of relish. Some even say it was Morita's baleful influence that resolved Mishima to die. But it is unlikely that Mishima needed prodding. What does seem certain is that the new student captain's taste for death was no less keen than Mishima's.

During the last year of their lives, Mishima and Morita were together frequently. In Mishima's company Morita was quiet and assured, in the words of one friend, "like a confident fiancée." Mishima played the role of proud protector, always careful to see that Morita got the attention and respect he thought Morita deserved. Often when he introduced Morita to friends he told them, "I've pledged my life to the emperor and Morita has pledged his life to me." He told others, "Remember him; he's the one who'll kill me."

There were a number of bizarre episodes. In the spring of 1970, when Mishima and Morita had already resolved to die together, the manager of the theater where *The Rite of Love and Death* had premiered was invited to dinner with Mishima, Yoko, and Morita. The purpose of the dinner at the French restaurant Moustache was to familiarize Morita with western table manners. According to the friend, the meal was consumed with ritual seriousness, Mishima and Yoko together intent on improving Morita's style and Morita no less determined. In September 1970 a young poet friend received a call from Mishima asking him to come to dinner at a Japanese inn in Shinbashi. When the poet arrived, he was shown to a private room where Mishima was waiting with a young man in society uniform. Mishima introduced him as Morita and requested the poet to attend and remember the story of Morita's life, "an exemplary life and one of value," in case something should happen to Morita. The poet swears that Morita then quietly related the story of his life from childhood to the present, pausing occasionally for Mishima's suggested interpretations of critical moments.

One view of Mishima and Morita's death was that they had

committed "lovers' suicide." It was maintained that Mishima
had finally found the lover he had been awaiting all his life,
and had contrived to die a violent warrior's death with him, as
in "Patriotism." There is no evidence of this. But surely it was
true for Mishima, whether or not he and Morita were physical
lovers. At the very least, Mishima must have felt a strong
sexual attraction to Morita or he would not have chosen him
for his executioner. What is not clear, and must have been
decisive, is Morita's attitude. Presumably, Morita's death was
less complicated than Mishima's; presumably he was conscious
of dying only as a warrior and a patriot. If that was the case,
then the faintest suggestion that he and Mishima were being
driven to die together by an unmanageable passion is likely to
have been repugnant to him. On the other hand, the Japanese
warrior code included a perfectly orthodox tradition of homosexuality. Thus a physical relationship with Mishima need not
have conflicted with Morita's scrupulous sense of propriety, so
long as he was not conscious of a connection between their
physical love and their deaths.

There is no knowing when Mishima and Morita resolved to
die an "admonitory death" together in the name of the emperor. But it seems likely they had reached their understanding
even before the roof parade on November 3, 1969. By that
time Mishima had definitely abandoned his fantasy about
kirijini. At least he had decided by then that the excuse for
final action he had built into all his plans, mobilization of the
Self-Defense Force, would never occur. He had been led to this
conclusion by what had happened to the demonstrations
against Prime Minister Sato's departure for Washington to
issue the Sato-Nixon communiqué in October. It was generally
anticipated that these would become the largest and most
destructive riots to date. But when the student and worker

crowds took to the streets on October 21, 1969, they were confronted by an immensely enlarged riot force of fifteen thousand specially trained policemen equipped with shields and antimob weaponry, and ready to kill. There were a few clashes and arrests and a certain number of wounded. But relative to their explosive potential, the demonstrations were a dud.

Mishima seems to have expected that if ever there was to be a time when the Self-Defense Force must be called up, this would be it; when the riot police were more than adequate to the job, he despaired. His singular reading of the day, according to the manifesto he announced just before his death one year later, was that the government, "having anticipated the maximum strength of the extreme Left and anticipated the reaction of the general public to police restraint on a scale tantamount to martial law . . . had gained confidence that it could defend the political system with police force alone, without coming into conflict with the constitution." Mishima reasoned that since the government was now "confident" it did not have to mobilize the Self-Defense Force, it would no longer consider itself obliged to raise the question of the constitutionality of mobilization. In other words, the government could now be counted on to shift to full and unabashed support of the constitution since constitutional reform, always a dangerous subject, had been proven unnecessary to maintaining its own interests. In Mishima's view a corollary was that the only possibilities for constitutional reform hereafter were a coup d'état from the Right or a revolution from the Left.

On the last day of October, at a meeting at his home of the nine group leaders of the society, Mishima presented his gloomy conclusions about Japan's future and asked what the society ought to do. Morita proposed surrounding the Diet with the Self-Defense Force and demanding a discussion of constitutional reforms. Mishima was skeptical; he mentioned the problem of weapons and the difficulty of occupying the Diet while it was in session. Finally he expressed his view that the Self-Defense Force could not be expected to stand up and fight for its rights as a national army. This is important. It is evidence that Mishima knew all along from firsthand experience that there was no possibility of a coup d'état originating in the ranks. It means that the appeal to the Self-Defense Force to rise and join them which Mishima and Morita now began to plan and finally executed a year later was conceived by Mishima as merely formal, a gesture without meaning or value in the logic of the warrior, unless it was ratified by *seppuku*.

eight

1970

By the end of March 1970, Mishima and Morita had decided they would need help in the action they planned to take and had agreed on two cadets they trusted sufficiently to include. One was group leader Masayoshi Koga, twenty-two, a senior at Kanagawa University studying industrial managment. Koga had entered the society in August 1968, in the same group as Morita. Because he was four feet eleven inches and wrote his last name with the character "little," Koga was known in the society as "Chibi-Koga" — "tiny-Koga" — to distinguish him from another comrade of the same name. On April 3, 1970, in the coffee shop at the Imperial Hotel, Mishima asked Chibi-Koga if he was prepared to join him and Morita in "final action." Koga replied he was.

A week later Mishima confronted group leader Masahiro Ogawa, twenty-two, with the same question. Ogawa, a senior at Meiji Gakuin University, had been brought into the society by Morita, whom he regarded as a big brother. At the Student Seminar House in May 1968, Ogawa had heard Mishima discuss the new nationalism with Fusao Hayashi and Takeshi Muramatsu and had been deeply moved when Mishima remarked that "the Right was not theory but feeling." Later he would testify that he had acted out of "love for the emperor."

During this same week in April, Mishima quietly began to close accounts. On the pretext that he was behind schedule on *The Sea of Fertility* (secretly he was far ahead), he asked Hiroshi Nitta to "forget" the new projects they had been discussing. These included a novel based on the life of the great court poet Teika Fujiwara and some pornography. Puzzled by his abruptness, Nitta asked uneasily about the diaries Mishima had often told him he might publish someday. Mishima laughed and said he had decided to burn them.

Early in May, Mishima informed Muramatsu that he wished to resign from the Board of Directors of the Japan Symposium on Culture, and suggested they discontinue the magazine they had been coediting. He did not offer explanations and Muramatsu was offended. Mishima intended him to be; he was beginning to sever the few associations that still connected him to the literary world.

At a meeting at his house in the middle of May, Mishima suggested to his lieutenants that the ideal action would be precisely the plan Morita had proposed in October, occupying the Diet together with the Self-Defense Force and demanding revision of the constitution. In his view however, the ASDF could not be counted on to join them; accordingly, they would have to plan on acting alone. He proposed that they force the Ichigaya division to assemble either by occupying the arsenal and threatening to blow it up or by taking the commandant hostage. When the troops had gathered, they could plead their case and hope that men from the ranks would join them in a march on the Diet. At a second meeting at the Hotel Okura it was agreed that the more effective alternative would be to take the commandant prisoner. Mishima proposed luring him within easy reach with an invitation to attend a dress parade in November on the second anniversary of the society. On June 21, at a third meeting at the Yamanoue Hotel (where he had "canned" himself during the writing of *Kyoko's House*), Mishima reported that he had received permission from the commandant to hold November military drill at the heliport on the Ichigaya base. Since the heliport was distant from the commandant's office, he suggested that the next in command, the regimental commander, be taken prisoner instead. It was agreed that Japanese swords would be the only weapons used, and that a car would be needed, to be driven by Chibi-Koga. Mishima would provide the swords.

In June, Mishima met with his lawyer to transfer the rights to *Confessions of a Mask* and *Thirst for Love* to Shizue. It was a careful choice. *Confessions* had been selling steadily at a hundred thousand copies a year and, next to *Temple of the Golden Pavilion*, was the most frequently anthologized of the novels. *Thirst for Love* was not a very big seller relatively; therefore, no one could say that Mishima had deeded only the richest properties to his mother. Moreover, both novels had been written before his marriage; they were, in fact, the first and second novels of his professional career. Shizue would feel most attached to them, and for Yoko they would hold no personal significance.

In June Mishima also began saying goodbye. After his death various people thought back to the last time they had seen or heard from him and semed to remember some word or gesture that should have warned them something was not right. The producer Fujii, for example, received a phone call "well after midnight" about the possibility of entering *The Rite of Love and Death* in the Milan Film Festival. It was unlike Mishima to call so late at night, when he would be writing in his study, and even stranger for him to remain on the phone for twenty minutes, reminiscing about the making of the film. Fujii was mildly surprised, but realized only afterward that Mishima had ended the conversation by saying goodbye — *sayonara* — instead of the more idiomatic "see you again soon." Other friends were abruptly invited out to drink or to have dinner. In June alone Mishima spent final evenings with half a dozen critics and writers including the three he most respected, Jun Ishikawa, Taijun Takeda, and Kobo Abe (all leftists who had agreed with Mishima when he founded the society that they would not again discuss politics). Late in July, Mishima invited his friend Date of NHK (Japan National Broadcasting) to dinner at Hamasaku, and abruptly asked if Date thought it would be "big news" if he died. Date supposed it would. Mishima asked, "If I decided to commit *seppuku*, could you televise that live?" For just an instant Date thought Mishima might be serious. Then Mishima burst out laughing and Date laughed too. But surely he was serious. Like the narcissist Osamu in *Kyoko's House*, there must have been a place somewhere in consciousness where there was no distinction between death as a reality and death as a *coup de théâtre* on which the curtain would never fall.

On August 1, Mishima and the family went to Shimoda for their annual month at the beach, and there Mishima completed the final volume of *The Sea of Fertility*, *The Decay of the Angel*. No one suspected: serialization had begun only in July and he was actually more than a year ahead of the schedule he had announced. Those who were close enough to him to be worried — Yoko, Nitta, possibly Muramatsu — were certain that he would not attempt anything drastic until the tetralogy had been completed. It is hard to imagine how even Mishima was able to accelerate to the end of his masterwork even while he was laying the plans for his death. In fact, it is clear that whole sections of this final volume were written in distraction. The strain also took a physical toll. When Mishima returned to Tokyo, Shizue remarked that he looked haggard. He admitted he was exhausted, and told his mother this was the last time he would go to Shimoda with the family.

Late in August, Mishima and his comrades met to see if they could settle on any other members of the society to include in their plan. Chibi-Koga felt strongly, and Morita agreed, that only Hiromasa Koga (known in the society as Furu-Koga), a recent graduate of Kanagawa College, could be trusted. In his first year at college, Furu-Koga had written to a friend in his native Hokkaido urging him to read "an important story" by Yukio Mishima called "Patriotism." The hero of "Patriotism," he wrote, had indicated to him the direction he wanted to take in his own life.

On September 1, Chibi-Koga and Morita met with Furu-Koga at a coffee shop in Shinjuku and asked him to "lend them his life." Morita told him only that "Mishima-*sensei*" planned to take action at Ichigaya. Furu-Koga bowed to his comrades and thanked them for having included him. On September 9 Mishima took him to dinner at a French restaurant on the Ginza to explain that there was "no possibility" of the Self-Defense Forces joining them. Furu-Koga understood at once that Mishima was telling him the plan called for *kirijini*. He pledged his readiness to die and asked if there was time for him to travel to Hokkaido, for a last look. Mishima told him the date had been set for November 25, urged him to go in early October, and gave him half his travel expenses.

In mid-September Mishima posed for the young photographer Kishin Shinoyama for the first of a series of photographs to be called "Death of a Man." The series was Mishima's inspiration and Mishima designed the scenes. They included Mishima drowning in mud, Mishima with a hatchet in his brain, Mishima beneath the wheels of a cement truck, and of course Mishima as Saint Sebastian, arms roped above his head to a tree branch and arrows burning deliciously into his armpit and flank. The photographs were intended for publication in a magazine called *Blood and Roses,* but when Mishima died, Shinoyama could not bring himself to release them. The photograph that most unnerved him was one he had taken in jest; Mishima sits naked on the floor with a short sword buried in his abdomen, and standing behind him, with a long sword raised waiting to behead him on his signal, is Shinoyama. What can Mishima have been thinking? Were these moments when stage blood and the real thing became confused in his mind and he looked forward to his actual death as simply another more sensational pose? In all the hours of talk about each scene while it was being planned and photographed, Shinoyama's only impression was that Mishima was intensely serious about the project, "the most demanding and the most cooperative" model he had ever had.

On October 19, the day after Furu-Koga returned from his trip to Hokkaido, Mishima and the others posed for a formal, memorial photograph. Mishima's choice of a photographer was consistent with the grand design of his fantasy: the Tojo Studios were famous originally as photographers to Meiji generals. The atmosphere of the picture, including the pose and the antique chair, was definitely Restoration Japan.

On November 3, at the Misty Sauna Baths in Roppongi, Mishima informed Ogawa and the two Kogas that it would be their duty to deliver the hostage safely (insuring that he did not attempt to assume responsibility for the incident by committing *seppuku* himself), and to submit to arrest in order to explain the spirit of the Shield Society in a court of law. Furu-Koga later testified how difficult it was at this time, having prepared for death even to saying goodbye to Hokkaido, to resign himself to life. Morita comforted him and the others, assuring them, "Death can't separate us; we'll meet again somewhere." Later he told his comrades that performing his *kaishaku* (beheading him on his signal after he had beheaded Mishima and then had committed *seppuku*) would be "the ultimate act of friendship."

During the first week of November, Mishima designed and mounted at the Tobu department store a photographic retrospective of himself called "An Exhibit of Yukio Mishima." It began with baby pictures he had hunted out of old family albums and moved down through Mishima history to the present moment, including even a few of the photographs from the "Death of a Man" series. Predictably there was a good deal of nude photography; curiosity about this latest "indecent" display drew large crowds for a week.

Mishima had draped the gallery walls in black and grouped the photographs in four "rivers." First was the "river of books." In the catalogue he wrote, "If the agitated nights and desperate, despairing hours that I have given to these books were accumulated in my memory, I would surely go mad." Next came the "river of the theater," then the "river of the body," and finally the "river of action":

This is a terrifying river through a jungle. There are crocodiles and piranha, and poison arrows come flying from the enemy camp. This river and the river of books collide head-on. It is one thing to talk of the dual way of the pen and the sword, but the true merger can be achieved only in the instant of death.

But in this river of action are tears and blood and sweat unknown along the river of books. Here souls can touch without the agency of words, making this the most dangerous river. . . . But to be a man is to find this river irresistible.

The four rivers were designed to empty into *The Sea of Fertility*. Inasmuch as no one knew at the time how the final volume ended, the significance of this cannot have been entirely clear; in the last scene of *The Decay of the Angel* the tetralogy is abruptly bereft of substance and its reality made to seem a dream. Thus a part of what Mishima seems to have been saying in the exhibit — to himself — was that his entire life to the present moment, this side of death, had been an illusion merely, without substance. In fact, in a newspaper article written in July, he had said the very thing, "When I think of the past twenty-five years within myself [i.e., since 1945] I am astonished at their emptiness. I can scarcely say that I have lived."

And there was something more. Mishima spent the day before the opening checking the titles beneath the photographs with Hiroshi Nitta. (It was the last time Nitta saw him.) As they left the building he asked Nitta if he thought the time might soon be right to bring out his complete works. Nitta wasn't sure. Mishima knew of course that the time would be right long before his publisher imagined; he would see to that. What he said was that he wanted his "complete works" to include not only his writing but tapes of all the readings he had recorded, photographs, even a print of *The Rite of Love and Death*. Nitta pointed out the impossibility of packaging such a product; Mishima insisted that a "complete complete works" must include all of himself. In the exhibit he had represented his entire life as emptying into his final work, as if he was anticipating the satisfaction, by *seppuku*, of his lifelong need to become his masterpiece. "The murderer knows," he had written at eighteen, meaning the artist, himself, "that only by being murdered can he be completed, realized."

On November 14 Mishima met again with the others at the Misty Sauna Baths to secure their approval of the manifesto he had drafted. "What has driven us to this ungrateful action?" it began.

Our love for the Self-Defense Forces. You were our only haven in this lukewarm land where biting air could be breathed. . . . We watched Japan become drunk on prosperity and fall into an emptiness of the spirit. . . . Grinding our teeth we had to watch Japanese profaning Japan's history and traditions. . . . And we believed that only in the Self-Defense Force was the real Japan, the real Japanese, the true spirit of the samurai, preserved. When you awakened, we believed Japan would awaken with you. . . .

The document proclaimed the importance of revising the "dishonorable" constitution in order to restore the Self-Defense Force to its rightful place as a national army rather than a mere police force; it lamented the "tragic day" in October 1969 when the Self-Defense Force, until then a "bastard under the constitution," had been turned into an army to defend the constitution. From that day on, "We listened with breathless expectation. but nowhere in the Self-Defense Force did we hear the manly voice of protest against the humiliating

order to defend a constitution which denied its existence."
The manifesto ended with an appeal:

For the past year we have waited ardently. We can wait no
longer for those who defile themselves. But let us wait another
thirty minutes, the last thirty minutes. Rise with us and, for
righteousness and honor, die with us.

We will restore Japan to her true form, and in the restoration,
die. Will you abide a world in which the spirit is dead and there
is only a reverence for life? In a few minutes we will show you
where to find a greater value. It is not liberalism or democracy. It
is Japan. The land of the history and the tradition we love, Japan.
Are none of you willing to die by hurling yourselves against the
constitution that has torn the bones and heart from that which
we love? If you are there, let us stand and die together. We know
your souls are pure; it is our fierce desire that you revive as true
men, as true samurai, that has driven us to this action.

Morita and the others approved the manifesto unamended.
Then they determined an approximate timetable for the day:
twenty minutes for the division to assemble after the commandant had been captured; thirty minutes for Mishima's
speech, based on the manifesto; five minutes each for the four
others to speak their hearts; five minutes for instructions to
the Shield Society; a proclamation disbanding the Shield
Society (because action must be final and therefore occur only
once); and, finally, three cheers for the emperor.

On November 20, Mishima went to Shinoyama's studio to
make final selections from contact sheets for the "Death of
a Man" series. With him, in uniform, was Morita. While
Shinoyama looked on, Mishima marked with a grease pencil
those versions of his violent death he wanted in the series,
frequently asking Morita for his quiet opinion.

The next day Morita and Chibi-Koga, on the pretext of

delivering a book of Mishima's, went to the office of the regimental commander to verify that he would be in his office on the twenty-fifth, and discovered he would be away. When Mishima heard the news he said they would have to revert to their original plan of capturing the commandant, since it was too late to postpone the date. That same night he made an appointment to see Commandant (General) Masuda in his office at 11:00 on the morning of the twenty-fifth. The following day, Morita and the others purchased rope to bind the commandant, wire and pliers to barricade the doors of his office, cloth on which to write the "demands" they intended to hang from the office balcony, canteens, and brandy as a stimulant. On the way home that night, Morita asked Chibi-Koga to act in his place should anything prevent him from performing Mishima's *kaishaku*. Chibi-Koga agreed.

For the next two days Mishima and the others rehearsed in a room at the Palace Hotel (in view of the Imperial Palace). Mishima stood in for the commandant. They also wrote their demands on the canvas cloth and prepared headbands bearing the four-character slogan "All lives to the Fatherland" (one of those "ready-made concepts" denying all individuality which constituted the "language of the hero"). Late in the afternoon of the twenty-fourth, each composed the traditional "poem on leaving the world" in the classical form of thirty-one syllables. Although the plan called for the two Kogas and Ogawa to live, there was always the possibility of something unforeseen developing which might require them also to die. Mishima encouraged the students to write what came to mind without worrying about technique; before they copied the verses on formal paper he helped them polish a phrase here and there. At four o'clock they left the hotel and went to a small restaurant in nearby Shinbashi to drink a final toast with beer. Ogawa and Furu-Koga went with Chibi-Koga to spend the night in his room in Tozuka. Morita went to his room in Shinjuku. Mishima went home.

It had been roughly a year since Mishima had resolved to die with Morita, eight months since he had begun to lay plans for his death. In that time he had dispatched all his numberless commitments and had taken care to contract no more. Though no one realized it, Mishima's accounts were closed. A few last preparations remained. He telephoned the reporters Date and Tokuoka, told them he would like to meet them the following day, and asked where he might reach them between 10:00 and 10:05 in the morning. Then he sat down to some writing. He wrote letters to Donald Keene and Ivan Morris in New York, asking them jointly to oversee the translation of *The Sea of Fertility*, about which he had reason to be gravely worried. And he wrote other letters, nine or ten in all, last words of various kinds to people in his life of various importance. Whether there was one to Yoko is unclear; one was certainly addressed to his parents, one to a cadet named Kuramochi, instructing him to disband the society. Another long letter went to Kanemaro Izawa, Mishima's intelligence officer. According to Izawa, it read in part, "Dress my body in a Shield Society uniform, give me white gloves and a soldier's sword in my hand, and then do me the favor of taking a photograph. My family may object, but I want evidence that I died not as a literary man but as a warrior." Azusa quoted a similar passage from the family letter: "I have thrown the pen away. Since I die not as a literary man but entirely as a military man I would like the character for sword — *bu* — to be included in my Buddhist [posthumous] name. The character for the pen — *bun* —need not appear." These words

273

from a man who spent every night of his life, including this last one, writing in his study!

At about ten o'clock Mishima crossed the terrace to his parents' wing of the house. It was earlier than he usually appeared; Shizue asked if he was finished work so early. Mishima replied that he was "very tired"; Shizue urged him to go right to bed. Mishima nodded and bade her good night. He said good night to Azusa, who was reading in the next room. Then he left the way he had come, through the sliding doors that opened on the terrace.

On the morning of the twenty-fifth, Morita and the others left Shinjuku just after nine. Chibi-Koga was driving a white 1966 sedan he had purchased in July in preparation for this day. On the way they stopped to have the car washed, reaching Mishima's house at 10:15. Mishima came out to meet them in his society uniform. He carried a Japanese long sword and, in an attaché case, two short swords. At the car he handed Chibi-Koga an envelope containing 90,000 yen ($300) for lawyers' fees and a letter in which he took responsibility for the Incident and ordered the three students to live and to represent the society faithfully in court. Chibi-Koga and the others read the letter and swore to obey Mishima's order. Then they set out. Their route took them past Peers' School Elementary, where Mishima's daughter was in class. On the way Mishima joked about the kind of music that would begin at this point in a gangster film. He began to sing and the others joined in.

They arrived at the Ichigaya headquarters of the Army Self-Defense Force at 10:50 and were shown at once to Commandant Masuda's second-floor office. Mishima explained that he was in uniform because the society's monthly meeting was being held that day. He introduced Morita and the others as young men who were to be commended at the meeting. General Masuda was impressed with their bearing and comportment, and complimented them on the smartness of their uniforms. Then he noticed Mishima's long sword and asked if it were "edged." Mishima replied that indeed it was; the commandant asked if the police permitted him to carry such a weapon. Mishima smiled and unsheathed the sword, explaining that it was a certified blade by the famous swordsmith Seki no Magoroku. "Koga," he said to Chibi-Koga, "a handkerchief." This was the signal. Chibi-Koga stood up and moved behind the commandant as if to hand Mishima a handkerchief with which to "clear" the blade before presenting it for inspection. As he passed behind the commandant he seized him and covered his mouth with one hand. Ogawa and Furu-Koga sprang up and bound his arms behind him and tied his legs to the chair. Then they gagged him with the handkerchief, taking care that he could breathe.

While Chibi-Koga guarded the prisoner with one of the short swords, the others barricaded the three entrances to the office. It was now 11:20. Almost at once, aides in the adjoining office heard the noise and tried to enter. Mishima told them to go away or he would kill the commandant, and pushed the "demands" beneath the door. There were four: (1) that the entire Eastern Division be assembled in front of the headquarters building by twelve noon; (2) that a speech by Mishima and brief remarks by four students be "attended quietly"; (3) that the members of the Shield Society gathered for a meeting at the Ichigaya Kaikan be brought to the base to listen to Mishima and the others; (4) that no offensive action or interference take place from eleven o'clock to ten minutes past one. In the event of interference of any kind, Mishima promised to kill the commandant at once and to commit *seppuku*. He defined "interference" as "gas, water, ranger rope tactics, noise, blinding lights, speeches through loudspeakers, attempts at dissuasion, any and all psychological offensives." If all the demands were met the commandant would be delivered unharmed in two hours' time. The last article was very likely an intentional adaptation of a famous remark by the leaders of the February Rebellion to the effect that discussion of any kind was unthinkable. As Mishima put it:

4: With regard to the above demands,
    a: no modifications will be considered.
    b: no explanations will be offered.
    c: no questions will be answered.
    d: no meetings or dialogue of any kind will be accepted.

It took roughly ten minutes for the officer in charge to decide that Mishima meant business. In the meantime, about a dozen junior officers managed to push their way past the barricades into the room a few at a time. Mishima and Morita drove these men back with their swords. During the trial the defense would establish that Mishima had "thrust" with his sword so as to cut arms and legs but had not swung down with it in such a way as to kill. Nonetheless he and Morita wounded seven men before the senior officer called a halt and promised from the hall to assemble the division. The time was 11:35.

Meanwhile Date and Tokuoka had arrived at the Ichigaya Kaikan next door at eleven o'clock. Just before leaving his house, Mishima had requested them by phone to wait for him in the lobby with their cameras and press armbands. Date had had a premonition that something bad was afoot. As he left his house he had told his wife that he might be struck by a stray bullet and die that day. At the Kaikan the two newsmen met for the first time, although they had known Mishima well for two and a half years. They waited in the lobby until 11:20. Then someone from the society, acting on instructions he had received by telephone, came downstairs from the third floor where his fellows were gathered for their monthly meeting, unaware of what was happening. When Date and Tokuoka had identified themselves he handed them envelopes addressed to them. Each contained a copy of the memorial photograph, a copy of the manifesto, and an identical letter. The letter demonstrated the precision and foresight with which Mishima laid his plans. It was designed not to incriminate the reporters by making them privy to any of the details:

I will come right to the point.

I did not bring you here away from your work seeking publicity for myself. Since the matter will take place within the Self-Defense Force I was afraid that it might be hushed up, or that our real intention might not be communicated. Moreover, since it will not be clear until the last moment whether we shall succeed or be kept from our purpose, and since serious consequences would result should something force us to abandon our plan after it were known to the press, I am taking advantage of our friendship to ask you a personal favor.

Everything there is to say is contained in the manifesto, which will also be the general outline for my speech. Just how I intend to make that speech I cannot tell you at this time.

Until something happens the safest thing will be for you to wait in the lobby of the Ichigaya Kaikan. Please do not attempt to contact Self-Defense Force Headquarters.

On the third floor of the Kaikan the Shield Society, with no knowledge of this plan, is assembled for its monthly meeting. You will know that something has happened when they are ordered to move elsewhere, either by the Self-Defense Forces or the police. At that time, if you put on your armbands and enter the Ichigaya Base as if you just happened to be there, you will grasp the situation. Possibly you may get some idea of what is happening from the roof of the Kaikan.

In any event, understand that this is a minor incident, merely a private play of our own.

I have enclosed the manifesto and the photograph of our group because I am afraid of confiscation by the police. Please conceal them well and feel free to publish them. Do me the very great favor of publishing the manifesto uncut.

We expect the Incident to take two hours. But during that time anything could happen to foil us. To others this will seem lunacy; but I hope you will understand that as far as we are concerned, we act purely out of patriotic ardor.

If something has obliged me to abandon my plan I will be back at the Ichigaya Kaikan no later than twenty minutes to twelve. At that time I would appreciate the return of this letter, the manifesto, and the photograph, and I ask you to forget the entire matter.

Finally, please do not contact my home directly until the Incident is at an end. I apologize for my arbitrariness. I only desire that our purpose be communicated accurately to the public.

Apologizing for the inconvenience I have caused you, let me also express my gratitude for the warm friendship you have shown me for two and a half years.

In haste, Yukio Mishima.

P.S. I have sent one other letter only, identical with this, to Atsuo Tokuoka of the *Sunday Mainichi.*

Even as Date read the letter and skimmed the manifesto he could hear sirens approaching. With Tokuoka he dashed from the building and down the block to the entrance of Eastern Division Headquarters (police did not arrive to lead the society away until later). Eight hundred men from the 32 Regiment were assembled in front of the main building. Thirty feet above their heads, on the balcony outside the commandant's office, Mishima paced back and forth, sword in hand. He glanced at his watch repeatedly. At five minutes to twelve

Morita emerged and hung from the balcony the cloth banner
bearing the demands. At twelve noon Mishima faced the men
beneath him and began his speech. No one was listening, and
if they had been they could not have heard above the jeers
from the rest of the men. "Come down off there!" "Stop trying
to be a hero!" "Let the commandant go!" the angry soldiers
shouted. Crouched inside the office, one of the three cadets
whispered through the door that they would kill the commandant if the men below were not ordered to be silent. The
command went down but it did no good. And while the men
continued to shout below, three helicopters circled above
Mishima's head. Ironically, they were police helicopters; even
as Mishima reproached the Self-Defense Force for not demanding its rights as a proud national army, the Self-Defense
Force had called on the metropolitan police for help.

Mishima raced through the substance of the manifesto in
hoarse bursts of shouted rhetoric, repeatedly glancing at his
watch. He had intended to speak for thirty minutes, but after
seven he apparently decided it was pointless to go on. He
jumped to the final appeal to the men to join him and his
comrades in death, and the phrases he barked were swallowed
up in the din: "No more waiting," "thirty minutes more,"
"rise and die," "true men and Samurai." Naturally, there was
no response, not even an increase in the level of jeering.
Mishima motioned to Morita, who moved to his side. Three
times they shouted *"Tennō Heika banzai"* (Long live his
imperial Majesty)! Then abruptly they withdrew. Just as
abruptly the crowd beneath the balcony fell silent.

Mishima was unbuttoning his uniform jacket as he stepped
in from the balcony. He said only, "I don't think they even
heard me." Then he sat down on the floor, facing the balcony,
his jacket open. Morita took his place behind him and slightly

to his left, the Magoroku sword raised above his head. Mishima grasped the short sword with both hands, grunted, and drove the blade into his left side. Slowly he drew the steel across his abdomen to his right side. A writing brush and special paper were in readiness: he had intended to write the character for "sword" with his own blood. The pain proved too debilitating. He slumped forward. Morita struck his neck. Furu-Koga called out "again!" Morita struck again. "Koga!" he pleaded. Furu-Koga took the sword from his hand and beheaded Mishima with a third stroke. Morita kneeled and drove the short sword into his abdomen. Standing behind him Furu-Koga heard him say "wait," then "now!" He beheaded Morita with a single stroke.

The students righted the heads and bowed to them, hands clasped together. They removed the commandant's gag and allowed him to bow. They began to cry and the commandant urged them to "cry it all out." The students freed the commandant's legs only, saying Mishima had ordered them to keep him under guard until they had delivered him safely. "I won't attempt anything," he said. "Do you intend to let my subordinates see me with my hands tied?" The students untied the commandant's hands and led him into the corridor where they released him to his men. They held their arms out in front of them to be handcuffed. The time was 12:20.

The only one home was Azusa, who learned of the Incident when he turned on the twelve o'clock news. Yoko was in a taxi on her way to a luncheon when the same report came over the radio.

That night the press was out in force in front of the house, the garden bright as noon under the television lights. The house was dark, the cast-iron gate padlocked. A neatly written notice on the gate announced that the late Kimitake Hiraoka would be mourned by immediate family only, and asked people not to leave flowers or money. Rightist students in traditional kimono and hakama skirts walked up to the gate, bowed toward the house, and clomped off in their wooden clogs.

The body did not come home until four the following afternoon, and since the crematorium closed at five, there was scarcely time for the final "leave-taking." As he had requested in his will, Mishima was dressed in his Shield Society uniform, a military sword laid across his chest. At the last moment Yoko placed some manuscript paper and his fountain pen in the coffin with him. Only Azusa and Yoko's father, Nei Sugiyama, accompanied the body to the crematorium.

The following day the house was open to friends who came to light incense to Mishima's memory. Yoko greeted and looked after the guests whose acquaintance with the house had begun after Mishima's marriage; Shizue took care of older friends. One had come with a bouquet of white roses. As he stood in front of the Buddhist altar looking up at Mishima's photograph, Shizue said from behind him, "You should have brought red roses for a celebration. This was the first time in his life Kimitake did something he always wanted to do. Be happy for him."

It is not easy to be happy for a man who, as his brother put it, "always wanted to exist but never could." But perhaps it is possible, with Shizue, to see Mishima's *seppuku* as the "hero's death" he had longed for all his life and not the ghastly, needless waste it must otherwise appear. Perhaps we can even hope, however helplessly, that he found what he expected to find inside and beyond the pain.

The Major Plays and Novels of Yukio Mishima

1944 A Forest in Full Flower (Hanazakari no mori)
1948 Thieves (Tōzoku)
1949 *Confessions of a Mask (Kamen no kokuhaku)
1950 *Thirst for Love (Ai no kawaki)
       The Green Years (Ao no jidai)
1951 *Forbidden Colors, Part I (Kinjiki)
1953 *Death in Midsummer (Manatsu no shi)
       *Forbidden Colors, Part II (Higyō)
       Sunflowers at Night (Yoro no himawari)   (play)
1954 *The Sound of Waves (Shiosai)
       Young Men, Revive! (Wakaudo yo, yomigaere!) (play)
1955 Death Beneath the Falls (Shizumeru taki)
1956 *The Temple of the Golden Pavilion (Kinkakuji)
       *Five Modern Nō Plays (Kindai Nōgakushū)
1957 A Misstepping of Virtue (Bitoku no yoromeki)
       The Hall of the Crying Deer (Rokumeikan)   (play)
1958 Roses and Pirates (Bara to kaizoku)   (play)
1959 Kyoko's House (Kyōko no ie)
1960 *After the Banquet (Utage no ato)

* Translated into English.

1961   *Beasts' Game (Kemono no tawamure)*
1962   *Beautiful Star (Utsukushii hoshi)*
1963   *Sword (Ken)*
         *The Sailor Who Fell from Grace with the Sea (Gogo no eikō)
1964   *Silk and Insight (Kinu to meisatsu)*
         The Harp of Happiness (Yorokobi no koto)   (play)
1965   **Madame de Sade (Sado kōshaku fujin)*   (play)
1966   *The Voice of the Hero Spirits (Eirei no koe)*
         *Spring Snow (Haru no yuki) (serialized September 1965–
         January 1967)
1967   *The Fall of the House of Suzaku (Suzakke no metsubō)*
         (play)
1968   **Runaway Horses (Honba)*   (serialized February 1967–
         August 1968)
         My Friend Hitler (Waga tomo Hittora)   (play)
1969   *The Terrace of the Leper King (Raiō no terasu)*   (play)
         The Black Lizard (Kurotokage)   (play)
         Tale of a Moon Like a Drawn Bow (Chinsetsu yumiharizuki)
         (play)
         *The Temple of Dawn (Akatsuki no tera)   (serialized
         September 1968–April 1970)
1970   **The Decay of the Angel (Tennin gosui)*

Index